Fat Chance

Fat Chance

DIET MANIA, GREED, AND THE INFAMOUS FEN-PHEN SWINDLE

RICK CHRISTMAN

south limestone

Published by South Limestone
An imprint of the University Press of Kentucky

Copyright © 2021 by The University Press of Kentucky
All rights reserved.

Editorial and Sales Offices: The University Press of Kentucky
663 South Limestone Street, Lexington, Kentucky 40508-4008
www.kentuckypress.com

Library of Congress Cataloging-in-Publication Data

Names: Christman, Rick, author.
Title: Fat chance : diet mania, greed, and the infamous fen-phen swindle /
  Rick Christman.
Description: Lexington : South Limestone, 2021. | Includes index.
Identifiers: LCCN 2020032963 | ISBN 9781949669305 (hardcover) | ISBN
  9781949669312 (pdf) | ISBN 9781949669329 (epub)
Subjects: LCSH: Weight loss. | Appetite depressants. | Fenfluramine. |
  Phentermine. | Products liability—Drugs—United States. | Weight loss
  preparations industry—Law and legislation—United States.
Classification: LCC RM222.2 .C4844 2021 | DDC 613.2—dc23
LC record available at https://lccn.loc.gov/2020032963

This book is printed on acid-free paper meeting
the requirements of the American National Standard
for Permanence in Paper for Printed Library Materials.

Manufactured in the United States of America.

This book is dedicated to my wife, Lindy Karns,
who consented to its publication despite her better judgment.

Contents

Preface and Acknowledgments

THIS BOOK IS ESSENTIALLY written in two parts. The first four chapters deal with the development, marketing, and demise of the diet drugs fen-phen (fenfluramine-phentermine) and Redux (dexfenfluramine). The remaining chapters cover in detail a bizarre, Kentucky-based class-action lawsuit against the manufacturer of these drugs. Those most interested in the legal aspects of the story may prefer to skip directly to chapter 5. Any reader who wishes to get right into the thick of the book may dispense with the introduction altogether.

Although I labored to make this book as readable as possible, it is by necessity a complicated story. Readers are urged to consult the timelines section at the end of this book, which will be helpful in that respect.

As the book developed, an underlying subtext emerged as to the openly cavalier ethical attitudes seemingly pervasive throughout the legal industry, including law schools, practicing attorneys, and judges. I will let the facts speak for themselves with regard to my opinion.

During my research I discovered evidence of malfeasance that heretofore had not been published. I have been careful not to present the evidence as conclusive, but rather to allow readers to make their own judgments. This book has been vetted by an attorney who specializes in media law specifically for that purpose.

I am not an attorney and I relied on the assistance of University of Kentucky professor of law Bill Fortune on at least one occasion, who helped me to better understand the rules of legal procedure.

Preface and Acknowledgments

Although I have no personal connection to the story, I find it fascinating and deserving of being told. I hope the reader will agree.

The author wishes to thank the following, who made this book possible: Patrick O'Dowd, Gary Matthews (for inspiration), Mike Cox, John Paine, Anthony Chiffolo, Bill Fortune, Melbourne Mills, Ila McEntire, B. M., B. K., D. D., and L. F.

Introduction

IF MONEY CAN BUY HAPPINESS, how much is enough? A 2010 Princeton University study of the relationship between money and the sense of well-being found that an annual household income of $75,000 is the satisfaction ceiling. The researchers determined that incomes above that level provide little to no appreciable increase in happiness.[1] A variant of this finding is known as the Easterlin paradox. Here, researchers found that a sense of national well-being is closely correlated with a rise in mean personal income, but only up to a certain point, after which the two diverge.[2] Yet most people persist in the belief that their discontent can be healed with the medicinal properties of cash. When this remedy fails, it is typically blamed on an insufficient dosage.

This book describes a collection of real-life characters who were so addicted to wealth that they needed huge fixes of other people's money to maintain their states of euphoric indulgence. Coincidently, their income sources were related to actual pharmaceuticals.

During the early 1990s, the breakthrough diet drugs fen-phen (fenfluramine-phentermine) and Redux (dexfenfluramine) achieved tremendous popularity. What's not to like about a pill that makes losing weight effortless? But when medical researchers became convinced that the drugs caused heart valve disease, the hopes of the overweight and obese were dashed, along with the potential fortunes of the drugmaker. In addition to the manufacturer, various others were keen to profit from sales of these drugs, including the doctors who prescribed them, the pharmacists who dispensed them, and, eventually, the many lawyers who sued over the consequences of taking them. This last group included several attorneys who attempted to amass personal fortunes from the ocean of cash generated by an improbably successful class-action lawsuit. Five of the major players were longtime members of the bar—four successful practicing attorneys and one gullible circuit court judge. Although they tried to abscond with nearly $95 million, their ultimate take was only about $45 million, arguably the largest theft in the United States, edging out the 1972 United California Bank robbery, which totaled $30 million.[3]

Fen-phen—a chemical cocktail that greatly depressed appetite—was discovered by chance, marketed with hyperbole, and prescribed to millions. Redux, a close derivative of fen-phen, was made by the same pharmaceutical giant: American Home Products. Redux was developed as a backstop to one of the components of fen-phen, as the patents for each had lapsed.

The tortuous journey taken to obtain US Food and Drug Administration (FDA) approval of Redux is just one example of the overly cozy relationships among science, money, and politics. In the case of Redux, American Home Products orchestrated the razor-thin vote by the medical panel necessary to obtain quick FDA approval of the drug. It enlisted the help of the majordomo of several Republican White Houses, General Alexander Haig, to seal the deal and also received support from Senator Ted Kennedy. In Kentucky, which served as the setting for much of the drama in this tale, intense lobbying efforts and an active fund-raiser for the state Democratic Party paved the way for the medical review panel's removal of the time limitation for the prescription of fen-phen.

The massive popularity of fen-phen and Redux was the result of the convergence of two truths: the centuries-old antipathy toward those who are overweight, and the contemporary assumption that obesity is a serious health crisis. Without question, the nation's craze for fen-phen and Redux was the wildest in Kentucky—not only because Kentucky had an overabundance of people categorized as overweight but also, and more significantly, because it was surrounded by states that tightly restricted or outright banned the sale of these drugs.

Attempts by the pharmaceutical industry (aka Big Pharma) to cash in big-time have hardly been limited to diet drugs. At its peak in 2012, more than 50 million prescriptions for OxyContin (oxycodone) were written in the United States. Kentuckians were especially fond of this inducer of euphoria. In Clay County, Kentucky, population 21,000, more than 617,000 oxycodone tablets and 2.2 million hydrocodone pills (oxycodone's first cousin) were sold in a twelve-month period—more than ten tablets per month for every man, woman, and child.[4]

According to *Kentucky Health News,* "In 2014 and 2015 opioid manufacturers paid hundreds of doctors who prescribed particularly large amounts of opioids six-figure sums, and thousands more than $25,000." Dr. Andrew Kolodny, a senior scientist at the Institute for Behavioral Health at Brandeis University, commented, "It seems like doctors being bribed to sell narcotics." In March 2018 a group of rural health care clinics in Kentucky filed a lawsuit against more than twenty opioid manufacturers and distributors for "creating and engineering" an epidemic of drug abusers. In one case, the drug company had provided literature to physicians that described the addictive qualities of opioids as a "myth."[5]

Having lit the flame of opiate demand with OxyContin and hydrocodone, Big Pharma is largely responsible for the wildfire of heroin addiction now sweeping the United States. One sad example, also with a Kentucky connection, is the very small town of Austin, Indiana, which is known as "Little Hazard." (Hazard being a small town in eastern Kentucky. A meatpacking plant that formerly operated in Austin imported a sizable portion of its workforce from Hazard, reportedly because one could travel from Hazard to Austin on a single tank of gas.) Austin has a population of 4,100, and at least 10 percent are addicted to illegal intravenous drugs. As a consequence, it had the dubious distinction of having the largest outbreak of HIV in the United States in 2015, growing from 3 cases to 180 that year.[6]

Following in the wake of this trail of misery, about $35 billion is spent each year by the government, insurers, and families for the treatment of drug abuse. As described by Gabrielle Glaser in the *Atlantic*, the majority of substance abuse treatment programs claim a success rate of around 30 percent—a figure that is likely inflated. In fact, a study by the Veterans Administration found that only 5 percent of persons undergoing facility-based detox and intensive counseling were off drugs after three months.[7]

But even if the statistics published by the treatment industry are correct, this means that 70 percent of people who enter drug treatment receive no benefit at all. And too often, treatment does more harm than good. Tragically, many people die from overdoses shortly after leaving a treatment facility. While in rehab, their tolerance for opiates diminishes, but not their cravings. As one rehab counselor reported to journalist Christopher Moraff, "People who die from overdoses if you look at their history, they were most likely either in rehab or jail."[8]

Today's rehab industry is reminiscent of the Wild West–like pharmaceutical industry before the creation of the Food and Drug Administration in 1927. As Glaser observed: "Nowhere in the field of medicine is treatment less grounded in modern science. Most treatment providers carry the credential of addiction counselor or substance-abuse counselor, for which many states require little more than a high-school diploma or a GED. Many counselors are in recovery themselves."[9] A 2012 report by the National Center on Addiction and Substance Abuse Disorder at Columbia University compared the current state of addiction medicine to general medicine in the early 1900s and stated, "The vast majority of people in need of addiction treatment do not receive anything that approximates evidence-based care."[10] As detailed in a report by Marketdata Enterprises, there are now more than 14,000 treatment facilities in the United States serving 2.5 million Americans.[11]

The for-profit rehab industry has been quick to innovate for the purpose of making a fast buck. The most disturbing practice is known as "body brokering." Body brokers, who represent residential treatment centers, pay halfway houses or "sober homes" for referrals. Once an individual has stayed at a particular rehab facility for the maximum time allowed by the insurer, the body broker moves the addict to yet another treatment center in a phenomenon known as the "Florida shuffle." Indeed, every brokered body is a potential gold mine. *Miami Herald* reporter Peter Haden spoke with Staci Katz about her son Dillon, a recovering drug addict. Staci had amassed three huge binders containing her son's medical bills over a five-year period. The cost of Dillon's stints in rehab exceeded $600,000, including $9,500 for five urine tests.[12]

Of course, not all drug treatment centers are for-profit operations. On December 12, 2017, Douglas Tieman, president and CEO of the nonprofit Caron Treatment Centers, testified before the US House Subcommittee on Oversight and Investigations. In addition to citing insufficient resources to deal with the opioid epidemic, Tieman noted, "The state of the treatment sector today is disconcerting as profiteering begins to outweigh the sacred trust of families in crisis." Tieman went on to assure members of the subcommittee that, "as a non-profit treatment provider, Caron is not bound by investor or profit motives."[13] In 2015 Tieman's compensation package totaled $736,244.[14]

The $35 billion rehab train shows no signs of slowing down. Demonstrating yet again that there is profit in poverty, within the past decade, most states have added substance abuse treatment as a reimbursable Medicaid service. In March 2018 the federal Omnibus Budget Act provided an additional $3.3 billion for opioid treatment and related programs.

Just as substance abuse treatment centers have sprung up throughout the United States to cash in on the opioid crisis, attorneys rushed in to take advantage of the financial opportunities offered by the deleterious health consequences of using fen-phen. In a very short time, a rash of lawsuits threated to ruin American Home Products. By the time the company was compelled to withdraw the drugs from the market, more than 18,000 lawsuits had already been filed. After losing several of the early rounds in these trials, including one featuring an overweight beautician in Texas who smoked and had been diagnosed with heart disease even before taking fen-phen, American Home Products succeeded in getting most of the cases combined in a national class action that would be heard in a federal district court in Philadelphia. However, former users of the diet drugs could "opt out" of the national settlement and seek restitution in state courts. One such lawsuit involving a group of opt-outs took place in Kentucky.

Kentucky attorney Melbourne Mills was contacted by more than 6,500 former fen-phen users who responded to his television ads. Of these thousands, 431 chose to pursue a Kentucky class action rather than participate in the national class action, gambling that they would win more in Kentucky than they would in Philadelphia. And indeed, they did! One woman was reportedly awarded $2 million for a claim that probably would have garnered no more than $100,000 in the national settlement. Such windfalls can do strange things to people, and she apparently purchased five Dodge Durangos with her settlement money.

After establishing the group of 431 former diet drug users, Mills and his two Kentucky colleagues, Bill Gallion and Shirley Cunningham, contrived to "forum shop" and move the trial to Covington, Kentucky. There, they hired "trial consultant" Mark Modlin, who had some sort of relationship with the presiding judge, Joseph "Jay" Bamberger. Meanwhile, Cincinnati attorney Stan Chesley was taking notice of what was happening across the Ohio River. Chesley, who at one time was arguably the most successful tort attorney in the world, elbowed his way into the Kentucky class-action suit, while still mediating the national class action in Philadelphia. According to the Kentucky Bar Association (KBA), this was accomplished by "multiple convoluted and dishonest machinations."[15]

Even though most of the plaintiffs in the lawsuit had suffered little or no permanent health damage from taking the drugs, and even though a neutral mediator had estimated the settlement value to be in the $30 million range, American Home Products agreed on May 1, 2001, to a negotiated settlement for the monumental sum of $200 million—seemingly a bonanza for the 431 claimants, except that none of them were told the amount of the settlement. The story gets even more shocking. Judge Bamberger would later testify, "Looking back, nothing that happened after May 1, 2001, was appropriate."[16] A settlement of this size would have generated legitimate legal fees of $61 million—more than enough for the attorneys to live in luxury for the rest of their lives. Yet they considered these millions insufficient and were determined to satisfy their desire for much more.

Of the three Kentucky lawyers, Melbourne Mills was the most unusual. Having flunked out of the University of Kentucky Law School twice, he eventually graduated from the University of Louisville and did not enter private practice until after he turned forty. Mills attained notoriety when he became the first person in the United States to take advantage of the US Supreme Court ruling that allowed attorneys to advertise their legal services. His ubiquitous "Call the Man" television ads rounded up workers' compensation claims and arguably made Melbourne Mills the most recognizable name in eastern Kentucky. Mills also struggled with alcoholism. According to Mills's key legal assistant, near the beginning of 2001 he "seemed to be drunk round the clock . . . he was really drinking first thing in the morning . . . if he was not drinking, his hand would be shaking real hard and staggering."[17]

Shirley Cunningham was the son of a sharecropper in western Kentucky. He would later gain infamy not only for his involvement in the fenphen case but also for a scandal at Florida A&M University that led to the resignation of the dean of its law school. Cunningham's fortunes fluctuated throughout his career, and at one point he had to pay for a legal seminar with quarters.

Bill Gallion was arguably the brains of the Kentucky trio. A devoted bon vivant, Gallion used his fleeting wealth to purchase a chalet in France, four Porsches, a home in an exclusive Florida development, and, with Cunningham, a Thoroughbred horse named Curlin. After being purchased for a mere $57,000, Curlin went on to great racing fame, earning the distinction of being named "American Horse of the Year" in 2007 and 2008. Despite standing on the verge of becoming a multimillionaire, Gallion once refused to pay for a lap dance at a strip club, resulting in bodily injury to himself.

Stan Chesley was by far the most fascinating of the lot. He first gained national attention after the tragic Beverly Hills Supper Club fire in Covington, Kentucky. Chesley subsequently became the primary negotiator for a host of high-dollar class actions, including those involving the Pan-Am jetliner explosion over Lockerbie, Scotland; Monsanto's Agent Orange; Dow Corning's silicone breast implants; and the monumental settlement with the big tobacco companies, to name just a few.

Chesley and his wife, a federal judge, lived in a 27,000-square-foot mansion in Cincinnati replete with an eight-car garage and a carriage house that held his collection of twenty luxury automobiles. Before becoming one of the most successful attorneys in the United States, Chesley created the doctrine of "enterprise liability," a stratagem of tort law that continues to be taught in law schools. Because of his considerable fund-raising abilities, he was also an eminent figure in national politics. He dined with members of Congress, rubbed elbows with Hollywood celebrities, and slept in the White House's Lincoln Bedroom on occasion. Chesley was ultimately disbarred for his many ethical abuses throughout the fen-phen debacle.

Following the $200 million settlement by American Home Products, awards were negotiated with each of the 431 claimants for amounts far less than would have been expected, given the settlement's total. Judge Bamberger was talked into approving attorneys' fees of nearly $100 million but was somehow oblivious to the fact that the three Kentucky attorneys had already been paid their 33 percent contingency fees under their client contracts. Bamberger later allowed $20 million to fund a bogus nonprofit company that paid various members of the legal team $60,000 per year as board members. After the KBA honored Bamberger as "Judge of the Year," he joined the board of this phony philanthropy and began to receive payments as well.

Despite attempts to keep the amount of the settlement secret, the law partners of Gallion and Mills eventually realized that they too had been cheated under their fee-sharing agreements and complained to the KBA. The KBA in turn alerted the FBI. During this time, Judge Bamberger was also investigated by the KBA and was eventually disrobed and disbarred. Following their federal indictments on charges of wire fraud, the three Kentucky attorneys were held in the county jail as they awaited trial, being considered flight risks. As they sat behind bars, Curlin won $2.2 million in the Dubai World Cup.

Chesley obtained immunity and testified against his former partners, but despite his testimony, the jury was unable to reach verdicts in the cases against Gallion and Cunningham. Mills was declared not guilty after the jury concluded that he was usually too drunk to be complicit. In a retrial, Gallion and Cunningham were convicted and sentenced to long prison terms.

Introduction

This tale also includes a $42 million civil suit filed against the four attorneys on behalf of their fleeced former clients by Lexington lawyer Angela Ford. Through a series of jaw-dropping machinations, millions of dollars of this settlement found their way into an illegal operation to manufacture and distribute synthetic marijuana. To add yet another dollop of absurdity to the tale, some of the clients for whom Ford won $42 million later sued her for allowing the statute of limitations to expire by a single day on a closely related and bizarre lawsuit.

The scheme by Gallion, Cunningham, Mills, and Chesley was breathtaking in its audacity and scope. Tens of millions of dollars were pocketed in a manner that was transparently wrong. Their attempt to keep upward of $95 million that rightfully belonged to their clients was one of the largest thefts in American history. Millions remain unrecovered to this day. One member of a later judicial tribunal described their behavior as "a tale worthy of the pen of Charles Dickens, alas this story is not fiction."[18] Readers, too, will need to remind themselves that this book is a work of nonfiction.

Along with the undisputed perfidies described, this book presents evidence of an even more massive conspiracy directly tied to the Kentucky class action. The blemishes in our justice system are particularly ugly in Kentucky. Those who occupy the bench in the Bluegrass State are too often elected because of their ability to garner campaign contributions rather than their competence. This unfortunate circumstance is exacerbated by a system of judicial oversight that allows judges to be monitored by well-acquainted peers, rather than neutral investigators dedicated to that sole purpose.

Sadly, this is a story packed with villains but nearly devoid of heroes. The company that made the drugs and the physicians who prescribed them were careless. The echocardiogram mills and tort attorneys that sought to capitalize on the drugs' health dangers were greedy. Significant numbers of the so-called victims were also out to game the system.

This book will both disgust and amuse. Readers will find passages that make them shake their heads in revulsion and others that make them laugh out loud. And it's all true.

1

A Prescription for Disaster

IN THE 1932 NOVEL *BRAVE NEW WORLD,* Aldous Huxley warns of a future run amok, of a society trapped in a Faustian bargain whereby the dignity of humanity in its natural state is exchanged for the beguiling comforts of palliative drugs. In at least one significant aspect, Huxley's dystopian classic was a harbinger of things to come. In the same decade as its publication, scientists learned how to synthesize psychotropic chemicals to regulate selected neurotransmitters in the human nervous system, in particular, dopamine and serotonin. After passing the minute synapses between neurons, these neurotransmitters temporarily flood the neocortex, carrying the power to ease melancholy, calm anxiety, and induce euphoria.

Certain refined and fabricated substances used to excite or repress neurotransmitters are so powerful that the government prohibits their production and sale; these include cocaine, heroin, speed, fentanyl, and ecstasy. Other less efficacious mood-altering drugs such as Xanax, Prozac, Ativan, and Lexapro, which also stimulate neurotransmitters, may be legally prescribed. But they all do essentially the same thing.

One of the first legal neurotransmitter agents created in a laboratory was phentermine. This substance triggers the release of dopamine throughout the brain's cortex, inducing the sensation of euphoric contentment. In the 1960s fenfluramine, another synthetic mood-altering chemical, was introduced. Fenfluramine elevates serotonin levels, bolstering the user's sense of well-being and confidence. Because these drugs also suppress the desire for food, they were believed to be safe and effective medications for weight loss, and eventually, the US Food and Drug Administration (FDA) approved both drugs for this purpose—phentermine in 1959 and fenfluramine in 1973. However, neither became popular in the United States. People using phentermine complained of the unpleasant side effects of sleeplessness and the jitters. Conversely, fenfluramine, which was eventually marketed as Pondimin, caused users to experience drowsiness and nausea.

The eureka moment occurred in 1983 when Michael Weintraub, a research pharmacologist at the University of Rochester, was struck by an inspiration while stranded at an iced-in Kansas City airport. Weintraub postulated that by combining the two drugs, each medication would essentially counterbalance the unpleasant side effects of the other. Drug company A. H. Robbins, which owned the license for Pondimin (the sales of which had become moribund), eventually commissioned Weintraub to test his serendipitous insight. Robbins already boasted a number of popular household products, including Robitussin cough syrup and ChapStick.

Weintraub's four-year study, partially funded by the National Institutes of Health (NIH), determined that subjects given the fenfluramine and phentermine cocktail, in combination with diet and exercise, lost an average of thirty-four pounds in eight months. This was three times the weight loss experienced by a control group that received placebos. Because the two drugs were administered in relatively low doses, the subjects in the experimental group did not suffer symptoms of withdrawal after the medications were discontinued. Weintraub's inspiration would soon be known as "fen-phen," a neologism formed by combining the first syllables of the drugs' names. Since both drugs had already been approved as diet medications, no further FDA approval was necessary.

Although Weintraub's study was concluded in 1988, for unknown reasons that later baffled reporters and attorneys, its findings were not published until 1992. The circumstances behind the study's eventual publication are murky as well. The study appeared as a special supplement to the May issue of *Clinical Pharmacology and Therapeutics* under the title "Long-Term Weight Control Study." This was highly unusual, making it likely that some person or corporate interest had paid for the extra printing costs. The NIH grant had already expired, and it is unlikely that Weintraub had the money to cover the costs. Although a pay-for-play arrangement with the journal was only alleged, it is clear that A. H. Robbins had much to gain from the study's publication. Later, a spokesperson for the journal refused to reveal the name of the benefactor, and although Weintraub recalled that the funds came from the "industry," he was unable to remember how much was paid or by whom.[1]

In an interview with the *Washington Post,* Arthur Frank, director of George Washington University's obesity management program, told a reporter, "The bonanza for drug companies could amount to a quintillion-dollar industry."[2] This statement, though hyperbolic, expressed the general excitement at A. H. Robbins. In fact, prospects were so good that Robbins was soon acquired by the pharmaceutical giant American Home Products (AHP). AHP already carried an impressive array of drugs, including America's most popular over-the-counter analgesic, Advil. AHP possessed the financial wherewithal to market fen-phen to a wide population.

According to Patrice Boussel, AHP's history dates to 1860, when John and Frank Wyeth opened a drugstore and a small research facility. Stuart Wyeth, John's only son, became president of the company in 1907. Upon Stuart's death in 1929, a controlling share of stock was donated to Harvard University. One year later, Harvard sold Wyeth to American Home Products, establishing AHP as a manufacturer of pharmaceuticals in addition to its many other products, which included Black Flag insecticide and Easy Off oven cleaner. AHP established a penicillin research facility in 1941, and by 1944, it had developed the technology to mass-produce this drug—the first effective means of controlling deadly infections. That same year, AHP began producing estrogen tablets that would later become the birth control pill. During World War II the company shipped sulfa drugs, plasma, quinine, and vaccines to the military. Over the next several decades, AHP continued to grow into a hegemon. Throughout this period, AHP intentionally kept a low profile and was wryly dubbed Anonymous Home Products by industry analysts.[3]

The potential demand for a pill that made losing weight relatively effortless was vast. The contemporary association between slenderness and beauty was succinctly phrased by Wallis Simpson, wife of the former Edward VIII, who renounced the throne of the United Kingdom for her: "You can never be too rich or too thin." The Western aversion to being overweight is nothing new. An old English proverb declares, "Gluttony kills more than the sword." In the *Divine Comedy,* Dante ranks gluttony as the second of the seven deadly sins.

In the early medieval period, because of ineffective agricultural practices and the collapse of the road system after the fall of the Roman Empire, most Europeans were ragged and hungry. Beginning in the early twentieth century, humankind's ability to produce food exploded. Thanks to technological advances such as the Haber-Bosch process, which collects nitrogen, a critical nutrient, from the atmosphere, humankind can now distill sufficient amounts of digestible caloric compounds from sunlight and the elements to render 1.9 billion adults living on the planet either overweight or obese.

In 1994 the *New York Times* reported that the portion of obese Americans had increased from one-fourth to one-third within a single decade.[4] A 2018 report by the US Centers for Disease Control and Prevention (CDC) determined that 70.7 percent of American adults were overweight or obese.[5] How did Americans grow so fat so fast?

The 1980s witnessed a boom in low-fat and fat-free "diet" foods; unfortunately, low fat does not equate to low calorie. For example, Swedish Fish, a product consisting primarily of sugar, corn syrup, cornstarch, red dye #40, and wax, is advertised as a "fat-free food." According to the nutrition label, a single forty-piece bag contains 60 grams of sugar and 60 milligrams of sodium. These translucent morsels are no more food than they are fish.

As the maker and distributor of fen-phen, American Home Products was not alone in seeking to capitalize on the perceived deleterious health consequences of being overweight. According to *New York Times* reporter Edward Wyatt, weight-loss products are a $66 billion industry. Unfortunately, many of the pills, potions, and powders that claim to melt away the pounds are scams. In fact, 13 percent of the fraud claims registered with the Federal Trade Commission involve diet products, more than double the claims in any other category.[6]

Foremost among the propagators of weight-loss flummery is television celebrity Dr. Mehmet Oz, who is also a top heart surgeon and director of Columbia University's Cardiovascular Institute. About the same time Oz was appointed director of the institute, the university launched its Center for Complementary and Alternative Medicine. Oz, whose wife is a Reiki master (the practice of touching the body with the hands to strengthen energy fields), saw this as a green light to merge medicine with metaphysics. This included inviting parapsychologists into his operating room to redirect life energies as he opened patients' chests and performed surgery on human hearts.

As related by author Kurt Anderson in his 2018 book *Fantasyland,* Oz caught the attention of fellow New Ager Oprah Winfrey and appeared on her daytime talk show dozens of times, often wearing surgical scrubs. With Winfrey's media masterstroke, these appearances were soon spun off as *The Dr. Oz Show,* where Oz gives advice on such topics as homeopathy, the channeling of cosmic energies, and necromancy. Unquestionably the most popular topics on *The Dr. Oz Show* are diets and weight-loss drugs, and it is in this realm that Anderson describes Oz as a "dispenser of make-believe."[7] Some of the many dubious diet products that Oz has shilled are the "amazing" weight-loss properties of the chlorogenic acids found in green coffee beans; Garcinia Cambogia, a "fat-busting" tropical fruit; and Raspberry Ketone, a "miracle fat burner in a bottle."

The path to stardom for "America's doctor" has not been an uninterrupted string of praise. The *Huffington Post* reported that "ten physicians penned a letter to Columbia University's dean of medicine calling for the University to oust Dr. Mehmet Oz." The doctors accused Oz of "manifesting an egregious lack of integrity by promoting quack treatments and cures in the interest of personal financial gain."[8] At a June 2014 congressional hearing on health and science, Missouri senator Claire McCaskill charged that Oz gave viewers "false hope" while promoting weight-loss products he knew to be ineffective. McCaskill pointedly remarked, "The scientific community is almost monolithically against you [Oz]."[9]

Showman P. T. Barnum famously declared, "There's a sucker born every minute." Barnum had only posters and carnival barkers to reel in his hapless marks. Today's purveyors of make-believe have television, the Internet, Facebook, and Twitter. In the time it takes to read this paragraph, hundreds more suckers will have been taken in.

In recent decades, Americans have spiraled into a vortex of self-loathing as the gulf between society's ideal body image and the reality in their mirrors grew wider. A study commissioned by the US Department of Health and Human Services found that "91% of all women are unhappy with their bodies and resort to dieting." The study also found that fear of fat is transmitted to children at a young age: "81% of 10-year-olds are afraid of being fat."[10] Consequently, the annual revenue of the weight-loss industry is a whopping $66 billion.[11] Thus, a pill that promised to help Americans shed unwanted pounds without the sacrifice of self-denial seemed like deliverance in a bottle.

But obesity alone was not sufficient for the medical community and the government to place its imprimatur on AHP's solution. Many skeptics remained. Typically, animal studies are performed first to test the safety of a drug, but Weintraub's study used human subjects, and he was focused exclusively on weight loss, not safety. Some researchers were concerned that during Weintraub's study the fen-phen combination had been administered for much longer periods than recommended by the FDA.

Harry Brandt, director of the Mercy Center for Eating Disorders in Baltimore, was an early critic of Weintraub. Brandt determined that the fen-phen study suffered from a very high subject dropout rate and led to weight gain among those who remained on the drug regimen during the entire four-year study. Brandt warned that fen-phen "was one of the worst developments in the care of people with obesity. . . these are not benign medications."[12]

To counter these threats to fen-phen's financial potential, AHP decided to market the drug in the context of obesity as pandemic. To prove this claim, AHP found willing clinicians at various public health agencies and universities to ring the alarm about the dire health consequences of being overweight. In March 1985 *Science* magazine carried the cover story "Obesity Declared a Disease." This seminal article, based on a study by the National Center for Health Statistics, warned that obesity was associated with a wide array of ailments, including hypertension, heart disease, arthritis, cancer, gallstones, and gout.[13]

The panic was turned up a notch when the CDC declared in 2001 that obesity-related ailments were killing 300,000 Americans a year. Dr. Xavier

Pi-Sunyer of St. Luke's Hospital in New York stated, "There is no reason to treat it [obesity] any differently than you would treat diabetes or high blood pressure . . . there is a new realization that obesity is a disease." Philip Lee, assistant secretary of the Department of Health and Human Services, solemnly intoned that the "government was not doing enough."[14]

In stark contrast to the death-by-food alarmists, Sylvia Tara, a biochemist and author of *The Secret Life of Fat,* states that our body's fat "secretes essential hormones . . . keeps us safe from disease, and may even help us live longer." Fat, in fact, produces the hormone adiponectin, which removes glucose, toxic lipids, and fat molecules from the bloodstream. According to Tara, doctors refer to the phenomenon of being fat *and* healthy as the "obesity paradox."[15]

While it is true that obesity is associated with many of the maladies described in the CDC study, association is not synonymous with causation. Simply said, the foods and lifestyles that can make us sick also happen to make us fat. Fat, in and of itself, is largely benign.

Gregg Fonarow of UCLA reported that having a higher body mass index (BMI) was associated with a substantially lower in-hospital mortality rate. In fact, for every 5 percent unit increase in body mass, the odds of dying decreased 10 percent.[16] Katherine Flegal, an epidemiologist at the CDC, combed through hundreds of studies comparing rates of early death to body mass index and concluded that Americans who fell into the categories of overweight to mildly obese had the lowest levels of premature death.[17] Although the widely held belief that Americans were digging their own graves with knives and forks appeared to be overstated, it is a stone-cold fact that no one wants to be fat and dieting is no picnic.

A 1990 Gallup poll titled "Mirror of America" found that 62 percent of women and 42 percent of men wanted to lose weight, but only 18 percent were doing so—results that had remained relatively unchanged for forty years.[18] The Sisyphean effort of dieting is almost always a failure, resulting in the return of every pound lost, plus more, within five years. As metabolism gradually slows with age, the pounds pile on, even with the same caloric intake. The average person burns 900,000 calories each year.[19] A metabolic slowdown of only ten calories per day results in a weight gain of one pound per year. Such grim biological facts make permanent weight loss seem well-nigh impossible.

Fen-phen was hardly the first chemical solution for weight control. In the 1950s and 1960s the answer was amphetamines. Benzedrine was first developed by American scientist Gordon Alles in 1928. The drug works by flooding the nervous system with dopamine, the same neurotransmitter released after sexual orgasm. Amphetamines were effective for weight loss but were also problematic. The FDA approved Obetrol, produced by Richwood Pharmaceuticals based in Florence, Kentucky, as a weight-loss drug in 1960. The 10-milligram dose was canary colored, like the "little yellow pill" in the Rolling Stones' song "Mother's Little Helper." Obetrol was also the drug of choice of pop artist Andy Warhol. Because of its recreational applications, it was only a matter of time before the federal government declared the drug illegal. Accordingly, Richwood reformulated Obetrol by removing methamphetamine from the recipe and renamed the resultant drug Adderall. Today, it is widely prescribed for children, mostly boys, diagnosed with attention-deficit disorders and is manufactured by the ton.

Despite the momentous potential of a diet drug without the negative effects of amphetamines, the initial public reaction to fen-phen was less than stellar, and sales were disappointing. Frustration turned to exhilaration in February 1995 when the fashion magazine *Allure* published "The Pill Seekers," an article about the nascent popularity of fen-phen. After the *Allure* article was reprinted in *Reader's Digest,* millions of Americans began to clamor for the miraculous drug. Regarding the resurgence of medication-assisted weight loss, Kelly Brownell, a Yale University psychologist, commented, "We went through a down period of 15 years when people did not consider drugs for obesity because of the amphetamine experience . . . [but] drugs are here to stay."[20]

To take advantage of the opportunity created by the *Allure* article, AHP launched a $21 million "1996 tactical plan" that included more than a thousand sales representatives who delivered copies of Weintraub's study to physicians' offices and the pressrooms of major newspapers.[21] In addition, cash grants to the American Diabetes Association, American Academy of Family Physicians, American Association for Obesity, and American Society of Bariatric Physicians helped cultivate the support of practicing physicians. Academia was also heavily recruited in AHP's public-relations onslaught.[22]

The exploitation of scientific journals for financial gain is not uncommon. A publication from the Hastings Center, a bioethics research institute, noted that the distinction between health care research and marketing has become nonexistent. To underscore that point, the author cited an article in the *New England Journal of Medicine* by Dr. Troyen Brennan, the chief medical officer for CVS Health. Brennan reported that he had been offered $2,500 to write an editorial for a peer-reviewed medical journal on behalf of a pharmaceutical company.[23]

The warnings of a smattering of skeptical scientists were quickly brushed away by AHP, which was eager to reap maximum profits as soon as possible. Its haste was driven by a fly in the ointment—the twenty-year patents on fenfluramine and phentermine had already lapsed. Within a few years, cheap generic knockoffs of the drugs would flood the market.

Even worse, the French pharmaceutical manufacturer Laboratories Servier had developed a new and refined version of fenfluramine for weight reduction. Fenfluramine has two components: dexfenfluramine and levofenfluramine. Servier had stripped out the levofenfluramine, creating a new patentable drug. Beginning in 1994, dexfenfluramine was marketed in Europe as a weight-loss drug under the name Isomeride. This new product would be introduced in the United States by Richard Wurtman, an enterprising professor at the Massachusetts Institute of Technology (MIT).

Wurtman had been monitoring developments in France with rapt and rapacious interest for some time. While majoring in philosophy at the University of Pennsylvania, Wurtman had become fascinated with the mind-body relationship, leading him to enroll at Harvard Medical School after graduating from Penn. Subsequently, Wurtman and his wife, Judith, became researchers at MIT, where they studied the relationship between mood and the consumption of carbohydrates. The Wurtmans' joint study, published in the January 1989 issue of *Scientific American,* closely monitored the total caloric intake of subjects with moderate to morbid obesity.[24] Their food intake was measured throughout the day during meals, and they had access to a specially designed snack machine that contained a selection of items divided between high-protein snacks and high-carbohydrate snacks that had relatively equal amounts of fat and calories. Contrary to popular assumptions, people with obesity tended not to overconsume at meals but used the snack machine often, especially in the late afternoon and early evening. The Wurtmans found a positive correlation between the consumption of high-carbohydrate snacks and weight above the ideal. During interviews, the subjects self-reported that their hankering for high-carbohydrate snacks was not merely to appease hunger but also to relieve stress and anxiety—which explains why, after a romantic breakup, spurned lovers are more likely to console themselves with a pint of Ben and Jerry's than a can of tuna.

There is a scientific explanation: Carbohydrates produce tryptophan, which, through a complex process, produces serotonin. Serotonin relieves stress and anxiety. For many, the relief is fleeting; as postsynaptic neurons absorb (uptake) the soothing serotonin, the brain is triggered to demand more carbohydrates, in the form of cravings. The Wurtmans concluded that if the uptake of serotonin could be blocked, its palliative effects would be extended, the feedback loop would be repressed, and the desire to consume even more carbohydrates would be diminished. Dexfenfluramine, with its powerful serotonin-enhancing qualities, appeared to offer a perfect, and patentable, solution.

Although Servier was interested in manufacturing dexfenfluramine for consumption in the United States, for whatever reason, it did not wish to market the product. That role would be assumed by Interneuron Pharmaceuticals, a company cofounded by prominent Wall Street investment banker J. Morton Davis and Richard Wurtman. Armed with a variety of studies on dexfenfluramine and, in particular, a study conducted in the Netherlands showing the drug's efficacy in reducing depression (and presumably carbohydrate intake) among people with obesity, Interneuron was ready to jump to the next level with its new drug, christened Redux.

Interneuron need to find a pharmaceutical company that would help its new drug negotiate the FDA labyrinth leading to approval. Although AHP seemed an obvious choice, Wurtman feared that AHP would continue to favor fen-phen, so Interneuron partnered with Lederle Laboratories instead. Lederle was part of a much larger conglomerate, American Cyanamid—a

Fortune 500 company with a sprawling product line that ran the gamut from animal feed additives to plastic resins to Old Spice cologne. Then in 1994, much to the dismay of Wurtman, American Cyanamid merged with AHP in what was at the time the second largest merger in US history. AHP sold off many of the Cyanamid subsidiaries, but it retained Lederle, bringing the rival formulas under the same roof.

Rather than picking a favorite, AHP decided to promote both drugs, at least for the time being. However, Redux still required FDA approval, and AHP was determined to leave no stone unturned in this effort. It wanted to corner the diet drug market.

2

Cashing In

THE FEDERAL GOVERNMENT'S DUTY to protect Americans from ineffective and dangerous medicines dates to the Food, Drug, and Cosmetic Act of 1938. This law created the Food and Drug Administration and imbued it with the authority to review the safety of all new drugs before they can be marketed. Considering the many thousands of medications developed since that time, protecting the public from their potentially harmful effects is a massive responsibility. Perhaps the most tragic example of the FDA's failure to adequately vet a new drug was thalidomide, used to ease morning sickness in pregnant women. It was eventually discovered that thalidomide caused birth defects, some quite severe, in an estimated 100,000 children in the early 1960s.

The desire to avert other such disasters led the FDA to create an exacting multiphase approval process involving both animal and human trials that can take as long as twelve years. However, as part of the 1993 Prescription User Free Act, pharmaceutical companies were allowed access to an expedited process known as the "fast track." The fast track allows medications that are necessary to treat "serious, unmet medical needs" to undergo a far more concentrated and expeditious approval process, granting manufacturers permission to skip human trials and replace them with postmarketing monitoring. Needless to say, the fast track also allows products to roll out, and profits to roll in, much faster.

American Home Products immediately sought a fast-track designation for Redux. The Centers for Disease Control had already warned that more than 300,000 overweight Americans were dying every year. AHP would use this statistic to insist that there was not a moment to spare.

Regardless of whether there was actually an unmet medical need for a new weight-loss drug, the likelihood of AHP obtaining FDA approval to fast-track Redux was uncertain. The arguments on both sides of the issue were virtually in equilibrium. In the end, the decision by the FDA Advisory Panel to recommend the fast-track designation was influenced by a series of wildly unusual events.[1] The pro-Redux contingent repeated the "obesity is a disease" mantra, insisting that obesity was killing hundreds of thousands of Americans annually and that the deadly carnage would become worse with each passing year. The Redux critics argued that the drug was a powerful psychotropic with associated hazards that outweighed any benefits.

Among Redux's detractors was Lewis Seiden, a pharmacologist at the University of Chicago. He testified before the FDA panel that after Redux was discontinued in animal tests, serotonin levels fell precipitously and remained low for extended periods. In addition, even a moderate overdose of Redux could damage or even destroy the neurons that produce serotonin.

In an interview for *Time* magazine, Dr. George Ricaurte of Johns Hopkins University stated that dexfenfluramine (Redux) was like the party drug ecstasy and "produced long-lasting toxic effects to the brain."[2] Ricaurte's research found that animals given slightly higher doses of Redux than those prescribed for humans suffered extensive brain damage consisting of the destruction of nerve fibers that convey serotonin to the brain. In humans, the absence of serotonin could plunge the unfortunate victims into deep and possibly permanent depression.

An additional warning was issued by Dr. Lewis J. Rubin of the University of Maryland Medical Center. He linked Redux to primary pulmonary hypertension (PPH), a particularly nasty condition in which the small arteries of the lungs become thick and constricted, increasing the internal pressure in the lungs; this, in turn, causes the heart to enlarge as it works harder to circulate blood, leading to fluid buildup. In most cases, patients become increasingly debilitated. In severe cases, lung transplants are necessary to avoid heart failure. PPH was initially reported in Europeans who had taken dexfenfluramine for six months or longer.[3] Because PPH is idiopathic, meaning of unknown origin, the ingestion of Redux could not be ruled out as a cause.

The risk-benefit trade-off was appreciably narrowed as it became evident that Redux was not the magic bullet it purported to be. As reported by CenterWatch, an online provider of clinical trial analysis, a yearlong study of 900 patients found that 64 percent of dieters who took Redux experienced a 5 percent weight loss, compared with 43 percent who attained the same weight loss using diet and exercise alone. Later, the *Journal of the American Medical Association* found that fen-phen and Redux resulted in only moderate weight loss that plateaued after six months.[4] In addition, during one of the first lawsuits against AHP, the lawyer for the plaintiff shared the results of a twelve-month study conducted by AHP itself, which found only a 3 percent difference in weight in the group taking Redux versus those taking a placebo.

The fast-track approval showdown took place on April 24, 1995, on the FDA's sprawling campus in Silver Spring, Maryland. If the panel recommended fast-track status, this would lead to swift FDA approval for Redux to enter the market as an effective and safe weight-control medication. Unfortunately for AHP, the possibility of brain damage and PPH, combined with its questionable efficacy, was sufficient for the panel to refuse to recommend fast-track status for Redux by a vote of five to three.

But the fight was far from over. According to an article that appeared in the *Wall Street Journal*, the pro-Redux contingent in the room stormed out but later regrouped and buttonholed one of the panel members who had voted no.[5] Although a switch of one vote would not have changed the outcome, panel chair James Bilstad, an FDA official, tried to reopen the discussion a few hours later, claiming that the panel member had misunderstood the question of whether Redux should receive fast-track status. However, three members had already left, and the panel now lacked a quorum. Dr. Bilstad decided to reschedule the discussion for another date to clear up any "ambiguity."

Conveniently for AHP and Interneuron, the next scheduled meeting in November had more members in attendance, but it also coincided with a neurosciences conference in San Diego that was attended by two of the anti-Redux voters on the panel. Most critically, panel members at the November meeting did not have an opportunity to hear the oral testimony of several Redux critics, including Dr. Seiden. To tip the scales even further in its favor, the newest member of Interneuron's board of directors, General Alexander Haig, worked the room prior to the hearing and the vote.[6] Haig had served three Republican presidents: Richard Nixon, Gerald Ford, and Ronald Reagan. He is best remembered for his attempt to reassure the public after the attempted assassination of President Reagan by John Hinckley, when Haig announced to reporters: "I am in control here." Haig's glowering countenance as he stared into the eyes of panel members was sufficiently unsettling to help win their acquiescence.

To convey the impression of bipartisanship, Interneuron also asked Senator Edward Kennedy to take an active role in promoting Redux's fast-track designation. Since Interneuron's corporate headquarters was in Lexington, Massachusetts, the Democrat's home state, Kennedy was happy to oblige. He worked the phones and persuaded seven of his congressional colleagues to join him in urging the FDA to approve Redux. Ralph Nader's organization, Public Citizen, found itself in the unusual position of opposing the Liberal Lion of the Senate as it fought the approval of Redux. One of Public Citizen's attorneys acidly remarked, "We expected more from Senator Kennedy."[7]

The panel's recommendation for fast-track status came on November 16, 1995, by the wafer-thin margin of six to five. The following day, one member tried to change his vote after talking with his son, a cardiologist, who scolded him, "Father, you have made a terrible mistake. This drug will kill people."[8] But the decision was final, and in April 1996 Redux received full FDA approval.

This marked the first approval of a diet drug in more than twenty years. Redux was also the first weight-loss medication approved for long-term use. Overnight, Interneuron's stock shot up 24 percent, increasing the value of cofounder Richard Wurtman's holdings by $1.68 million. Estimated sales at the time were $600 million. Interneuron's chief executive, Dr. Glenn L. Cooper, described the Advisory Committee's recommendation as a milestone, noting that Redux was now positioned to become the first obesity drug approved for long-term use in this country.[9]

Others considered the connivance to obtain FDA approval as a milestone in perfidy. In the December 1997 issue of *Life Enhancement Magazine*, the publisher questioned the genuineness of Wurtman's concern for obesity by pointing out his opposition to the now ubiquitous aspartame (NutraSweet). Wurtman had earlier supported the sweetener, the implication being that his about-face had been driven by personal business interests.[10]

The people charged with keeping the public safe can sometimes be beguiled by the prospect of earning much bigger bucks in the private sector. Lucrative job offers from pharmaceutical companies were more likely to accrue to those FDA officials who were not too exacting. Dr. Gerald Faich, an FDA employee at the time Redux was approved, piously remarked, "The last thing I'd want to do is deprive people of a drug that has a much larger chance of doing more good than harm." Faich was later hired as a spokesperson for AHP.[11]

Michael Weintraub, the man who first conceived of fen-phen, was hired by the FDA as director of oversight for over-the-counter medications. Despite his scholarly, drab appearance, Weintraub became a figure of cultish admiration at the FDA. In 1998, after just five years, Weintraub resigned and became a consultant to Advantage Weight Control, a string of weight-loss clinics based in Florida. The corporate officers of Advantage used Weintraub's name and connections to their own advantage. According to a September 1999 story by the Associated Press, Weintraub promoted fen-phen before a state medical panel, and on at least one occasion he reportedly wrote referral letters for an Advantage-affiliated marketing consultant using FDA letterhead.[12]

With both fen-phen and Redux approved for sale, AHP hired the international firm Burson-Marsteller to create a marketing strategy. By the 1990s, Burson-Marsteller had branches in twenty-eight countries on five continents and employed a workforce of 2,300. In addition to selling products, Burson-Marsteller deftly handled a host of public-relations (PR) calamities, including the Three Mile Island nuclear meltdown, the Tylenol poisonings, Union Carbide's Bhopal chemical disaster, and New Coke. In time, the firm's skills at damage control would be tested by AHP.

Burson-Marsteller counseled AHP to stress the "obesity is a disease" mantra. Accordingly, AHP salted a variety of advocacy organizations with large grants to garner their support, or at least their silence. These organizations included the American Academy of Family Physicians, the American Diabetes Association, the North American Society for the Study of Obesity, and the American Society of Bariatric Physicians. AHP also jumped on board the "Shape Up America" campaign, contributing $700,000 in support of Surgeon General C. Everett Koop's initiative.

AHP also hired Excerpta Medica, a Dutch firm specializing in medical communications, to solicit articles for medical journals at $20,000 apiece to promote drug-assisted obesity treatments. The doctors who lent their names to the publications received $1,500 honoraria. AHP retained ultimate editorial control, which it used to scrub the final products of any negativity related to fen-phen or Redux. In one example, AHP had Excerpta strike a sentence from a draft article that read, "individual case reports also suggest a link between dexfenfluramine and primary pulmonary hypertension." Among the publications in which Excerpta placed pro–diet drug studies were the *American Journal of Cardiology* and the *American Journal of Surgery*. Eventually, Dr. Robert Tenery, chairman of the American Medical Association's (AMA's) Council on Ethical and Judicial Affairs, called Excerpta out on these and other scientific inaccuracies. Tenery remarked to a reporter, "What they're doing is clearly an advertisement. But it is couched in a scientifically valid paper."[13]

The results of Excerpta's PR blitz were spectacular. More than 700,000 prescriptions were written in 1995, which represented a 90 percent increase over 1994. Demand was so great that the fenfluramine portion of the two-tablet cocktail was in short supply from January through October 1995. By 1996, the problem was resolved, and more than 18 million prescriptions were written for the fen-phen combination. The *Washington Post* predicted that annual sales of fen-phen would be at least $220 million in 1997 and projected that this would quadruple the following year.[14] Long-established weight-loss programs such as Nutrisystem decided it was better to switch than fight and established NutriRx, dispensing the two medications along with its usual packaged foods.

Wall Street analysts reported that the potential sales for Redux and fen-phen were "off the charts." AHP's profits reached nearly $180 million. At the peak of their popularity, 200,000 prescriptions for both diet drugs were being written each week.

Both fenfluramine and phentermine had long been FDA approved as diet medications, but because they were classified as Schedule III drugs and were being prescribed in combination, and thus in a manner considered "off label," states had the authority to control how they were prescribed. As defined by the Controlled Substances Act, there are five levels of scheduled drugs. Schedule I drugs, such as heroin and LSD, are considered to have no therapeutic value and may not be prescribed. All others are available by prescription with varying levels of caution, based on their potential for abuse. Schedule III drugs are considered to have a moderate potential for abuse. In some states, cautious health officials withheld approval of fen-phen and Redux in part or in whole.

In Indiana, fen-phen was approved but could be prescribed for a maximum of 30 days; Ohio limited prescriptions to 14 weeks; and in Kentucky, prescriptions were not to exceed 120 days. This led to the creation of several physicians' offices dedicated to the prescription of fen-phen in northern Kentucky, such as the Riverfront Diet Clinic in Covington. In Tennessee, which shares a 300-mile border with Kentucky, sale of the drug combination was outright forbidden.

Kentucky physicians were cautioned not to overprescribe, but as Ed Crews, director of the Drug Control Branch of the Kentucky Health Service, lamented, the state's lack of the necessary computer monitoring systems meant that it didn't "have the sales figures for controlled substances."[15] Thus, oversight and enforcement in the Bluegrass State were lax, and over time, the recommended prescription limitation would become even more lenient.

That Kentucky was one of the states with the fewest restrictions was not surprising. Two-thirds of its population was either overweight or obese. AHP considered Kentucky a rich target, as the percentage of obese Kentuckians had doubled in the past decade.

Among the reasons for Kentuckians' obesity is their striking lack of exercise. A 2009 publication of the Partnership for a Fit Kentucky found that "Kentucky is the fourth most sedentary state in the nation" and "more than two thirds of Kentucky adults are overweight or obese."[16] Kentuckians also have terrible diets. They consume snack food and fast food in epic proportions. They drink so much soda, especially in eastern Kentucky, that it has led to a dental epidemic known as "Mountain Dew mouth." Not surprisingly, some of the nation's most notorious calorie bombs are named for the Bluegrass State. The all-you-can-eat KFC luncheon buffet remains a popular choice for the morbidly obese. The proprietary Derby Pie (named for the Kentucky Derby) and its many knockoffs are based on the holy trinity of southern cuisine—eggs, butter, and sugar—with the addition of chocolate chips and nuts; these pies are sold by the hundreds of thousands. And, of course, there's the Kentucky Hot Brown, a concoction consisting of two slices of thick buttered toast, cheese sauce, and slabs of ham and sliced turkey, topped with several strips of bacon and more cheese.

Because fen-phen sales were restricted in bordering states, AHP enjoyed great sales in Kentucky not only from its own overfed residents but also from the many thousands who traveled from Indiana, Ohio, and Tennessee. Although advertising for the diet drug was restricted in Kentucky, enterprising doctors at the Diet Clinic of Louisville circumvented that restriction by changing "fen-phen" to "phen-fen" in its ads in the *Louisville Courier-Journal*. As word of mouth spread, Kentucky became the epicenter of fen-phen sales in a huge portion of the Ohio Valley. For instance, Mount Vernon, Kentucky, is just off Interstate 75, which runs south to Knoxville, Tennessee. Mount Vernon boasted a population of just 2,500, yet by the end of 1996, Dr. James Cunningham of the Mount Vernon Weight Loss Clinic was actively treating about 1,500 patients with fen-phen.

One string of weight-loss clinics in Kentucky owned by Dr. Rex Duff were particularly efficient operations. Patients were charged $85 for the initial office visit, which included a prescription; follow-up visits were $60 apiece, likewise including drugs. By some estimates, an astonishing 60,000 patients were served by Duff's clinics. AHP shipped the drugs to Duff's offices, where they were sold directly to eager patients, bypassing pharmacies altogether. This practice also kept pharmacists from warning their customers of the drugs' potential side effects.

Cashing In

Duff started his operation innocently enough. As a trusted, longtime family physician in Ashland, Duff was on the verge of retirement when he began to see fen-phen patients, generally after regular office hours. These patients were shown a video about the drugs and received a physical examination that included a blood pressure reading and check of the heart and lungs; then Duff would prescribe the drugs. His Ashland operation proved to be so popular that he opened a second clinic. One of Duff's patients, fifty-three-year old Reverend Jerry Gumm, made the improbable claim to a reporter for the *Lexington Herald-Leader* that he had lost seventy-five pounds in three weeks. As word of this miraculous success spread, Dr. Duff's bariatric clinics did too, soon totaling eight in all.

As the number of Duff's patients grew into the thousands, it became obvious that, as a single practitioner, Duff would not be able to purchase enough malpractice insurance to cover potential liabilities. AHP therefore agreed to assume responsibility for any damages related to the prescriptions Duff wrote. Once the doctor was given this blank check, the medical examinations at his clinics became more desultory. Eventually, the Kentucky Board of Medical Licensure took action to permanently suspend Duff's license to practice medicine for "improperly prescribing the weight loss drug phentermine (phen)," charging that he "failed to adequately monitor his patients and engaged in a uniform or rote approach to the treatment of his patients."[17] Duff would later be arrested for disorderly conduct after screaming and shaking his finger at a Greenup County deputy sheriff.

Many Kentucky pharmacists were also living large. In Monticello, the Daffron Pharmacy filled an average of sixty fen-phen prescriptions a day. Monticello is a town of 6,000 inhabitants within a few miles of the Tennessee border. Pharmacy owner Dan Daffron claimed that Monticello enjoyed more financial benefits from the Tennesseans who visited the many recently established diet drug clinics than from the tens of thousands of visitors who drove through Monticello on their way to nearby Lake Cumberland State Park each year. For those travelers who found their way to his pharmacy, Daffron thoughtfully provided maps showing the fastest route back to Nashville.[18]

In 1996 six new weight-loss centers opened in Lexington. The *Lexington Herald-Leader* reported that many physicians were happy to supplement the earnings from their medical practices with the easy money available through diet clinic operations. Anesthesiologist Efrim Moore opened a diet center in the summer of 1995, offering a "two patients for the price of one" special. Ronald Goble, a family practice physician, opened the Bluegrass Weight Loss Center and soon had three competitors on the same thoroughfare. One of these, the Beverly Hills Weight Loss Center, was operated by Dick Larumbe, a psychiatrist from Ashland, Kentucky.[19]

That same year, the Kentucky Board of Medical Licensure met to consider how to better manage the runaway phenomenon. Fen-phen sales were hot across the nation, but in Kentucky they were on fire. Diana Droz, a pharmacist with the Kentucky Cabinet for Health Services, concluded, "To me what's most significant is that sales tripled in Kentucky, while [in] the rest of the country they doubled . . . that's telling me what other states' laws are have influenced what's happening in Kentucky."[20] In a tepid effort to quell the demand, the board recommended that the drugs be prescribed only for persons with a body mass index (BMI) of 27 or higher (199 pounds for someone six feet tall). But soon the board would negate that easy-to-ignore guideline by essentially eliminating the time limit on prescriptions.

The board's December 18, 1996, decision to lift Kentucky's already generous 120-day limit was significantly influenced by the testimony of Dr. Matt Vuskovich, co-owner of the Medweight Weight Loss Clinic in Lexington. Droz introduced Vuskovich to the board as a "very, very ethical" practitioner. His business partner at Medweight, Jim Parsons, was a prominent organizer of fund-raising events for the state's Democratic Party.[21] Although they still controlled both the state legislature and the governor's office in 1996, Kentucky Democrats were entering the twilight of their political hegemony, and the party needed money, which opened plenty of doors in state government for Parsons. While Parsons worked the room, Vuskovich testified that obesity was a "disease." As reported in the *Lexington Herald-Leader,* the review panel approved the relaxation of the 120-day restriction. This approval was granted despite the concerns of Ed Crews, executive director of the Drug Control Branch, who warned that the drugs were being prescribed without adequate physical examinations, not to mention the fact that the FDA had issued guidelines advising physicians to limit administration of the drugs to 120 days. But the pressure from physicians and pharmacists was impossible for the board to resist.[22]

Dr. Vuskovich's pronouncement neatly encapsulated the argument for drug-assisted weight control. For the board to sanction the removal of the 120-day limit on fen-phen and Redux, it first had to accept the paradigm of obesity as a disease. This was not a particularly difficult argument to make at the time. The American Medical Association defines disease as an impairment of the normal functioning of some aspect of the body with characteristic signs or symptoms leading to harm or morbidity. In a published resolution, the AMA recognized obesity as a "disease state with multiple pathophysiological aspects requiring a range of interventions to advance obesity treatment and prevention."[23]

With the tacit go-ahead to prescribe these medications for indefinite periods, it became tantalizingly common for Kentucky physicians to provide them to patients who were not obese but wanted to drop a few pounds. The results could be deadly. On January 13, 1997, forty-five-year-old Mary Spurgas was found dead in her Nashville home. At the time of her death she weighed just 120 pounds and had a BMI less than 23, far below the recommended guidelines, especially for a person with diabetes.

In the ensuing investigation, several receipts as well as a canceled check dated January 4 issued to Arnold's Drug Company in Franklin, Kentucky, were found in Spurgas's residence. Pharmacist Jim Arnold claimed the receipts were in error and declined to discuss the matter. The prescriptions were traced to Dr. Michael Talbot, who worked for Diet Doctors Clinics in Franklin. Talbot, who had a medical practice in Gallatin, Tennessee, had recently obtained a medical license from the Kentucky Board of Medical Licensure after agreeing to abide by the board's recommendations on medical monitoring and BMI guidelines for the use of fen-phen and Redux. During a telephone interview from his Gallatin office, Talbot claimed that he worked in Franklin one evening a week, where he saw as many as forty of his fellow Tennesseans in as little as four hours. He denied any knowledge of Spurgas.[24]

The attorney for Spurgas's estate, Ralph Mello, filed a complaint with the Kentucky Board of Pharmacy. According to Mello, Spurgas had been hospitalized for complications of diabetes four times in the five months before her death. Two months after Spurgas's death, Dr. Talbot received a letter from the Kentucky Board of Medical Licensure congratulating him for complying with state regulations after being visited by a state regulator. Interestingly, Talbot had previously testified before the same medical board that had approved lifting the 120-day prescription limit, admitting that he saw his patients only every six months, ignoring the two-month guideline. Despite this clear confirmation of the concerns of the director of the Drug Control Branch, the board ignored this red flag. Kentucky's commissioner of public health told reporters that he had talked with political operative Jim Parsons "while the regulations were being drafted" and concluded that fen-phen was "only a minor problem."[25]

The diet clinic industry and the public regarded the BMI guidelines as a mere nuisance to be ignored, and they hailed the lifting of the 120-day restriction. The results were immediate and staggering. In Harlan County, an area of high unemployment and poverty in the southeastern corner of Kentucky, fen-phen prescriptions jumped from 98 in one twelve-month period to 3,893 the following year—an increase of more than 4,000 percent. For the same period, statewide prescriptions for fen-phen shot up from 84,049 to 258,480. The metropolitan areas of Kentucky experienced the frenzy as well. To keep up with daily demand, Lexington pharmacists resorted to prefilling prescriptions and lining the bottles up like rows of dominoes on dispensary tables before the start of business to keep up with the crush of eager customers.[26]

Elsewhere in the United States, fen-phen and Redux were also being prescribed to an increasing number of patients who were not clinically obese. This, of course, was contrary to the rationalization that had enabled the drugs to be approved in the first place. Jim Merker, executive director of the American Society of Bariatric Physicians, worried that the pills were being used by women who wanted to "get from a size 10 to a size 8."[27]

One woman in Massachusetts tried to do just that, with tragic consequences. Mary Linnen of Quincy took fen-phen so that she could fit into her wedding dress and died from a heart-lung disorder thought to be associated with the drugs. Her mother told a reporter, "Instead of walking down the aisle before the bride, I walked behind a casket."[28] Even Michael Weintraub began to worry about the irrational exuberance surrounding his innovation. By the time the music stopped, approximately 4 million people had taken fen-phen, and another 2 million had used Redux.

As sales continued to skyrocket, accounts of the negative health consequences of the diet drugs had not abated. Reports of primary pulmonary hypertension were continuing to arrive from Europe, where the drugs had been introduced years earlier. In 1996 the *New England Journal of Medicine* published an article based on these reports, which linked fenfluramine to a "23 times greater risk of PPH."[29]

The FDA raised the possibility of issuing a "black box warning" for fen-phen—the strictest warning that exists, implemented when there is "reasonable evidence for a serious hazard with a drug." After a review of the proposed language of the warning, AHP counterattacked with a pack of lobbyists armed with friendlier statistics. AHP took exception to the proposed statement that PPH "is invariably lethal," noting with cold comfort that 55 percent of those diagnosed with PPH could expect to live for at least four years.[30]

When Interneuron's stock fell from $44 per share to $28, based on this news, Richard Wurtman groused in an internal email: "Now everything is clear. The coordinated attack on Redux during the past few weeks is a conspiracy—led by fat women . . . to keep everyone fat."[31] Wurtman's rationalization was misleading. Mark Moliver of Johns Hopkins University and a former Harvard Medical School classmate said of Wurtman, "He refuses to listen to facts. And he's misrepresented what we have presented."[32]

Gerald Faich, the former FDA epidemiologist who had resigned to work for AHP, insisted that the risk of PPH was small or absent. Because of pressure from physicians and pharmacists who were profiting from the pills and patients who demanded that the government stay out of their health care decisions, the likelihood of an FDA warning grew more remote.

AHP and Interneuron assured stockholders that they could quash the prospect of a black box warning. Accordingly, stock prices leveled off and began to trend upward again. Unfortunately for AHP, this turnaround proved to be temporary. A fatal reckoning was about to be delivered from the lonely plains of North Dakota.

3

It Hits the Fan

WITH RECORD HIGH TEMPERATURES of 114 degrees and record lows of −48 degrees, residents of Fargo, North Dakota, must endure what is arguably the worst weather in the United States. So isolated that it doesn't even merit designation as a flyover state during cross-country flights, North Dakota seems an unlikely place for a seismic epidemiological discovery. Yet one of its inhabitants would initiate a cascade of events that would eventually cost AHP billions of dollars.

Beginning in December 1994, sonographer Pam Ruff of the MeritCare Medical Center noticed an increasing number of patients with alarming heart valve abnormalities. Heart valves function much like the valves in an internal combustion engine, which open and close to allow gas to be drawn into a piston, compressed, and ignited, thus creating a force that is sufficient to power a vehicle. In the human heart, valves allow blood to be drawn into a chamber, where it is compressed through muscle contractions and ultimately released by another valve to circulate through the body. When the valves in a human heart no longer close tightly, the individual experiences fatigue and eventually incapacity. If seriously malfunctioning heart valves are not replaced, death can result.

Sonograms were ordered for these patients after they complained of shortness of breath and constant fatigue. Mysteriously, none of these relatively young individuals had a history of rheumatic fever, the most likely cause of heart valve damage. Upon further questioning, Ruff found a single common denominator: all the patients had taken fen-phen. Initially, the physicians at MeritCare considered this connection a mere coincidence, as neither current medical journals nor past drug trials had established any connection between valve disease and either of the components of fen-phen. But Ruff's curiosity was piqued, so she used her off-duty time to examine thousands of sonograms in MeritCare's massive patient base, looking for similar abnormalities, and she cross-referenced these with fen-phen or Redux consumption. She amassed a database of twenty patients with heart valve abnormalities who shared no etiological commonalties other than the ingestion of fen-phen, but the cardiologists at MeritCare were still not impressed. Frustrated, Ruff finally lost her temper one day and told a cardiologist, as he ducked a sheaf of papers she had thrown at him, that he already would have conducted a board of review if fen-phen was being linked to prostate disease.

Eventually, a MeritCare cardiologist who had initially doubted Ruff's theory saw the light. A female patient who had had normal heart function prior to being prescribed fen-phen revisited Dr. Jack Crary with complaints of fatigue and shortness of breath. Upon examining her, he detected a murmur and other signs of heart failure and knew that Ruff had been right all along. Crary later stated: "I went back and reviewed the cases that Pam had collected, it was the same story over and over."[1] Crary's epiphany on December 16, 1996, occurred exactly two years to the day after Ruff first detected abnormalities in the sonogram of a fen-phen user.[2]

Crary possessed both the competence and the credibility to unravel the threads of this medical mystery. As a pillar of the Fargo community, he was known not only as a trusted physician but also as the coach of the high school's championship soccer team and the founder of a mentoring program for young people considering medical careers. He feared that if the small population around Fargo had already experienced twenty cases of drug-induced heart valve damage, the rest of the country might soon be inundated by a tsunami of cardiac disease.

Crary was momentarily sidetracked when his son was seriously injured in a car wreck. But in mid-January, soon after his son was out of intensive care, Crary phoned Dr. Heidi Connolly, a friend and colleague at the

Mayo Clinic in Rochester, Minnesota. Established in 1863 by William Mayo, the famous clinic's annual revenue now exceeds $10 billion. It specializes in primary care, education, and research and often tackles the most difficult medical issues.

Dr. Connolly would discover the connection between heart disease and fen-phen. She happened to know of a similar case involving a forty-one-year-old woman who had used fen-phen and now required a heart valve replacement. The surgeon who performed the procedure described the defective valve as waxy and encased in glistening white plaques of a leaflet-like material that appeared to be stuck on. Such valve abnormalities had previously been found only in patients who had taken the migraine medication ergotamine. Although the woman in question had never taken this drug, it was known that ergotamine's chemical properties are similar to those of serotonin. Since fenfluramine elevates serotonin levels, a connection was plausible. Soon thereafter, Dr. Lauralyn Cannistra of the Brown University School of Medicine discovered damaged heart valves in a thirty-one-year-old woman who had taken dexfenfluramine, thus establishing a connection to Redux as well.

Further research determined that the phentermine in fen-phen also raises serotonin levels by inhibiting the action of monoamine oxidase (MAO), an enzyme that destroys serotonin. The serotonin-enhancing properties of phentermine had not been fully understood twenty years ago, the last time anyone had tested the drug's potential side effects. As reported in a publication of the Massachusetts Institute of Technology (MIT), the combination drug fen-phen unintentionally resulted in a double dose of serotonin: one from phentermine's MAO-inhibiting properties, and one from fenfluramine's inhibition of serotonin reuptake, thus "destroying the body's ability to control the amount of serotonin in blood plasma."[3] In addition to being a mood stabilizer, serotonin helps blood platelets bind and clot. Excess serotonin forms plaques that adhere to heart valves, as observed at the Mayo Clinic.

Since Redux did not contain phentermine, it was arguably less toxic than fen-phen, but it might have been equally damaging because it had been approved by the FDA for longer-term use. In fact, the findings of Dr.

Cannistra and others, along with the likely relationship to PPH, led already skeptical medical practitioners such as George Ricaurte and Lewis Seiden to conclude that both drugs were dangerous.

From that point forward, the bad news for AHP continued to fall like hammer blows. July 1997 was the cruelest month. The Mayo Clinic completed its study of the women from Fargo and its own clinic who had developed heart valve issues. By then, the number had risen to twenty-four. On July 8 Dr. Connolly delivered a speech to a meeting of the FDA describing the possible link between fen-phen and heart valve disease.

On the same day, the FDA sent letters to physicians requesting information on heart valve disease in patients taking these diet drugs. Within weeks, a total of 101 new reports had been received. More disturbingly, of 291 diet drug users who were asymptomatic, 30 percent had abnormal electrocardiograms. If their conditions worsened, the result could be congestive heart failure from the accumulation of fluid in the lungs, sending the patient into a downward spiral until the heart ultimately failed. Although an abnormal electrocardiogram alone is not sufficient for a diagnosis of heart disease, the Mayo study appeared to link the two.

The grim outlook for AHP grew even worse on August 28 when *Science Daily* published a report that the National Institutes of Mental Health had warned that fenfluramine and dexfenfluramine "have been demonstrated to damage brain serotonin neurons in animal studies."[4] That same day, the *New England Journal of Medicine* published an article by Dr. Connolly titled "Valvular Heart Disease Associated with Fenfluramine and Phentermine," which described the possible relationship between fen-phen and the "concentration of circulating serotonin and the resultant valvar injury." The article was deemed of such major consequence that the journal broke its long-standing policy and released details in advance of publication.[5]

On September 2, in a presentation at the International Congress of Obesity, researchers from the Massachusetts College of Pharmacology and MIT stated that fen-phen was potentially toxic because, taken in combination, the drugs destroyed the body's ability to control serotonin, causing damage to blood vessels, lungs, and heart valves. Finally, on September 15, 1997, the FDA publicly announced that both fenfluramine and dexfenflu-

FAT CHANCE

ramine should be withdrawn from the market. AHP had no choice but to comply.

Somewhat ironically, the Tennessee house of representatives had recently voted 72–22 to allow fen-phen and Redux to be prescribed in the Volunteer State. The Tennessee Board of Medical Examiners had strenuously objected, but physicians and pharmacists in the state were sick and tired of forfeiting income to their neighbor to the north. Governor Sundquist signed the new fen-phen law just four months before AHP pulled it from the market.[6]

Obviously, AHP's problems were far from over. Personal injury lawyers began prodding AHP for its interoffice correspondence and laboratory studies. The opportunities for litigation presented a wide array of targets. Many diet clinics had passed out medications without the proper safeguards, such as physical examinations and ongoing medical monitoring. Most had also prescribed the drugs to persons who were not obese. For its part, the FDA bore responsibility for approving Redux under questionable circumstances and for not acting soon enough to rein in the sales of fen-phen. The biggest culprit, of course, was AHP, which had benefited the most from sales of these products. The *Pink Sheet,* a publication for the pharmaceutical industry, noted that, according to the FDA, "363,000 to 725,000 U.S. patients may have associated valvopathy" from fen-phen and Redux.[7]

In response, AHP launched yet another public-relations campaign, this time for $90 million.[8] To cast doubt on the number of cases contained in the Mayo Clinic study, AHP hired Arthur Weyman, a cardiologist from Harvard University and Massachusetts General Hospital, to examine the data generated at Fargo. He found no fault with the information or how it was gathered. Dr. Weyman reportedly told Dr. Crary, after learning about Pam Ruff's herculean efforts, "If this had happened at Mass General, we would have never figured it out."[9] It became critical for AHP to generate its own studies to counter the growing acceptance of the relationship between its diet drugs and PPH and coronary disease. Accordingly, on April 1, 1998, a front-page headline in *USA Today* declared: "Study: No Damage from Diet Drug." The $18 million study had been conducted by Neil Weissman of Georgetown University.[10] Although *USA Today* did not carry the same cachet as the *New England Journal of Medicine,* AHP hoped it would serve as a counterbalance.

It Hits the Fan

The April Fool's Day date of the publication proved to be appropriate, as the study was not accurate. In fact, *New England Journal of Medicine* editor Gregory Curfman discovered a glaring flaw. Weissman's study featured women who had taken Redux for 2.5 months and were found to have no statistically significant increase in coronary valve disease, but the number of women with some form of valve disease had been miscounted. When the numbers were corrected, Curfman concluded that fen-phen posed a significant hazard.

AHP's downward spiral gained momentum when it was learned that the Mayo Clinic had provided its data to AHP as early as March 1997. In a move that would later prove devastating for AHP, employee Amy Meyers had wiped out the data from Mayo through a computer file overwrite. (Later, during her trial testimony, Meyers was described as "hovering between nervous and catatonic."[11]) Whether Meyers intentionally deleted this information or not, it significantly increased AHP's liability. Also, for reasons unknown, the Mayo Clinic did not immediately share its findings with the FDA. According to *Brown et al. v. AHP* (the lawsuit seeking a national settlement), the findings were not made public until July. During this four-month interval, AHP sold millions of the toxic tablets.

AHP's effort to stem the tide of lawsuits was an abject failure. By September 1997, more than 18,000 lawsuits had been filed. In December the *Drug Litigation Reporter* published "Fen-Phen: A Primer on Diet Drug Litigation." In January 1998 the *ABA Journal* published an article titled "Fen-Phenomenal Tort Battle Brewing." For many experienced litigators, the hunt for plaintiffs required no effort at all. Paul Rheingold, an attorney in New York, signed up more than 3,000 potential plaintiffs simply by placing ads in *TV Guide.*

The first attorney who managed to put AHP on the defensive was Kip Petroff of Dallas, Texas. Petroff began his legal career handling workers' compensation claims but later raised both his professional and financial profile by successfully representing unhappy breast implant recipients. He was introduced to fen-phen litigation through a referral by one of his former breast implant clients. Petroff forged a path to fortune that dozens of other trial attorneys would soon follow.

The plaintiff referred to Petroff was Mary Perez. After taking the diet drugs for only three months, Perez was so incapacitated by PPH that a catheter had been inserted to constantly feed medications directly into her heart. She had been forced to close her day care business and ultimately declared bankruptcy.

Rather than follow the usual routine of pretrial discovery—that is, requesting specific documents prior to taking depositions—Petroff jumped ahead and immediately deposed Dr. Marc Deitch, a senior medical officer at AHP. During a deposition, the witness answers questions under oath but outside of a courtroom. Written transcripts of the deposition are created, which may be used later in a formal trial. Deitch had been AHP's front man after the devastating 1997 *New England Journal of Medicine* article, and under withering questioning, Petroff was able to wring Deitch's confession that the company had failed to follow up on initial reports of cardiac damage in an effort to maintain sales.

Petroff then obtained a court order for AHP to provide copies of all its diet drug–related documents. Hoping to overwhelm Petroff, who lacked the massive infrastructure of an established multipartner law firm, AHP dropped off two truckloads of unsorted documents at Petroff's doorstep in the spring of 1998. Undaunted, he rented two floors of office space in a building close to the courthouse, hired a small army of law students who were beginning their summer break, and went to work. Preparing for litigation is tedious, and this was certainly the case as Petroff and his team of young assistants sifted through mountains of files, most of which were irrelevant. Over several weeks, however, the paper trail of AHP's duplicity gradually took shape. The first damning piece of evidence to emerge was a draft of a marketing flyer that had been vetted by AHP lawyers. In a preliminary version of the document, the original phrase "has been used safely and effectively" had strike marks through the word "safely."

Perhaps the greatest liability for AHP was its willful disregard of the numerous reports of PPH from Europe. The first report was received in 1994, and they totaled no fewer than ninety-three by June 1996, after which AHP finally informed the FDA. In the twenty-five-month interim, an estimated 3 million people had been prescribed the drugs, garnering AHP at least $50 million in profits. Had these warnings been made public, per federal regulations, many physicians would have refused to prescribe the pills.

According to the files Petroff had uncovered, AHP's motivation for turning a blind eye was more than the $50 million in profits. Its main fear was that prospects for Redux would be negatively affected as it walked the tightrope through the FDA approval process. Any more reports of PPH related to fenfluramine would raise questions about dexfenfluramine, perhaps resulting in denial of fast-track status for Redux.

Knowing that Petroff was holding a hot hand, AHP folded six days before the scheduled trial in Little Rock, Arkansas, and settled out of court for a reported $4.5 million. One month later, AHP settled out of court with another of Petroff's clients in Dallas. But AHP was just biding its time. It was waiting for a case in which the facts could convince a jury that the aggrieved party was a fraud and Petroff was an ambulance chaser.

As Petroff prepared to go to trial with his next client, thirty-six-year-old manicurist Debbie Lovett, AHP was ready to spring its trap. Lovett was an overweight smoker who had first been diagnosed with a heart abnormality back in 1989. After losing forty-five pounds on fen-phen, Lovett complained of shortness of breath but lost no work time. Although an electrocardiogram showed moderate to severe valve damage, her own physician did not believe it had been caused by fen-phen. Lovett's medical bills totaled only $2,000. She was a defense team's dream. Perhaps more significantly, the trial was being held in the East Texas town of Canton. The inhabitants there did not cotton to out-of-town lawyers from Dallas, and they were unlikely to award a big civil settlement. Defense attorneys believed they had finally bested Petroff and thought he would be more than happy to accept a token settlement to avoid a trial. Yet AHP managed to snatch defeat from the jaws of victory.

Much to the shock of AHP, Petroff was eager to bring Lovett's case to trial. He had wisely reasoned that he had nothing to lose. If the jury sided with AHP, Petroff had plenty of other, more favorable cases yet to come. However, if AHP lost against Lovett, it would consider any future legal battles with Petroff untenable.

During the trial, Petroff focused not on his client's ailments but on

AHP's deceit and greed, which posed a menace to society. In a strategic error, AHP sent a team of five attorneys against the lone Petroff. To the Texans on the jury, Petroff looked like Gary Cooper in *High Noon.* The jury deliberated for three days and returned on August 6 with a recommended judgment of $23.4 million against AHP. Of this amount, $3.4 million was to cover Lovett's pain and future medical bills, and a full $20 million represented punitive damages—proof of Petroff's masterful portrayal of AHP executives as public enemies. The next day, AHP's stock prices tumbled nearly 12 percent, causing stockholders a paper loss of $8 billion. AHP was now in full panic mode.

Indeed, panic was the order of the day, and not only because of what had just transpired in a Texas courtroom. So little was known about the etiology of diet drug–induced heart disease that medical professionals could not be certain how long users needed to take the drugs before experiencing ill effects or how long it might take for any latent ill effects to manifest after the drugs were discontinued. A case in New Jersey sought medical monitoring in the form of an echocardiogram for every person who had ever taken fen-phen. At $1,000 per test, the total could have ranged from $6 billion to as much as $24 billion. Moreover, the number of fraudulent claims of heart disease was likely to explode. About 2 percent of the general population naturally has some amount of heart valve leakage, and the testing process itself can be manipulated. An echocardiogram, sometimes referred to as a sonogram of the heart, uses reflected sound waves to create an image of the heart. This image can reveal damage and, using Doppler technology, can detect blood flow through the heart. However, depending on the settings used by the sonographer, even healthy hearts can appear to be damaged.

As word spread about the opportunity to profit at AHP's expense, a number of attorneys and physicians apparently colluded to manipulate sonograms. A case in point is cardiologist Linda Crouse of Kansas City, Missouri. Crouse tested 725 patients who had taken the drugs and found that 60 percent had evidence of heart damage. Yet a few months later, only 5 percent of those patients had any medical evidence of damage. Crouse also diagnosed heart damage without ever seeing the patients or reviewing their histories. A judge commented that the high-volume efficiency of her sonogram mill operation would have been the envy of Henry Ford. Crouse managed to bill $2.5 million in just ten months.

Other physicians were not so willing to cash in. One court-appointed cardiologist reviewed a sample of 1,000 electrocardiograms and concluded, "Thousands of people have been defrauded into believing they have heart valve disease when in fact they do not." Michael Fishbein, a well-known tort lawyer, cited "an intentional effort to game the system." He believed that 70 percent of the most serious claims were "medically unfounded and unjustified because the claimant doesn't have the condition." Fishbein worried that if too much of AHP's rapidly dwindling resources was eaten up by bogus lawsuits, there would be nothing left to compensate those who had genuinely been injured.[12]

Notwithstanding these cautions, the legal onslaught against AHP was relentless. Sol Weiss, the lead attorney for the New Jersey plaintiffs, piled the evidence so high, citing the many instances in which AHP had disregarded, destroyed, or otherwise discredited the medical evidence, that superior court judge Marina Corodemus advised AHP to seek to consolidate all the lawsuits against it—known as a class action. AHP took this advice. Certainly, the settlement would be in the billions, but whether in the single-digit billions or in the ruinous tens of billions was still to be determined.

By this time, Interneuron (the "pimple on the ass" of AHP, according to one Wall Street analyst) offered to pay AHP $100 million to join as defendants in the class action. But then Interneuron's leadership sued AHP for failing to inform them earlier about the drugs' health risks. Amid this donnybrook, Richard Wurtman resigned in 1999, having lost much of his $26 million.

AHP hoped the class action would be a safe harbor of sorts. Hundreds of separate lawsuits from multiple federal jurisdictions could be combined into one all-encompassing settlement. Such settlement negotiations are managed by a single federal judge, and the corporate defendants believed a judge would be more likely to base his or her decision on facts and reason, rather than the emotional appeals that often sway juries.

When there are multiple class actions or single lawsuits with the same complaint from two or more states, there is a mechanism to prevent the federal court system from getting bogged down in redundancy. In such instances, the matter is referred to the US Judicial Panel on Multidistrict Litigation. This panel is composed of seven federal judges from throughout the United States chosen by the chief justice of the US Supreme Court. The panel meets on a regular basis in Washington, DC, where attorneys file petitions for multidistrict litigation status. The panel then selects one federal district to handle all these essentially identical lawsuits. In the case of AHP, the panel's choice was the US District Court for the Eastern District of Pennsylvania, presided over by Judge Louis Bechtle.

January 15, 1998, was an unusually raw and blustery day in Philadelphia. After shedding their expensive overcoats, roughly 100 of the most prominent tort lawyers from all over the country packed into one of the conference rooms at the Ritz Carlton to hammer out a plan for filing a national class action against AHP.

By the time of this gathering in Philadelphia, shares of AHP stock had fallen from $70 to $40. Even more ominous, AHP executives were beginning to unload their own shares, an indication that AHP's stock value was in danger of an even deeper decline very soon. If the national settlement proved to be as large as feared, these executives would have to act fast before there was nothing left to save.

It was likely that the selection of Judge Bechtle was not entirely objective. Tort attorneys are notorious for "forum shopping"—actively seeking venues where the judge will be sympathetic. Those attorneys who had relationships with members of the Judicial Panel no doubt lobbied for the appointment of a judge who was unsympathetic to corporate interests. But regardless of how Bechtle was chosen, one of his most anticipated duties was selecting members of the Plaintiffs Management Committee (PMC). Appointments to the PMC are highly coveted. One function of PMC members is to bankroll the litigation of a national class action in exchange for a return of several times their investment, usually taken off the top before any additional legal fees are distributed. Among tort attorneys, membership on a PMC is considered a "license to print money."[13]

PMC members in major class actions are typically selected from a relatively small group of premier attorneys known colloquially as the "Class

Action Club." Members of the Class Action Club battle for seats on PMCs, especially when the prize is as big as it was in the case against AHP. Once the case is settled, a disproportionate amount of the attorneys' fees granted by the judge flows to one of the dozen or so members of the PMC, while the bulk of the actual work is performed by less senior attorneys who have yet to achieve a sufficient level of prominence. The PMC takes a big slice of the settlement, leaving the many other attorneys to vie for the residual. This can be a contentious process, with each attorney inflating his or her own contributions while denigrating the work of others. Not surprisingly, these negotiations often dissolve into acrimonious shouting matches. Bill Gallion, who referred 4,500 Kentucky plaintiffs to the AHP national settlement (in addition to organizing a much smaller, separate class action), called this whole fee-seeking process embarrassing. And this judgment came from a man who, as the reader will soon learn, was a scoundrel himself. But among the members of the Class Action Club, the one with the sharpest elbows was an attorney from Cincinnati known by his colleagues as the "Master of Disaster."

4

The Master

NO ONE FAMILIAR WITH THE power players in the legal world was surprised when Stan Chesley, aka the "Prince of Torts," was invited to join the Plaintiffs Management Committee for the AHP class action in Philadelphia. He had definitely earned the privilege. One could argue that Chesley was to mass tort litigation what Elvis Presley was to rock and roll. Chesley's ascent to top of this hierarchy was as swift as it was improbable.

The son of Ukrainian immigrant parents, Chesley grew up in a rented apartment, where the family lived on the income his father earned at his modest typewriter repair shop. While in high school, Stan sold women's shoes at Shillito's Department Store in the evenings and on weekends to help support his family. He was born with a gift for persuasion, and at his suggestion, the store's general manger changed the name of his department from "Budget Shoes" to "Fashion Shoes." The immediate uptick in sales earned the astute young Chesley a bonus of $25—and so began his ascent into riches. Despite being told that he was not college material, Chesley managed to earn undergraduate and law degrees from the University of Cincinnati. After seventeen years as a garden-variety trial attorney and a self-described "unknown quantity," Chesley rocketed to prominence after his smashing legal victories related to the tragic Beverly Hills Supper Club fire.[1]

The Beverly Hills Supper Club was located in Southgate, Kentucky, just across the Ohio River from Cincinnati. A popular nightspot since the 1920s, it drew talent from Las Vegas, Hollywood, Nashville, and New York. A young

Dean Martin dealt blackjack at its illegal casino before that operation was closed in the early 1960s. With time, the club grew into a sprawling complex that the state fire marshal had approved for 1,500 occupants.

On the night of May 28, 1977, an estimated 3,200 people were packed into the velvet palace. In the elaborate Cabaret Room, between 900 and 1,300 occupied a space approved for only 600. Singer John Davidson was the headliner that night. A regular on the popular TV game show *Hollywood Squares,* Davidson was known for his elaborate fabricated stories that usually fooled contestants. Just before Davidson was set to go onstage at 9:00, the staff smelled faint whiffs of smoke from the adjoining Zebra Room. By coincidence, the room was empty after a faulty roof air conditioner had driven out a wedding reception scheduled for that evening. When club workers opened the door to investigate, the rush of fresh air ignited a stack of drapes that had been smoldering owing to an electrical short circuit, and the room erupted into flames.

Busboy Walter Bailey ran through a side door and leaped onto the stage. He grabbed the microphone and shouted for the audience to evacuate. Bailey's quick thinking was credited with saving hundreds of lives. Many people began to file, unhurriedly, toward the main doors, but many others remained seated, likely assuming that Bailey's cries were part Davidson's routine. When the main doors to the Cabaret Room were opened, smoke from the blaze in the Zebra Room rolled in, leading to pandemonium. Because the Zebra Room was located between the Cabaret Room and the nearest exit, guests were forced to navigate the warren-like hallways, looking for alternative ways out.

As dozens of patrons rushed toward the exits, people tripped, and bodies began to pile up in front of the doorways. One woman whose cocktail dress was ablaze jumped from table to table, screaming. Others swung chairs in a vain attempt to clear a path through the crowd and to safety. John Davidson left his dressing room and led a number of audience members to safety through the backstage exit, barely escaping with his own life.

Firefighters arrived on the scene within minutes, only to find black smoke, illuminated by the blaze, billowing from the stricken building. The flames, unhampered by firewalls, flashed above the suspended ceilings, accelerating the spread of the conflagration. By this point, the lights had gone dark throughout much of the building. The shrieks of those trapped inside filled the night air as they attempted to escape. Many of the doomed tried to exit via the main entrance but could not escape as hot, thick smoke began to roll up the spiral staircase. As the panic reached a crescendo, the bodies of the dead and nearly dead piled up; firefighters would later discover that the bodies reached to the top of one doorway. Around midnight the roof collapsed, but by then, the terrifying cries of those trapped inside had long gone silent.

At midmorning the next day, 134 corpses were laid side by side, covered by white sheets, on the surrounding hillside. The charred ruins continued to smolder for two days. The temperature in what had been the Cabaret Room reportedly reached into the thousands of degrees, reducing bodies to greasy cinders. The unforgettable stench of burnt flesh, accentuated by the sticky humidity, assaulted the nostrils of the shocked recovery personnel. Their grisly work included the often difficult task of separating the victims by gender.

An unshaven Governor Julian Carroll rushed to the scene from Frankfort to observe the carnage and comfort the families of the victims. By June 1, after the heat and smoke had finally subsided, 31 additional charred bodies had been pulled from the ashes, bringing the total number of dead to 165, not counting two unborn fetuses. Barbara Thornhill lingered in agony until March 1, 1978, before succumbing to her burns. Among those who perished were Thornhill's husband and his two sisters, one of whom was pregnant.[2]

Many, including Governor Carroll, believed that criminal indictments would be forthcoming, but after five months of deliberations, a grand jury found no reason to press charges for criminal negligence. The grand jury concluded in August 1978 that, "even though notified to evacuate [the patrons] failed to react and remained seated until the conditions of the room itself indicated the need to exit. By this time in some instances it was too late."[3] This meant that the families of the victims could now attain justice only through a civil lawsuit.

Despite this horrendous human tragedy, attorneys were not clamoring to represent the victims. The overcrowding, the insufficient exits, and the faulty wiring clearly singled out the club owners for an enormous share of the blame. Unfortunately, the property carried only $1 million of insurance, and the site itself was, for all practical purposes, unsalable after such a calamity. With very little money available to compensate the families of the victims, the legal fees would likewise be small.

But Chesley rushed in where others had demurred. With characteristic bravado, he invested $300,000 of his own funds to pay for expert witnesses and other out-of-pocket expenses in an audacious gambit to bring a class-action lawsuit. As described by New Orleans lawyer Wendell Gauthier, "the difference between Stanley and a pit bull is that a pit bull lets go."[4] Within five days after the fire, Chesley had obtained an emergency order to stop demolition of the ruins. The evidence for Chesley's yet to be revealed legal innovation lay among the ashes.

Soon after attaining the writ to cease cleanup activities, Chesley and his investigators began to sift through the cinders—critics called him ghoulish. The cause of the fire was determined to be electrical in nature, and a report described the wiring as an electrician's nightmare. Chesley's focus, however, was not the workmanship of the wiring but the wire itself. Although it was acknowledged that overheated aluminum wire might have been responsible for the blaze, virtually all other attorneys considered this a dead end. There were dozens of wire manufacturers, and it was impossible to determine which company had produced the wiring used in the club. Chesley's idea was not to ferret out the particular wire manufacturer but rather to indict the entire aluminum wiring industry. He would argue that the cheaper aluminum wire, unlike copper, was less pliant and more likely to short out and cause a fire. This legal tactic is now known as "enterprise liability." Jacob Stein, one of Chesley's opponents who represented an aluminum wire manufacturer, described the enterprise liability strategy as suing "a large number of people who had no liability and are willing to pay you several thousands of dollars to make you go away."[5] Despite these dubious qualities, the doctrine of enterprise liability became a landmark of jurisprudence and is now taught in law schools throughout the United States.

Chesley may have been a first-rate intimidator, but his skills before a jury were less than spectacular. At trial, his best efforts failed to convince the jury of the logic and application of the enterprise liability argument. After only two hours of deliberation, the jury sided with the defendants. Chesley lost both the case and the $300,000 he had invested in it. Fortunately for him, he was going to be granted a second bite at the apple.

The heart-wrenching stories told by the victims' families remained a topic of conversation in the community. The public's general dismay about the verdict led one of the jurors to write an anonymous letter to the *Kentucky Enquirer* defending the jury's decision. He explained that he had conducted home experiments with aluminum wire and electric current, and his results squared with the arguments of the wiring industry's attorneys. When it was learned that this juror had shared his findings with his fellow jury members, the verdict was set aside, and a new trial was ordered. Federal district judge Wilhoit referred to this turn of events as "one of the most bizarre occurrences in anyone's memory."[6]

But by this time, many of the defendants were unwilling to pay the expenses of another trial. Nor did they want to subject themselves again to Chesley waving photos of charred and contorted corpses. The manufacturers were also strongly advised by their attorneys not to trust their fates a second time to a capricious jury in an angry town. To avoid a complex and emotional legal ordeal against a courtroom demagogue, fourteen wire manufacturers, most of which were no doubt blameless, settled for a combined total of $4.2 million. Only General Electric refused to settle.

Having dunned the aluminum wire manufactures out of millions, Chesley next trained his sights on the manufacturers of the club's furnishings. Rather than settle, the furniture makers went to trial. This seemed to be a risk worth taking until the day Chesley held up a piece of foam padding from the cushion of one of the club's chairs. When he lit the foam, an acrid odor filled the air. Chesley told the jury they were smelling cyanide gas. This type of foam padding continues to be widely used in home and commercial applications. It is not the foam that creates the toxic gases but rather the flame retardant applied to make the furnishings safer. Without a fire retardant, polyurethane foam is referred to by the National Association of Fire Marshals as solid gasoline, as it is easily ignited and burns at very high temperatures. Although toxic gases likely did result from the incineration of the flame-retardant chemicals, all the victims died of smoke inhalation or carbon monoxide poisoning, making the furnishings a nonfactor in the death toll. Nonetheless, Chesley's dramatics visibly moved the jury and cowed the defense teams. With one exception, all the defendants settled before the jury began its deliberations, marking yet another huge victory for Chesley. As reported by television station WCPO, throughout the remainder of his legal career, Chesley kept a large envelope in his desk filled with the foam from one of the chairs used in the Beverly Hills Supper Club. He would regale visitors with a parlor trick, lighting a small sample of the foam and, as a tendril of smoke rose, saying in a stage whisper, "cyanide."[7]

The one attorney who refused to back down was Robert Gettys, a young lawyer from Covington. He represented Rash-Saville-Crawford, a small company that installed heating and ventilation equipment, as Chesley was also planning to force settlements from the HVAC industry. Throughout the battles with the wire and furniture industries, Chesley became more adept at proclaiming the righteousness of his cause. Stomach-turning photographs of bodily fluids bubbling out of charred lips and skin were displayed during the defendants' depositions. Each day, Gettys sat in the back of the auditorium where the depositions were being conducted and studied Chesley's words and mannerisms. Gettys concluded that although Chesley's arguments were empty bombast, he delivered them with such confidence that no one was willing to challenge his facts. Gettys called Chesley's bluff and made it clear that he would not agree to settle. As a result, Chesley backed down and never took Gettys's client to trial. Uncharacteristically, Chesley was not miffed, and Gettys earned his grudging respect.

Gettys later remembered a scene in a hallway where Chesley was confronting a much taller defense attorney. Chesley was jabbing the other man's chest with his finger while threatening to bankrupt his client's company if he did not settle. As described by Gettys, "The man withered and settled while I'm standing there watching." Once the other lawyer was gone, Chesley turned to Gettys and said, "I know I'm full of shit and you know I'm full of shit, but they don't."[8]

Every day, another young attorney made the eighty-minute round-trip drive from Lexington to Covington to observe the depositions. Like Gettys, he always sat in the back of the room, taking notes and studying Chesley's performance with rapt interest and admiration. Decades later, this same man would play an integral part in the series of events that led to the demise of them both.

Returning to the lone holdout on the aluminum wire issue, Chesley eventually settled with General Electric for a whopping $10 million. The combined settlement from all the defendants totaled about $43 million. From this incredible amount, Chesley reportedly received a fee of $1.8 million. His failure to win in the courtroom taught Chesley to adopt the strategy he used to great effect throughout the remainder of his legal career—avoid trials by intimidating the defendants into settling out of court. This strategy vaulted him into the stratosphere of multibillion-dollar national tort litigation. Starting with the Beverly Hills Supper Club case, Chesley demonstrated a Zelig-like ability (a reference to the opportunistic character in the Woody Allen film) to be the key player in a string of high-profile class actions.

Chesley was the first to file a class-action suit against Dow Corning, the maker of silicone breast implants. David Kessler, commissioner of the FDA under both George H. W. Bush and Bill Clinton, became convinced that the silicone gel used in breast implants posed a serious health risk, despite the lack of scientific research and the widespread and successful use of silicone in other medical devices for more than four decades. Kessler classified silicone breast implants in the highest category of risk and eventually issued a moratorium on their manufacture. As a result, many thousands of women were unnecessarily panicked and had their implants surgically removed. In a 2016 article, Dr. Jack Fisher, a professor of plastic surgery, describes these events, including how misinformation and greed brought down a major corporation.[9]

Trial attorneys, most prominently Chesley, jumped at the opportunity to file a class action and claim a share of the legal fees from the Dow Corning settlement. The initial group of about 250,000 women won a record $4.25 billion settlement, from which lawyers likely kept about $1 billion. Hundreds of plastic surgeons also faced financial calamity. In 1995, after paying $11 billion in settlements, Dow Corning filed for bankruptcy protection.

In 1999 Congress finally commissioned a study on the adverse effects of silicone breast implants, conducted by the prestigious Institute of Medicine. Among its conclusions was the following: "There are more than 1.5 million adult women of all ages in the United States with silicone breast implants, and some of these women would be expected to develop connective tissue diseases, cancer, neurological diseases or conditions. Evidence suggests that such diseases or conditions are not more common in women with breast implants than in women without implants."[10] Of course, the study came too late to help Dow Corning and not soon enough to prevent Chesley from reaping millions in legal fees. The American Enterprise Institute opined that much of Chesley's fortune had been made through the clever application of "junk science."[11]

Another of Chesley's high-profile lawsuits involved the manufacturers of the herbicide Agent Orange, which included Monsanto. Aircraft sprayed 20 million gallons of Agent Orange (so named because it was transported in barrels that bore wide orange stripes) during the Vietnam War to clear away the jungle foliage used to hide North Vietnamese positions. In addition to the catastrophic, lingering impact on the Vietnamese people, the chemical was believed to cause respiratory, nerve, skin, and digestive disorders, as well as elevated rates of cancer, in American servicemen. The plaintiffs' attorneys (which included Chesley) had originally sought billions, but in May 1984 they settled for $180 million. Although 200,000 GIs claimed to have been exposed to Agent Orange, the bulk of the fund went to 10,000 to 12,000 former soldiers who were deemed totally disabled, which amounted to $2,500 per year for ten years for each of them. Another $45 million was used to establish a foundation to assist the remainder with counseling and vocational rehabilitation services through what is known as a cy pres fund. Attorneys' fees totaled $9.3 million.

Chesley ventured into international affairs when he represented a group whose family members had died when Pan-American flight 103 exploded over Lockerbie, Scotland. On December 21, 1988, a suitcase bomb exploded on board, sending the stricken airliner and its 259 passengers plummeting to the ground, where 11 inhabitants of Lockerbie, a town on Scotland's southern border, were also killed. Compensation for the family members was not expected to be significant, since a 1929 international agreement known as the Warsaw Convention limited damages to $75,000 unless it could be proved that a crash was the result of "willful misconduct." This was the chink where Chesley applied his legal lever.

The suitcase containing the bomb had been loaded as cargo in Frankfurt, Germany, before the plane landed in London and then continued to its final destination of New York City. Prior to the flight, carriers had been informed of a possible terrorist threat that had been called in anonymously, claiming that a Finnish woman intended to bring a bomb on board an international flight.[12] Chesley argued that this knowledge should have compelled Pan-Am to X-ray all items taken on board, rather than rely on metal detectors. The call was later shown to be a hoax, and it is unlikely that the plastic explosive hidden in a tape recorder would have been discovered by X-ray or even by a physical search. Nonetheless, Chesley had managed to plant a seed of suspicion in the minds of the jury, which grew into a guilty verdict. The ultimate out-of-court settlement was rumored to be nearly $300 million. Along with the loss of customer confidence, that blow pushed Pan-Am into bankruptcy and, in December 1991, led to its ultimate demise. The iconic airline that had pioneered international travel and the use of jet aircraft was no more.[13]

Without a doubt, the largest lawsuit in which Chesley played an instrumental role was the 1998 settlement with the tobacco industry. The case had originated in 1994, when Dianne Castano sued nine tobacco companies over the smoking-related lung cancer suffered by her brother David, after he had made several unsuccessful attempts to quit. The tobacco industry was still reeling from events at the Democratic National Convention, where Vice President Al Gore had tearfully recalled his sister's death from lung cancer. Soon after, seven tobacco industry CEOs were brought before Congress, and they all implausibly testified that they believed tobacco was not addictive. By then, the public had had more than enough, and the stage was set for a huge financial reckoning. Chesley was at the front of the line.

The class-action lawsuit came to be known as *Castano et al. v. American Tobacco Company et al.* When Hugh Rodham, Hillary Clinton's brother, joined the legal team, this provided a direct link to the White House, which would be crucial in obtaining passage of the federal legislation that made the terms of the settlement possible. The ultimate settlement provided states with annual payments in perpetuity, with a guaranteed $206 billion in the first twenty-five years. A *New York Times* op-ed grumbled that "only a small fraction has gone into the prevention of smoking." An enormous portion of the money was used to finance pork-barrel projects such as a golf course sprinkler system in New York and, ironically, $42 million for the marketing and modernization of the tobacco industry in North Carolina.[14]

During the push for the necessary legislation, Chesley held a fund-raiser in his home for the Democratic National Committee that far exceeded $500,000. Consumer advocate Ralph Nader called this event "grossly inappropriate." As reported by the *Cincinnati Enquirer,* based on the amount of time Chesley actually spent on the case, he earned as much as $92,000 per hour. Across the river in Kentucky, Senator Mitch McConnell caustically remarked, "The national tobacco settlement has turned into the national lawyer enrichment deal." Chesley countered by telling reporters, "No one ever asked Bill Gates the hourly rate for his success."[15]

The billions of dollars paid in all these lawsuits did not come out of the pockets of the executives of Dow Corning, Monsanto, Pan-Am, or American Tobacco, who either kept their jobs or were granted healthy severance packages. According to a report by Tillinghast-Towers Perrin, a risk management consulting firm for the insurance and financial services industries, in 2002 the cost of tort lawsuits in the United States was $233 billion.[16] This equates to a per capita cost of $809, or the equivalent of a 5 percent tax on all Americans. This "tax" is paid indirectly, as corporations merely add such costs to the price of goods and services. It also diminishes stock values, which adversely affects the 401(k) retirement funds of middle-class Americans.

Chesley estimated that he won more than $350 billion in legal settlements, which in turn brought him enormous wealth and prestige.[17] Chesley became the sole stockholder of the twenty-lawyer firm Waite, Schneider, Bayless & Chesley. The offices of WSB&C were in downtown Cincinnati in a thirty-one-story edifice constructed of two-foot-thick chiseled limestone; the top was crowned with a pyramidal pediment surrounded by six huge Corinthian columns on each side. When it was completed in 1913, it was the fifth tallest building in the world. Chesley occupied an office on the top floor with a grand view of the Ohio riverfront. The interior had the dimensions and the appearance of a Manhattan ballroom, replete with leather uphol- stery, oil paintings, and an ornate gilded ceiling.

Twenty-five years after the Beverly Hills Supper Club fire, Chesley was living in an $8 million, 27,000-square-foot slate-roofed French château- style home set on 300 wooded acres, the most expensive home ever sold in Cincinnati. Other features included an eight-car garage and a carriage house to store his collection of twenty luxury automobiles, including Jag- uars, Rolls-Royces, Bentleys, Ferraris, and Aston Martins.[18]

Chesley and his wife became the quintessential power couple. Like her husband, Susan Dlott was the child of immigrant parents from eastern Europe. The couple derived much of their power from their political activ- ism. As demonstrated by his lavish fund-raiser, Chesley was a generous con- tributor to the Democratic Party, which granted him considerable access to the political class. The millions Chesley raised for the Democratic Party was thought to be responsible for Dlott's 1995 appointment to a federal judgeship in the Southern District of Ohio by a grateful President Clinton.[19]

President Clinton attended fund-raisers in the couple's home, includ- ing a $2,300-per-person event to benefit Hillary. Chesley and Dlott fre- quently visited the White House and slept in the Lincoln Bedroom on more than one occasion. For Chesley's granddaughter's birthday party, President Clinton visited the Cincinnati mansion and presented her with a cake with thirteen candles. At the 2000 Democratic National Convention, Chesley bragged about appearing in a TV shot with John Travolta. In fact, Chesley's cozy relationship with the entertainment media ran deep. In 2002, during one *Sunday Night Football* broadcast, announcers Chris Collingsworth and Al Michaels mentioned that Chesley had been hired to clear the way for wide receiver Chris Henry to be drafted by the Cincinnati Bengals.

As a federal judge, Chesley's wife earned considerable notoriety for two things: a preternatural affection for her dogs and a ruling that defined and prohibited racial profiling in Cincinnati. As might be expected, Dlott's judicial chambers were festooned with photos of herself and her husband and various political luminaries, including Bill and Hillary Clinton, Al Gore, and John Glenn. Also on display was a menagerie of dog-themed keepsakes, including stuffed animals, dog clocks, dog prints, dog bowls, bones, and beds, as well as a dog cart for her two Cavalier King Charles spaniels, Dickens and Crumpet. According to an editorial in the *Cincinnati Enquirer,* Judge Dlott was so smitten with her pair of pooches that she swore them in as federal marshals.[20] Her official photograph as a federal judge shows her with Dickens and Crumpet on her lap.

Cincinnati's Fraternal Order of Police publicly disparaged the judge after her landmark April 2003 ruling that the police in Cincinnati had routinely been violating the rights of African Americans for decades. Dlott's logic was based on her contention that blacks and whites commit crimes with the same frequency, but since the police spent a disproportionate amount of time in predominantly African American neighborhoods, a higher percentage of blacks were being questioned, arrested, convicted, and jailed. Coming on the heels of a 2001 race riot, Dlott's ruling was praised in some circles, but others believed that by discouraging vigorous policing in crime-prone areas, many more people were being victimized, especially African Americans.

Mayor Charlie Luken was quoted in the *Cincinnati Enquirer* as saying, "Our men and women in blue have been consistently attacked by Judge Dlott." Describing a "collaborative" of attorneys organized by Dlott to combat supposed racial profiling, Luken went on to condemn "lawsuits which use the existence of the collaborative as evidence against individual police officers and against the police department." Keith Fangman, vice president of the Fraternal Order of Police, fumed, "Most federal judges have some prior judicial experience. She has not even heard a parking ticket as a city magistrate. She's in over her head. Let's face it, her appointment by President Clinton was payback for all the fund-raisers by her husband, Stan Chesley."[21]

Ironically, Dlott's theory that crime was being ignored in the suburbs was confirmed years later. On the evening of December 15, 2015, three young African American men—Darrell Kinney, Terry Jackson, and Demetrius Williams—were cruising downtown when a late-model Rolls Royce pulled up beside them at a stoplight. They followed the Rolls out of town to Indian Hill, an affluent community. They trailed at a discreet distance as the Rolls meandered among mansions that shimmered with holiday lighting. At the end of a long, narrow lane, the trio beheld a prize beyond anything they could have imagined. It was the largest house any of them had ever seen, let alone robbed—the home of Stan Chesley and Susan Dlott. After a quiet break-in, Dlott and Chesley awoke at 10:45 p.m. to find three handguns leveled at their heads. One of the men held a gun to Chesley's temple and demanded jewelry and cars. At one point, they threw Chesley down a flight of stairs, fracturing several vertebrae. When a shaken Dlott managed to convince them that a silent alarm had already summoned the police, the three tried to make their escape, but it was too late. The thieves were apprehended by members of the police department that Dlott had denigrated twelve years earlier. Both Dlott and Chesley were in the courtroom when the three were sentenced to thirty-four years each. Chesley loudly chastised the malefactors, shaking his fists in rage.

Success breeds envy, and Chesley was not without his detractors. Although attorneys in the Cincinnati area were generally loath to say anything negative about Chesley for fear of retaliation by Dlott, others outside of her district were not so reticent. Dick Scruggs, a Mississippian who represented the state attorneys general in the Big Tobacco settlement, said of Chesley, "I didn't know him five minutes and I wanted to hit him."[22] According to journalist Peter Pringle, among the members of the Plaintiffs Management Committee, Chesley was "one of the least liked members . . . mainly because of his seemingly uncontrolled vanity and endless name dropping."[23]

Attorney Leonard Schroeter found that Chesley's insistence on prolonged mediation in a class-action suit involving workers injured in a Washington State nuclear plant, rather than proceeding to trial, needlessly delayed compensation to the victims. Schroeter went on to describe Chesley to *American Lawyer* magazine as "the ultimate grotesque, exaggerated perversion of what it means to be a lawyer." He later added, "I've known him for 40 years, and I've always thought he was an opportunist and just a nasty son of a bitch."[24]

In between wrapping up the AHP case and a class-action suit against the Catholic Diocese of Covington, Chesley represented the Kentucky Speedway racetrack in an antitrust lawsuit against NASCAR, a lease dispute between the Cincinnati Bengals and Hamilton County, and a probate case involving the children of late multimillionaire and construction magnate

Dutch Knowlton and the Knowlton Foundation over ownership of the Bengals. In each of these cases, the reward was so high that it would have been the case of a lifetime for most attorneys.

By anyone's measure, Chesley had attained the summit of fortune, success, and prestige. Yet his Icarian ambition was still not satisfied. Just across the river in Kentucky, three Lexington attorneys had convinced a few hundred former fen-phen users to opt out of the national settlement and take a risk with them in a separate legal action. Chesley was not about to sit idly by while millions were at stake in a courthouse he could practically see from his own office. He connived to get a piece of that action as well.[25]

5

The Troika

BILL GALLION, SHIRLEY CUNNINGHAM, and Melbourne Mills were well known in Lexington's legal community, where all three had practiced for years. Cunningham and Gallion developed a relationship after opposing each other in several civil suits, which meant they often traveled on the same out-of-town flights. The two had ample opportunity to talk shop while sitting around various airport terminals. One afternoon they discussed the vast opportunities involved in pursuing fen-phen litigation. Cunningham had already signed up a few former diet drug users. Since Gallion possessed a fair degree of medical knowledge, Cunningham realized they could both profit by working together in a lawsuit against AHP.[1]

Mills joined the business arrangement from a different direction. His highly successful workers' compensation practice was beginning to wind down after Governor Patton signed into law a reform measure that created fixed awards for all types of injures, thus obviating the need for attorneys to argue how injuries impacted various occupations. Soon his office staff dwindled from a high of twenty to half a dozen. Then one day, Mills came upon a magazine article that would have a profound impact on his life. The July 21, 1997, issue of *Time* magazine carried the headline "Danger in the Pills." The article detailed the discovery of a possible connection between heart valve disease and the use of the popular diet drug fen-phen. Mills believed he had found the solution to his financial woes.[2]

In late September 1997 Mills began advertising on television for fen-phen plaintiffs. In a comment related to the FDA's decision to grant fast-track status to Redux, Mills told reporters, "If I'm reading this right, the liability for the manufacturer and distributor may be greater than in your typical class action. This seems to be a case where they rushed the drugs to market without much testing."[3] Thousands of former fen-phen users lived within range of the TV stations on which Mills broadcast his ads, and the response far exceeded his expectations. Soon Mills had agreements with 311 potential plaintiffs to represent them in a lawsuit against AHP. However, because Mills typically negotiated out-of-court settlements, he had limited courtroom experience. He also had another distinct disadvantage: he lacked the necessary relationships with the medical community, especially cardiologists, to make the argument that his clients faced heart valve damage. Enter Gallion, who had the opposite problem: he had many physician friends at the University of Kentucky (UK) Hospital who could provide medical expertise, but very few clients. Once Gallion became aware of Mills's ad campaign, he paid Mills a visit, and Mills agreed to join forces with Gallion and Cunningham. Each of the trio brought his own unique history and personality into the gambit.

The Brains

Of the three, Bill Gallion was the most imposing. His square jaw and piercing eyes gave him the appearance of a snapping turtle, which, to a large extent, also described his tendency to seize whatever he wanted and hold on.

Gallion's mother and father were devout Catholics from Ashland, a small town along the Ohio River in the far northeastern corner of Kentucky. Bill was the seventh of nine children, and the family lived on the income generated from a liquor store they owned. After graduating from Holy Family School, Bill attended Ashland Community College while working in the family business. He initially enrolled at Marshall University in West Virginia but later transferred to the University of Kentucky in Lexington, where he graduated with a degree in political science and history. Believing that a career as a lawyer would get him out of the grimness of eastern Kentucky and keep him out for good, he enrolled at UK's School of Law in the fall of 1973.

By taking courses during the summer, Gallion graduated early and passed the bar in February 1976.

Despite his decidedly modest upbringing, Gallion was smitten by a desire for luxury at a relatively young age. One of his brothers was an executive at Opel, the German sports car manufacturer, and while visiting him, Gallion sipped fine wines, drove fast cars, and slept on sheets of Egyptian cotton. He longed to wear designer suits, dine in the best restaurants, and lounge by the pool of a massive home, just like his older brother. Prone to self-indulgence, Gallion loved to travel and never missed the annual Oktoberfest in Germany.[4]

Gallion landed his first job with Fowler, Measle, and Bell, a well-established Lexington law firm. One of the partners mentored Gallion, teaching him the techniques of trial law from both the plaintiff's and the defendant's perspectives. This partner also provided a prophetic nudge toward the future when he urged Gallion to travel to Covington to watch and learn from Stan Chesley as he conducted the famous Beverly Hills Supper Club trial.

Around this time, Gallion's wife, Holly, gave birth to a son with severe intellectual disabilities. By all accounts, Holly was a devoted mother, and while raising her son, she also enrolled at the UK School of Medicine. Through his wife's studies, Gallion acquired an extensive amount of knowledge about medical terminology and practice. Holly was eventually hired as an instructor of gynecological oncology at the UK School of Medicine, and Gallion's charm ingratiated him with many of the physicians there.

Within a short time, Gallion became a major rainmaker for his law firm by defending physicians being sued for malpractice. His prowess was especially appreciated after UK Hospital decided to become self-insured. As described by a former associate, Gallion was not particularly effective in the courtroom. His real forte was wearing down his opponents. He questioned every document, no matter how trivial, and every deposition, no matter how routine. In many cases, the plaintiffs' attorneys became so frustrated that they settled out of court rather than go to trial. But Gallion was merely the ringmaster; he let others do the heavy lifting. His reputation raised his status among the UK physicians and administrators to that of a folk hero. It was during this time that Gallion first met Mark Modlin—a name that would loom large in his later career.

As a consequence of his success, Gallion decided to establish his own law firm. He organized a group of law school classmates and other acquaintances to create Gallion, Baker, and Bray (GBB), a small firm with only three partners and a handful of associates. In addition to his UK connections, Gallion had his premier client: Liberty Mutual Life Insurance. This helped make GBB immediately successful, raising Gallion's lifestyle to one that matched his older brother's.

Gallion had an eye for talent and a knack for engendering deep loyalty. Beginning at age eighteen, Liz Overton worked with him for ten years. With Gallion's encouragement and financial assistance, she attended the University of Kentucky and graduated with honors; she then enrolled in law school and graduated first in her class. Overton's gratitude toward her employer and mentor was palpable. Given Gallion's passion for playing the bon vivant, he did not have much time for the practice of law, and according to a former colleague, he only managed to darken the door at GBB perhaps twice a month. This left Overton to pick up the slack, and she was more than happy to do so.

Overton was not the only one who found Gallion extremely charismatic. Many considered him shallow and insincere, but others were captivated by his dominant personality. He had a natural ability to put strangers at ease, and he could beguile a guest into believing that he or she was the only other person in the room. He was a lavish entertainer; at restaurants, nothing was too good for his tablemates, and he always insisted on picking up the check. Gallion liked to live large.

According to former associates, Gallion's charms worked particularly well with women, leading to several intense affairs. One romantic partner was a hospital administrator who fell deeply in love with Gallion. He had the odd compulsion to provide his paramours with trinkets and other luxuries identical to those he had purchased for his wife. Holly was so devoted to her husband that she managed to endure his infidelities, although she was known to divulge secrets after several glasses of wine. When the hospital administrator fell out of favor and onto hard times, Holly bought the gifts her husband had lavished on her rival, including fur coats, jewelry, and even lingerie.

The Wanderer

Shirley Cunningham was raised in Trigg County, where his father was a sharecropper and his mother a schoolteacher. Trigg, like the rest of western Kentucky, is culturally part of the Deep South. Cunningham had planned to play minor league baseball after high school and then return to the farm, believing that he would be granted an agricultural deferment to avoid the draft and a tour in Vietnam. Upon learning that agricultural exemptions no longer applied, he enrolled at Tennessee State University, a historically black college and his mother's alma mater. While working his way through college as a janitor and a bus driver, he caught the eye of the university president, Fredrick Humphries, who helped him enroll at the University of Kentucky School of Law.

After passing the bar in 1980, Cunningham's early endeavors were oddly varied. These professional forays included assistant county attorney, assistant professor of agricultural economics at UK, talk-show producer, host for a local news station, and vice president and general counsel for a bank. For those who worked with Cunningham, these disparate occupations were connected by a common thread: Cunningham was less than competent in all of them.

Despite his shortcomings, Cunningham aspired to be the first African American elected to the Kentucky legislature. In this effort he faced Jerry Lundergan, a perennially unsuccessful candidate, in the Democratic primary. The ensuing campaign was an ugly one in which Cunningham accused Lundergan of voter intimidation and civil rights violations. Lundergan won the primary but lost the general election by twenty-seven votes. An embittered Cunningham went on to join the Republican Party, while Lundergan went on to become chairman of the Kentucky Democratic Party.

By 1987, Cunningham had opened his own law office; he represented injured workers and small-time drug traffickers and handled other low-end legal matters, staying just ahead of his creditors. One afternoon, a colleague invited Cunningham to join him at a legal conference in Lexington. Cunningham had no money in his wallet and no checking account, so he stopped off at a laundromat he owned and paid his registration fee in quarters. At one point, Cunningham was forced to declare bankruptcy, leaving many creditors, including a local bank, in the lurch.

Eventually, Cunningham's fortunes began to look up when he started representing plaintiffs in medical malpractice suits. In this capacity, he and Gallion first met during the wrongful-death suit of Emily Withers, who had been treated at the UK Hospital. As he had done many times to delay proceedings, Gallion argued that UK, as a public entity, had sovereign immunity against lawsuits. This was based on the long-standing concept of common law that "the king can do no wrong." Cunningham represented the family of the deceased in an appeal before the Supreme Court, and he and the Withers family prevailed.

Cunningham's first wife, Annette, was also a UK Law School graduate. Together they had one son, but given the pressures of a two-career family, they divorced in 1985.[5] Cunningham's second marriage was to a schoolteacher, with whom he had two children. The couple also raised Cunningham's son from his first marriage. Throughout his second marriage, the dutiful Cunningham often made the three-hour drive to visit his ailing mother. When she died, the entire family attended the funeral service in Trigg County. At the funeral home, photographs of various family members were displayed, including the mother's deceased husband, her two sons, and several grandchildren. Oddly, there was also a photo of an unidentified child about four years old. Much to the shock of Cunningham's wife, the child in the photograph belonged to Cunningham and a secret lover. Soon thereafter, Cunningham had two ex-wives.[6]

The Man

Melbourne Mills was born and raised in Lexington, where his father was an architect. After two failed attempts to complete law school at the University of Kentucky, he later served in a noncombat role during the Korean War. Mills eventually graduated from the law school at the University of Louisville; he then worked for the Kentucky legislature as a researcher and spent two years in Hawaii. He and his first wife, Nancy, raised two daughters. After turning forty, Mills opened a private practice in Versailles, Kentucky. Just a fifteen-minute drive from Lexington, Versailles's picturesque downtown consists of well-kept storefronts, many dating from the nineteenth century.

Long before his involvement with the fen-phen litigation, Mills left an indelible mark on the practice of law in Kentucky. At one time, both statutes and codes of ethics prohibited attorneys from advertising their services. It was considered improper for attorneys to describe their abilities or legal specialties. In 1977, in *Bates v. The State Bar of Arizona,* the US Supreme Court held that the disciplinary rules imposed by state bar associations to prohibit attorneys from advertising were unconstitutional.

In this landmark case, the appellants, John R. Bates and Van O'Steen, were young attorneys in Phoenix. Because their profit margins were so low, they needed substantial volume to stay in business. After two years of struggling, the partners concluded that if they were to survive, they needed to advertise both themselves and their fee schedule. Someone complained to the Arizona Bar, which determined that the two must cease advertising, and each was suspended from the practice of law for six months. The case was eventually appealed to the US Supreme Court. The high court rejected the argument that the public was incapable of making reasoned determinations of their own legal needs. In a split decision, the court upheld attorneys' right to market their services. In his dissenting opinion, Justice Lewis Powell wrote, "Today's decision will have a profound effect on the practice of law" and will be "injurious to those whom the ban on legal advertising was meant to protect." Powell was prescient on both counts.

Mills had long believed that legal services should be marketed like every other business and that, by shrouding the law in mystery, minorities and the poor were ill prepared to obtain competent representation. Accordingly, he watched closely as *Bates* progressed through the court system. When the Supreme Court issued its ruling on June 27, 1977, this was precisely the break Mills needed. The very next day, he ran an ad in the *Lexington Herald-Leader* seeking clients and touting his knowledge of no-fault divorce. Thus Mills arguably became the first attorney to legally advertise his services in the United States.

Mills's television ads promoting his legal services relative to workers' compensation claims were the first to be viewed in Kentucky, and four decades later, they are still remembered as cringe-worthy. Images of Mills facing a fearsome T. rex were transposed next to the courthouse steps, and when Mills reached out to touch the dinosaur, it shrank way. During this magical transformation, an excited voice exhorted viewers to "Call the Man." Mills promised the aggressive pursuit of just recompense.

Mills realized that to be successful, one had to be patient. Initially, the public response was tepid at best, but with time and money, Mills eventually achieved a name recognition that was virtually 100 percent—a status usually reserved only for celebrities like his idol Elvis Presley. Because most of his business consisted of work-related disability claims, he also sponsored and heavily advertised the $10,000 Melbourne Mills Rehabilitation Award, bestowed on an individual who had prevailed over an acquired impairment. In these early years, the Kentucky legal profession looked down its nose at the philistine arriviste, but over the next decades, they would all pile on the advertising train. Imitation is the sincerest form of flattery.

As the years passed, Mills's shock of hair turned snow white, and he slowly succumbed to the dissipation caused by excessive alcohol consumption. Yet even at his lowest point, Mills stayed remarkably well informed, reading a stack of newspapers each morning. At age eighty-nine, although his body has suffered the ravages of hard living, his memory remains clear.

The team of Gallion, Cunningham, and Mills certainly had disparate backgrounds. Gallion was raised in the mountains of eastern Kentucky by parents who operated a liquor store, Cunningham was an African American whose father was a sharecropper in western Kentucky, and Mills grew up in the heart of the genteel bluegrass country of central Kentucky. Within this loose confederacy, Gallion and Cunningham formed the closest relationship, later becoming partners in a spectacularly successful business venture. Because of his heavy drinking and questionable reliability, Mills would remain the third wheel. In the fullness of time, Mills's status as the outcast would prove to be his salvation.

6

Brothers in Arms

BY 1998, EVENTS WERE UNFOLDING in a relatively promising manner for the three newly allied attorneys Gallion, Cunningham, and Mills (here, referred to collectively as GCM). Calls rolled into Mills's office in response to his ads on television, eventually attracting interest from more than 6,500 potential plaintiffs. About 4,500 of them decided to join the national class-action suit in Philadelphia, which was considered a sure way to collect damages.

However, 574 Kentuckians chose to "opt out" of the national settlement and signed a document, informally known as the Orange Form (for the color of the paper it was printed on), to that effect. These 574 thought their chances for a big payout would be better in Kentucky than in Philadelphia. Of these, 431 hired one of the three Kentucky lawyers to represent them. The overwhelming majority, 311, signed with Mills, followed by Cunningham with 117 and Gallion with only 3. The contracts used by Gallion and Cunningham used identical language and did not mention that the clients would be part of a class action. This omission was contrary to Rule 1.8(g) of the ethics code, which requires attorneys to obtain their clients' consent if the proposed legal action will be conducted as an aggregate with multiple plaintiffs rather than as an individual lawsuit. Mills's contract did state that a class action was anticipated, as well as noting that if attorneys' fees were awarded by the court, they "shall not be more than 30% [of] the client's net recovery."[1]

The resultant lawsuit, *Darla S. Guard et al. v. American Home Products* (or, more commonly, *Guard*), was filed in Boone County Circuit Court as civil action number 98-CI-75, with Judge Jay Bamberger presiding. *Guard* was entered as a class-action complaint with 431 named plaintiffs, as well as all "similarly situated" persons in Kentucky who had been injured by the diet drugs. GCM were hoping to obtain class-action status for all other affected Kentuckians before other attorneys could beat them to the punch. This nearly happened.

Complicating matters, Cletus Maricle, a circuit court judge in Leslie County, certified a similar class action known as *Feltner v. AHP* on the same day *Guard* was filed. Representatives of AHP disparagingly referred to *Feltner* as a drive-by class-action certification. The suit listed a man named Feltner, three other individuals, and "all Kentuckians who had consumed fenphen or Redux." Four attorneys filed this class action: Kenneth Buckle and Alva Hollon of Kentucky; Michael Gallagher of Houston, Texas; and Robert Aldridge of Vicksburg, Mississippi.

Meanwhile, Chesley was in the final stages of negotiating the national settlement in Philadelphia and would soon be casting about for potential claimants in Kentucky. It was only a matter of time before Chesley, GCM, and the *Feltner* quartet would engage in an all-or-nothing courtroom battle to determine whose class-action effort would represent Kentucky's opt-outs.

Chesley struck first. On July 30, 1999, the Prince of Torts filed his own class-action complaint in Boone County Circuit Court known as *Courtney v. AHP*. His class consisted of only three individuals, and Chesley soon filed a motion to consolidate *Guard* and *Courtney*. Chesley's sole purpose in creating *Courtney* had been to combine it with *Guard* and thus get his hands into GCM's potential money pot, which already contained 431 plaintiffs.[2]

The existence of *Feltner* complicated Chesley's plot, but he was a master of contrivances. He soon reached an undisclosed deal with the *Feltner* attorneys to transfer their clients to a separate class action in West Virginia. The order to that effect, signed by Judge Maricle and attorney Kenneth Buckle, also contained Chesley's initials: SMC. And in a bizarre twist of events, Chesley appeared in person as cocounsel at the *Feltner* preliminary hearing. Later, Chesley would deny having anything to do with the order or even knowing Buckle and Hollon.

Gallion was particularly upset when he learned that Chesley was trying to consolidate *Courtney* and *Guard*.[3] He saw Chesley as looking to take a big slice from the money pie while contributing only three plaintiffs. However, because of Chesley's vaunted reputation, it would be difficult for Judge Bamberger to deny Chesley's request to consolidate these two overlapping class-action suits. The impending courtroom drama would soon be resolved in a most unusual fashion.

The circumstances behind the initial face-to-face meeting between Gallion and Chesley are somewhat murky. According to Chesley, Gallion reached out to him through Richard Lawrence, a Cincinnati attorney who had helped Chesley organize fund-raising events for the Democratic Party. Lawrence also represented a few people seeking to sue American Home Products for fen-phen–related damages. In Gallion's more likely version of events, Gallion spotted Chesley by chance at a restaurant in downtown Cincinnati. Gallion was sitting at the bar and turned around to find Chesley standing next to him. Gallion immediately recognized the famous Beverly Hills Supper Club attorney, although his previous admiration for Chesley had soured somewhat. After brusquely introducing himself, Gallion informed Chesley that he did not want him involved in *Guard*. Chesley imperiously cocked his head and replied, "Well, you're going to have to get used to it." As it turned out, Chesley was correct.

Gallion believed he had an excellent working relationship with Helen Madonick, a key in-house attorney at AHP. He spoke with her frequently about the settlements for several of his clients who had developed primary pulmonary hypertension from taking the diet drugs. AHP was settling PPH claims throughout the United States separately from the more numerous cases involving heart valve damage. When Madonick suddenly stopped returning Gallion's phone calls, he learned the disturbing news that AHP executives had decided that all future communications would go through Chesley. Even though Chesley had been AHP's nemesis in the national settlement, he had somehow managed to outmaneuver Gallion with the inexplicable assistance of AHP.

Accordingly, GCM reluctantly relented and did not object when Judge Bamberger rolled *Guard* and *Courtney* into a single lawsuit, with Chesley as cocounsel. Chesley then advised his three plaintiffs from *Courtney* to join the national class action in Philadelphia. The treatment of the *Feltner* and *Courtney* plaintiffs is an example of what a later court would describe as Chesley's willingness to use people, including some of his own clients, merely as pawns to enhance his own fortune. Chesley would later describe these machinations as a power play.

Chesley then hammered out an agreement with GCM that provided himself with 27 percent of the attorneys' fees generated in the event of a settlement based on a successful mediation; that would be reduced to 15 percent if the case went to trial and the plaintiffs prevailed. In that case, Gallion was to be the lead trial attorney. In either event, GCM would receive the balance, except for 5 percent, which would go to Richard Lawrence. This agreement carried an expiration date of December 31, 1999, as Chesley was confident there would be plenty of time to negotiate the *Guard* settlement before the end of the year. Unfortunately for Chesley, the national settlement was not finalized until August 2000.

Just before Christmas 1999, at Lexington's busy Fayette Mall, a red-faced man in a Burberry coat was engaged in an intense cell phone conversation while pacing outside the entrance. That man was Gallion, and at the other end of the conversation was Chesley. Chesley had called to request an extension of their deal. But Gallion was now in the driver's seat, and he was unwilling to concede a 27 percent share. Driving down Chesley was something many had attempted but few had pulled off. However, when the negotiation was over, Chesley's percentage for a successful settlement had been reduced to 21 percent, with GCM sharing 74 percent and Lawrence again receiving the 5 percent balance. Lawrence's 5 percent stands out as exceptionally generous for a person who had no role other than recruiting a handful of plaintiffs. Gallion would later testify that Lawrence was allotted this portion in exchange for helping to select jurors should *Guard* be tried in court.

The new agreement again named Chesley as cocounsel, along with GCM. Accordingly, Chesley was not just a hireling to be used for the singular purpose of conducting the settlement negotiations. Rather, he was responsible for honoring all the contingency agreements GCM had signed with the 431 plaintiffs. These agreements limited legal fees to 30 to 33 percent of the clients' settlement amounts. Chesley would later testify that he had not received these simple, single-page documents, and he incorrectly asserted that he had no responsibility to the 431 *Guard* plaintiffs other than to negotiate a settlement.[4]

In preparation for a possible trial, David Helmers, a young associate of Gallion's, was sent across the country to find all the documents and all the successful strategies used by other lawyers against AHP. Apparently, many of these veteran attorneys empathized with his youth and inexperience, and Helmers returned with cache of court documents from other successful lawsuits against AHP.

Helmers had begun working for Gallion as a law school intern and remained after graduation. He was assigned this critical task of gathering strategic information even before passing the bar. Unlike most attorneys, Helmers did not attend law school immediately after graduating from college. He spent a few years in Washington, DC, as a staff member for Republican senator Mitch McConnell.

Of paramount importance for the GCM and Chesley team was obtaining certification as a class action from Judge Bamberger. Absent this class-action certification, their 431 clients were likely to relinquish their opt-out status and join the national class action. Ostensibly, AHP was opposed to the certification of *Guard* from the beginning. Bamberger would later testify that AHP virtually pleaded with him on multiple occasions, using the best legal representation it could muster, not to certify *Guard* as a class action. But based on ensuing events, Bamberger's assertion does not seem likely.

Oddly, despite his ignorance of class-action law, Helmers was tasked with the crucial responsibility of convincing Bamberger to certify *Guard*. Helmers's main argument was that because some of the *Guard* claimants had received their drugs from Dr. Duff's bariatric clinics, and AHP had supplied the drugs directly to the irresponsible Duff, *Guard* raised a new issue that was separate from the national class action. Because this was strictly a Kentucky issue, there was no cause to move the 431 plaintiffs out of state to the national action, since there were no overlapping jurisdictions between states. However, because Duff and some of the *Guard* plaintiffs lived outside of Kentucky, this was a slender reed on which to base an argument. Helmers would later testify that, apart from Gallion, the other attorneys at GBB considered *Guard* to be a lost cause—a "black hole."[5]

Yet Helmers ultimately prevailed. He described the proceedings as a battle of David and Goliath; however, this particular Goliath (AHP) was fighting with his sword sheathed and one hand tied behind his back. AHP seemed not particularly interested in prevailing. Just as critical to Helmers's "victory" was the presence in the courtroom of someone from Bamberger's past who made it likely that he would rule in Helmers's favor. That person was Mark Modlin.

Modlin was a psychologist who worked as a trial consultant. In this capacity, his role was to assist attorneys with client relations, jury selection, and the hiring of expert witnesses. But in this case, Modlin's real value was in his unusual relationship with Bamberger—a relationship founded on guilt. As longtime friends, Modlin and Bamberger were frequent golf partners. On a warm, sunny day in early 1987, the threesome of Bamberger, Modlin, and Judge Stanley Billingsley was golfing at Kenton County's public course.[6] After finishing the seventeenth hole, Bamberger noticed that he had left his club cover on the green, and he asked Modlin to retrieve the mislaid item. As Modlin drove his golf cart back to the green, he failed to notice a tightly stretched rope about one foot above the ground protecting a patch of newly laid sod. The rope slid up the front of the cart, "clotheslining" Modlin squarely on the neck. Although he might have been decapitated, Modlin finished the round! Nonetheless, he later learned that he had fractured several vertebrae.

The staff at the golf course recalled that the incident had occurred in March 1987, but Modlin insisted that it happened on May 27. A personal-injury lawsuit charging the Kenton County Parks Corporation with negligence was filed on May 28, 1988, just two days before the expiration of the statute of limitations. In the ensuing trial, the jury awarded Modlin $2,666,348 in damages, but the decision was later overturned by the Kentucky Court of Appeals, which found that Kenton County enjoyed sovereign immunity.[7]

Immediately after the accident, a distraught Bamberger made sure that Modlin had the help he needed to return to health. Neither of them fully recovered from the accident, which left them both with permanent impairments: Modlin to his gait, and Bamberger to his judgment. His lingering guilt would cloud his decision making whenever Modlin was involved. This was well known to several attorneys, including Chesley, who used Modlin as a "trial consultant" whenever Bamberger was the presiding judge in a case.[8] With that backdrop, Helmers's win was perhaps less a triumph than a foregone conclusion.

Throughout much of 2000, Chesley, as the key member of the Plaintiffs Management Committee in Philadelphia, continued to negotiate the national settlement with AHP. During these negotiations, AHP's defense team included Jack Vardaman, a graduate of Harvard Law School and a partner in the prestigious New York law firm of Williams and Connolly. Law was not Vardaman's original career objective, however; he had hoped to be a professional golfer. But, after facing Jack Nicklaus at a tournament in 1957 and witnessing Nicklaus's long, high drives, Vardaman came to the stark realization that the law would be a better profession for him.

According to Chesley, he and Vardaman maintained a long, mutually respectful professional relationship that spanned twenty years. It began when they sat on opposite sides of the table during mediations in the Dow Corning silicone breast implant class action. In fact, they became quite chummy. As Chesley later testified, long before the AHP national class action was initiated, he and Vardaman had conferred over breakfast in DC, discussing the prospects of legal action against AHP.

After the national settlement received preliminary approval from Judge Bechtle on August 28, 2000, Chesley and Vardaman were together again, this time as opposing sides in the *Guard* settlement. In a departure from Chesley's usual role as bête noir, his demeanor was much more congenial than caustic. However, within a few days, the two attorneys informed Judge Bamberger that their negotiations had reached an impasse. Consequently, Bamberger asked each party to hire a mediator to resolve their differences. Professional mediators are neutral participants enlisted for the sole purpose of facilitating an agreement and avoiding a trial. They are professionally bound to observe strict confidentiality.

The mediator selected by AHP was Daniel Weinstein, a retired judge from California. Weinstein, a founder of JAMS, the world's largest arbitration and mediation service, had played a key role in the settlement of several large-scale, complicated tort cases, including the one related to the Union Carbide chemical spill that killed 15,000 in Bhopal, India. Weinstein had also mediated settlements between AHP and PPH victims in the Golden State. AHP was paying Weinstein $10,000 a day to come to Lexington and act as its mediator. Gallion hired Pierce Hamblin, an attorney with a Lexington law firm, as the plaintiffs' mediator, paying him an undisclosed sum that was certainly much less than Weinstein's.

Based on his review of the records, his consideration of the arguments, and his vast experience, Weinstein's nonbinding assessment was that total damages for the 431 plaintiffs ranged between $20 million and $40 million. Gallion later testified that this settlement would have been fair. However, this amount was nowhere near what Chesley likely knew would be forthcoming from AHP.

Gallion and Helmers had worked assiduously to obtain a speedy trial, which was set to begin in July 2001. That date was now a mere two months away, making this the final opportunity for a settlement. It is unlikely that Gallion's urgency in obtaining a trial date was to obtain the funds necessary to address the deteriorating health conditions of their clients. Rather, their clients' medical conditions were likely to steadily improve over time, and with each passing month, it would be increasingly difficult to argue that the plaintiffs suffered from latent heart damage. Even more difficult would be seating a jury that empathized with the plaintiffs. Perhaps the *Guard* plaintiffs had erred in pinning their hopes on GCM and eschewing the national settlement.

In the national settlement (*Brown v. AHP*), AHP agreed to set up a $3.75 billion trust: $2.5 billion for medical compensation, $1 billion for medical monitoring, and the remaining $250 million for attorneys' fees.[9] (Later, another $1.275 billion would be added to the trust.) AHP considered itself fortunate that the settlement did not include punitive damages, which might have added several billion to its losses.

The national settlement had other complicating factors. More than 650,500 former users of the diet drugs had signed up. As an agreement appeared imminent, it looked like the deal might be blown to pieces when 88,000 of those individuals claimed to have serious valve damage, significantly more than AHP and the court had assumed. With surgical procedures for valve replacement costing $400,000, this could add up to a devastating $35 billion. Fortunately for AHP, Judge Bechtle concluded that the diagnoses of valve disease were based on questionable findings by the many shoddy echocardiogram clinics that had sprung up around the country to cash in on AHP's woes. For example, Echo Motion, a clinic in Chapel Hill, North Carolina, cleared $10 million after conducting 70,000 echocardiograms in one year, not one of which was reviewed by a cardiologist. Assuming that Echo Motion operated six days a week, it would have had to perform more than 200 procedures a day. Although the "echo mill' moniker is certainly fitting for Echo Motion, it pales in comparison to an operation in Kansas City (described later).

After a ruling that 100 percent of echocardiograms had to be reviewed by cardiologists (up from 15 percent), the number of valve damage claims fell dramatically. In the five years after the settlement, AHP paid $1.6 billion for the relatively small number of claims (4,391) involving serious heart damage. This represented only 0.007 percent of the claimants. That still left about 50,000 former diet drug users who had opted out of the national settlement and decided to take their chances with individual or state-based class actions. By this time, the highly paid AHP legal team was beginning to get its mojo back. In Mississippi, it managed to settle nearly 3,000 claims for $216 million, or roughly $72,000 each. AHP settled a slew of other cases for the modest amount of $350 million.

However, the national settlement proved to be even more parsimonious. The roughly $5 billion was divided among 650,000 actual claimants (out of 6 million total users), amounting to less than $8,000 each. According to an October 8, 1999, *New York Times* article, those who took the drugs for sixty days or less received only a refund of the cost of their prescriptions. Even for those with the most serious heart damage, awards did not exceed $1.5 million. Stock analyst David Saks was quoted as saying, "You have to say American Home Products pulled off a pretty good settlement."[10]

Some early estimates of the national settlement had been as high as $10 billion, and Chesley was notorious for extracting ruinous settlements that took corporate defendants to the brink of bankruptcy and beyond—witness Dow Corning and Pan-Am. In contrast, the value of AHP stock rose 7.8 percent immediately after the national settlement, and analysts were optimistic for continued growth. Many were surprised by the PMC's leniency. In the *New York Post,* plaintiffs' attorney Ronald Benjamin declared, "I don't think it was an adequate enough settlement."[11]

Chesley informed reporters that the attorneys' fees from the $5 billion settlement would likely total $429 million—a princely sum—but it would have to be shared among well over 100 attorneys. In contrast, 95 percent of the *Guard* legal fees would be divided among only four attorneys. If the *Guard* settlement was sufficiently large, Chesley could earn a much bigger payday from *Guard* than from the national settlement.

Helmers, fresh out of law school, used the documents he had collected from other attorneys to devise a strategy for *Guard,* a case involving considerable medical complexity. He produced a chart—known as the "matrix"—that assigned each of the 431 plaintiffs to a designated category of injury and specified their attorneys' fee agreements. The matrix's categories of injury listed 263 as having negligible damage, 138 having mild to moderate damage, and 30 having the most serious damage. The validity of Helmers's matrix was questionable. Gallion, who had defended a number of malpractice suits for University of Kentucky Hospital, knew some of the finest board-certified cardiologists in Kentucky and could have called on their expertise, whereas Helmers was not even certified to perform CPR. It would later become evident that this matrix was merely intended to give the subsequent distribution of fees the illusion of medical validity, as it was largely ignored during the distribution of settlement funds.[12]

When mediation began on April 30, 2001, Pierce Hamblin, the mediator chosen by Gallion, ushered Gallion, Helmers, and Chesley, along with the AHP team of Jack Vardaman and Helen Madonick, into a large conference room at the law firm of Landrum Shouse, overlooking Lexington's busy Vine Street. Cunningham and Mills had not been invited. Their exclusion in favor of Helmers spoke volumes about the extent to which Gallion had taken control and his reliance on Helmers. Gallion described himself as the "captain" and Helmers as his "first mate."

As negotiations began, the prospects for a settlement agreement appeared hopeless. Vardaman offered $5 million; Chesley, hunched over the table in his usual slouch, countered with $500 million. The day featured much testosterone-fueled bravado. Chesley, who worked to convey a public image of the courtly liberal, was reportedly so abrasive that, according to Helmers, a woman in the room (perhaps Madonick) was "driven to tears." But as Chesley would later testify, all that drama was merely theater.[13]

Gradually, the gap narrowed, and by the end of the first day, Vardaman had placed an offer of $150 million on the table. Gallion, giddy with excitement, wanted to hold out for $300 million. But Chesley, who knew that was too much, warned him, "Pigs get fat and hogs get slaughtered." Cunningham, who was waiting in the wings after inviting himself to the second day of mediation, counseled Gallion to come down to earth. When Gallion called Mills and told him the offer, an ecstatic Mills shouted into the phone, "Take it, take it." But Chesley was not finished. In exchange for GCM signing an ill-defined "side letter" agreement (a codicil to the main agreement), Chesley was able to sweeten the pot by another $50 million. The potential liability attached to the codicil appeared to expose GCM to considerable risk, and Chesley described this potential liability to Gallion as "whatever else is out there in Kentucky." Chesley reportedly asked Gallion and Cunningham, "Are you guys willing to take the risk?" And they answered, "Yes." At GCM's criminal trial, Chesley would back away from this statement.[14]

The legitimacy of the risk GCM assumed in exchange for the additional $50 million would be a topic of enormous importance during future courtroom battles and legal tribunals. Of the estimated 200,000 fen-phen users in Kentucky, only 4,000 had joined the national settlement and another 574 had formally opted out, leaving thousands of potential plaintiffs looming. Gallion and Cunningham agreed to take this risk in exchange for the extra $50 million, but they did not tell Mills about it. By this time, Gallion and Cunningham had grown wary of Mills, who was drinking a fifth of bourbon every day and was often inebriated by 10:00 a.m. Mills's favorite bourbon was Old Crow, a decidedly plebian variety that he prized for its oaky flavor; he bought it by the case from a local Rite Aid pharmacy.[15] Former client W. L. Carter told reporters he was "shocked" when he went to Mills's Versailles office to sign certain papers related to *Guard* and found the lawyer dressed in a T-shirt, flip-flops, and boxer briefs. Carter said, "That image is burned in my mind forever. He was ultra-casual that morning." Mills later moved his office to Lexington, which Carter described as consisting of a desk and two metal folding chairs in the middle of a gutted office suite. Carter noted, "The place looked like it had been looted, you could still see where carpet had been ripped off the floor."[16]

May 1, 2001, was a gorgeous day in Lexington, with a clear sky, calm winds, and a forecast high of 80 degrees. The foliage of the trees lining Lexington's downtown was taking on the fullness of summer. It was going to be a particularly bounteous day for GCM and Chesley. Just the previous day, Vardaman had faxed the draft agreement to AHP's New York headquarters. Helmers remembered that Chesley hurried the process along, and the document came back with only minor changes. Madonick's boss, Lou Hoynes, authorized Vardaman to sign the $200 million agreement on behalf of AHP.

The finalized agreement was signed by Gallion, Cunningham, and Mills. Cunningham later told investigators that he did not bother to keep a copy. Notably missing was the signature of Chesley, who reportedly demurred because he was not the attorney for the *Guard* plaintiffs, which was not accurate.

Soon after, Chesley and his wife organized a celebratory dinner in downtown Cincinnati. In attendance were Gallion, Cunningham, Helmers, and Modlin, along with their spouses. Mills was absent. Chesley crowed that *Guard* was by far the largest per-plaintiff settlement for diet drug–related damages in the United States. Helmers would later reminisce from the witness stand that Chesley really knew how to throw a dinner party.

After settling on the magnificent sum of $200 million, the lawyers discovered that there was one additional plaintiff represented by GCM, a man named Greg Dixon. AHP was so anxious to close the books on the deal (for reasons suggested later) that it added another $450,000 to the settlement without a murmur of resistance, making the total settlement $200,450,000 (for simplicity's sake, the settlement amount is stated as $200 million throughout).

Under the agreement, GCM had to first decertify (dissolve) the class action and then distribute the net settlement proceeds among the 431 plaintiffs. This action was taken without giving the required notice to their clients. The remaining fen-phen users who had opted out of the now closed national settlement but had failed to join *Guard* were left with nothing.

Since AHP, in effect, settled with each of the 431 plaintiffs as individuals rather than a class, did this mean that *Guard* was never a class action? If it was not a class action, why was it necessary to have it decertified? Remarkably, the settlement document did not address this crucial issue.

GCM agreed to a confidentiality agreement that the trio later interpreted as also extending to the 431 plaintiffs (now claimants). Even more important, GCM agreed to obtain the signatures of 95 percent of the 431 claimants on statements affirming that all their claims against AHP had been satisfied. Absent these signatures, AHP would be entitled to keep the portion of the settlement belonging to the claimants who refused to sign the release, or it could walk away from the agreement altogether. Soon thereafter, during a meeting at Gallion's home, Helmers was instructed to revise his original matrix to base the percentages of the final settlement on the severity of each plaintiff's fen-phen–related damage. In this way, fewer signatures would be needed to earn most of the money. In the end, however, this tinkering proved unnecessary, as the vast majority of the 431 plaintiffs willingly provided their signatures.

The signatures of the claimants had to be delivered by September 1, 2001. This situation created the rationale for holding back a residual amount of the settlement funds. This is sometimes referred to as the "all or nothing" dilemma. As detailed by Howard Erichson, to avoid running out of funds before all the claimants are satisfied and their releases signed, it is prudent to settle with each one for as little as possible. If all goes as planned, all the claimants will be satisfied, and then the surplus is supposed to be distributed in proportion to the initial settlement amounts.[17] Chesley described this practice as a front-end-loaded, fluid settlement. Whatever the process, the surplus is not the attorneys' to keep.

Of crucial significance was the aforementioned "side letter" agreement, which *appeared* to obligate GCM to satisfy the claims of all the other Kentuckians who had taken fen-phen. AHP colorfully termed the settlement an "intergalactic peace." Most critically, the side letter also specified that GCM were to create a contingency fund of $7.5 million. The exact purpose of the contingency fund would be a major point of contention and had a significant bearing on the outcome of the later criminal trial. The relevant provision read: "Notwithstanding paragraph 1, the settling attorneys and settling claimants shall not be obligated to indemnify AHP for attorney's fees and expenses *nor* for any amount in excess of $7,500,000 [emphasis added]." Gallion would maintain that the "nor" in the sentence made no grammatical sense and, according to his recollection, the sentence should have read: "the settling attorneys and settling claimants shall not be obligated to indemnify AHP for attorney fees and expenses for any amount in excess of $7,500,000." Obviously, without this tiny conjunction, the purpose of the contingency fund changed radically. Was the side letter intended to indemnify AHP for legal fees in excess of $7.5 million *or* from the future claims of all other Kentuckians? According to Gallion, the contingency reserve was for the very limited purpose of paying for AHP's subsequent legal fees. Chesley maintained that he had insisted on the $7.5 million cap, fearing that Vardaman and his firm Williams and Connolly would take GCM to the cleaners, using the opportunity to rack up legal fees far beyond $7.5 million.

Gallion would also insist at his criminal trial that GCM needed to retain a large portion of the settlement because of the obligation to pay for ongoing medical monitoring of any Kentucky resident who was not part of the national settlement. Medical monitoring to diagnose any latent heart valve issues had been included in the national settlement, but such costs were not covered in Kentucky. Gallion rested his contention on *Wood v. Wyeth-Ayerst Laboratories*, which sought to allow an award for the presumed costs of medical monitoring. A ruling by the Kentucky Supreme Court rejected this position and explained: "a cause of tort requires a physical injury to the plaintiff. To find otherwise would stretch the limits of logic."[18]

This meant that an actual injury, not just the possibility of future injury, was necessary to award damages. *Wood* was appealed to the US Supreme Court, which ruled in August 2003 that residents of states that forbade the award of medical monitoring could not receive an award for medical monitoring in a national class action. Accordingly, Gallion's argument that GCM was obligated to bear the costs of ongoing medical monitoring was baseless.

It is important to note that the clock on the twelve-month statute of limitations began to tick with decertification of the class, which occurred the week following the May 2 settlement. (Class actions were relatively new to the scene, and the case law for class-action suits continues to be established. The important standard for setting the starting point for purposes of statutes of limitations was *American Pipe and Construction Company v. Utah*.) With each passing day, the window for additional claimants to come forward from elsewhere in Kentucky closed a bit.

On the face of it, the side letter merely awarded GCM an additional $50 million in exchange for a $7.5 million indemnity—an indemnity that AHP failed to take advantage of when it later settled with seventy additional plaintiffs after the *Guard* agreement was finalized![19] Did AHP senselessly give away $50 million, or was it intended to satisfy a previous understanding between Chesley and AHP to bring the settlement up to $200 million?

It is not clear to what extent Chesley encouraged the subsequent low-ball offers to the 431 plaintiffs named in the settlement. Although Chesley had his detractors, few critics doubted his intelligence. Law professor Arthur Miller, who worked with Chesley in many trials, noted that one of his greatest gifts was "enormous peripheral vision," calling Chesley a person who "sees things in their entirety."[20] But Chesley's usually infallible intuition apparently did not warn him of GCM's shameless attempt to take a double helping of legal fees. There appears to be no evidence that Chesley knew GCM had already taken their contingency fees when they asked Bamberger to approve a larger class-action legal fee.

By all accounts, the $200 million settlement was a triumph. It was more than ample to fairly compensate the 431 plaintiffs, given the size of the national settlement. However, this astonishing amount tempted GCM to conceal its size and keep most of the windfall for themselves. For GCM and the many others who coveted the $200 million, it would prove to be the proverbial "curse of the monkey's paw"—a classic story by W. W. Jacobs in which the paw's possessors are granted a wish, resulting in horrific unintended consequences.

7

A Very Strange Thing

WHY WERE VARDAMAN AND AHP willing to part with the incredibly large sum of $200 million for so few claimants? That is a most confounding question. On the first day of the mediation, Weinstein took a marker and wrote on a white board in large figures: $20–30 million and $30–40 million. He explained that, based on his considerable experience with fen-phen settlements, the first dollar range would be a fair settlement, and the second would be what the plaintiffs might receive on their best day. Helmers testified that Weinstein was so appalled as the size of the settlement continued to skyrocket, eventually reaching $200 million, that he stomped out of the room and slammed the door behind him.

New York University professor Arthur R. Miller, a renowned expert in civil procedure, testified at Chesley's disbarment hearing. He described the settlement amount in these terms: "That's alchemy. That's incredible . . . the value added was $175 million."[1]

The *Guard* settlement was so enormous and out of the ordinary that the decision makers at AHP took great pains to keep the amount secret. AHP wanted to ensure that no other group of litigants who opted out of the national settlement would try to seek as much per claimant. For this reason, the settlement agreement contained a provision that held GCM responsible for any disclosure by any of the claimants, assessing a $100,000 penalty per occurrence.

Equally mystifying, AHP would have been on very firm ground if the mediation had fallen through and the case had gone to trial. Gallion was a mediocre litigator and would not have been particularly intimidating to the now battle-tested AHP attorneys, referred to as the "war team." Further, Chesley was notorious for avoiding trials, preferring to settle even if it resulted in a less than optimal award. In addition, if GCM won after a trial, Chesley's portion would have been reduced from 21 to 15 percent, making him even more anxious to settle for whatever he could get.

Even more puzzling is the fact that, by the time of the settlement negotiations, both AHP and the four attorneys for the plaintiffs were aware that the purported health consequences of fen-phen use were not nearly as serious as previously assumed. By Gallion's own admission, at least 230 of the 431 plaintiffs had no evidence of heart valve damage, so the facts would have been against them in a trial. During GCM's criminal trial, Helen Madonick testified that 269 of the 431 had zero to mild heart regurgitation, a condition that occurs naturally in a significant portion of the general population. Even among the 30 serious cases in Helmers's matrix, there was no way to be certain, based on the medical evidence, that their conditions were the result of taking the diet medication. Helmers would acknowledge under oath that of the 431 plaintiffs, only 4 had undergone surgery to repair their heart valves. Among the remaining plaintiffs, any conditions caused by using fen-phen were very likely to subside and eventually disappear after they stopped taking the drugs. GCM had to concede that, of the four plaintiffs who had died, taking the diet drugs was a secondary cause at best.

Both Gallion and Chesley would later testify that AHP had been willing to part with such a staggering amount of money because the company had indemnified Dr. Duff, who purchased the drugs directly from AHP. However, during GCM's trial, it was learned that AHP had entered into written contractual agreements with other doctors around the country to indemnify them as well.

One theory was that AHP had concluded that a jury trial in northern Kentucky might be a disaster. Thus, despite having both the facts and the law in their favor, AHP's attorneys agreed to pay the *Guard* plaintiffs several times more per claimant than had just been awarded in the national settlement. On the surface, fear that a Covington, Kentucky, jury might deliver a punitive verdict of epic proportions was not completely far-fetched. After all, Chesley had orchestrated a similar outcome in the Beverly Hills Supper Club case.

Even though Madonick thought AHP had a pretty strong case, she claimed the company preferred to settle for $200 million rather than risk a trial in Covington. However, her alleged fear of a Covington jury seems to be a smoke screen. The truth is that Covington juries are notoriously conservative, and awards are generally small. For example, when a forty-four-year-old member of the Covington Fire Department was killed in a car wreck, leaving behind a wife and children, the jury awarded only $440,000.

Had GCM been genuinely interested in seeking a venue with a sympathetic jury pool, a much better choice would have been the federal court in Ashland, Gallion's hometown. Ashland is a major terminus for Highway 23, the "Hillbilly Highway" running from the extreme southeastern corner of Kentucky all the way to Ohio and beyond. Native Ashlanders are notoriously suspicious of outsiders, especially those who represent big corporations. Also, an Ashland jury would have been composed of folks familiar with Melbourne Mills's incessant television ads portraying himself as the champion who helped injured workers get their rightfully deserved workers' compensation checks from reckless employers.

So why did GCM choose to take *Guard* to a Covington courtroom? The likely answer is Judge Bamberger. They all knew Bamberger had an Achilles' heel in the form of Mark Modlin. In addition to Bamberger's guilt over the golfing accident, he and Modlin were partners in a real estate investment. Though there was no guarantee that the trial would be assigned to Bamberger, it was certainly worth a shot. So, perhaps at Chesley's urging, Gallion hired Modlin to serve on the plaintiffs' team as a "consultant." As such, Modlin's most important task was to be present in the courtroom and in the judge's chambers. He performed this function to perfection.

In the legal vernacular, GCM's strategy is known as "forum shopping"—that is, selecting a court where the plaintiff is likely to receive a favorable determination. Typically, forum shopping involves finding a venue where the jury is likely to decide against the defendants. The conclusion that GCM forum shopped is bolstered by the fact that all three attorneys were from Lexington. It would have made far more sense to try *Guard* in the courtrooms of that city. If nothing else, they would have saved themselves the trouble of driving an hour and a half to Covington every day.

The answer to the question posed at the beginning of this chapter—why AHP was willing to part with so much money—is far more nuanced. Two explanations have already been eliminated. First, juries in Covington tend to be conservative with their awards, so this was not a legitimate worry for AHP. Second, and more important, since it was AHP's intent and understanding (eventually affirmed at trial) that the *Guard* settlement was meant to satisfy the damages of only the 431 plaintiffs and was not an open-ended class action, there was no chance that Dr. Duff's former patients or anyone else from Kentucky could seek damages from GCM. In fact, Vardaman testified at GCM's trial, "This [Duff] was something that Mr. Chesley harped on. And to me, it didn't appear to me that this was going to be a terribly serious matter."[2]

The relationship between Chesley and Vardaman was suspicious. As described earlier, Gallion was initially very opposed to Chesley joining the *Guard* suit but was forced to relent after AHP directed that all communications go through Chesley.[3] It is also curious that, after the indictments of GCM, Vardaman made a point of disassociating himself from Chesley. Gallion recalled during his trial that, immediately after the *Guard* agreement was reached in May, Chesley and Vardaman paired up the far end of the conference table to share their mutual regard. Later, when Chesley was facing his own legal problems, he was so confident of their relationship that he casually dropped off an affidavit at Vardaman's office that backed up Chesley's false version of events, assuming that Vardaman would just go along. Chesley's presumption of Vardaman's acquiescence and Vardaman's efforts to dissociate himself from Chesley are two sides of the same coin—namely, a relationship that Chesley wished to exploit and Vardaman wished to forget.

Other evidence of collusion between AHP and Chesley was brought up by Gallion during his trial. Gallion described an AHP filing with the Securities and Exchange Commission as "cryptic." These filings are used by stockholders and potential stockholders to assess the financial health of a corporation, and AHP's filing contained the caveat that it might incur significant costs for ongoing medical monitoring, even though its legal team knew that this was unlikely after the recent *Wood v. Wyeth-Ayerst* decision by the Kentucky Supreme Court. Most curiously, AHP's annual stockholders' report included a description of the opt-out settlements in every other state in the country but made no mention of the *Guard* settlement in Kentucky. Gallion found this very strange. It appeared that AHP did not want its stockholders to learn about the vastly disproportionate settlement amount.

Even more strange was a story related by Mills. Gallion was seeking to negotiate a settlement with AHP for one of his PPH cases. When AHP refused to budge beyond $3 million, Gallion shared his frustration with Chesley. After one phone call from Chesley, AHP agreed to increase the award to $5 million.[4] If accurate, this is a stark example of Chesley's great influence within the higher echelons of AHP.

These facts suggest (but do not prove) a possible quid pro quo arrangement between Chesley and AHP in the form of a low-dollar national settlement in exchange for a massive *Guard* settlement. Had *Guard* been settled for $30 million, in line with Weinstein's estimate, GCM would have earned $10 million in attorneys' fees, and Chesley's share would have been $2.1 million. In contrast, GCM's contingency fee for a $200 million settlement was $61 million, of which Chesley's share (21 percent) was $12.8 million. If the arrangement between Chesley and AHP did in fact exist, there is no evidence that he shared the plan with GCM. However, based on his testimony, it is apparent that Gallion suspected some type of prearrangement between Chesley and AHP.

Another intriguing fact is contained in the 2013 report of the findings in *KBA v. Chesley.* Investigators concluded that Vardaman and Chesley had already agreed on a settlement before the negotiations of April 30 and May 1, 2001, and the mediation was merely for show. Further, in a brief for Chesley's appeal of his disbarment, his attorneys wrote, "Vardaman and Chesley knew before the mediation they could settle for $200 million," which led "Vardaman to believe the mediation would be over in 30 minutes." Based on a deposition by Vardaman, this astonishing brief went on to state: "However when the mediation began, Gallion took a much different tack than Vardaman expected and the mediation ultimately stretched over two days."[5]

Since Chesley testified that he had not read any of the attorneys' one-page contracts, he certainly never read 431 medical reports before coming to the $200 million agreement with Vardaman, further evidence that the monumental settlement had nothing to do with the plaintiffs' alleged injuries. By extension, the size of the *Guard* settlement was not an end in itself; rather, its purpose seemed to be to funnel a large fee to Chesley for the reasons already described.

Why did Chesley and Vardaman hide the fact that they had already come to an agreement before the formal mediation? More important, when did this agreement take place? Clearly, AHP executives had approved the settlement amount. So what did AHP receive in return for this obscenely generous award?

If all this were true, the scheme might have worked if not for the greed of GCM, which extended beyond even Chesley's imagination. The fact that GCM had already taken their 33 percent contingency fees before Bamberger later awarded much larger fees could have occurred without Chesley's knowledge. Accordingly, it appears that Chesley and GCM were working behind each other's backs—Chesley keeping mum about the nature of the settlement negotiations, and GCM not mentioning the taking of their contingency fees. Their mutual duplicity led to their mutual demise.

8

Lowering the Bar

SOON AFTER HIS *GUARD* VICTORY, the always restless Chesley once again took the short drive across the Ohio River into Covington to represent a group of plaintiffs in a scandal that was roiling the nation. Chesley's second legal foray into the Bluegrass State is relevant because it illustrates the unprincipled behavior occurring at the highest levels of the Kentucky legal community. In fact, it suggests that the venality described in this book is more the rule than the exception.

The cover of the July 2008 *Bench & Bar,* a publication of the Kentucky Bar Association (KBA), featured the smiling faces of its recently elected president, Barbara Bonar, and her family against a backdrop of rolling green hills and a picture-perfect sky. As is customary, the publication also contained a message from the new president to the KBA membership. Bonar's essay bemoaned how the media and the public had unfairly denigrated her cherished profession. She stated, "Although the professional road we travel is often harsh and fraught with pitfalls, most of us remain true to our oath, devoted to our clients and above all honorable in professionalism."[1] Incredibly, Bonar herself had just been publicly reprimanded by the KBA Board of Governors. Five years later, the *ABA Journal* would bear the heading "Ex-Ky Bar President Is Reprimanded for 'Brazen' Misrepresentations in Office."[2]

For several years, Bonar maintained a private legal practice in Covington. Because of her local connections and Chesley's experience with class-action law, the two formed a brief and tumultuous relationship in pursuit of

90

another landmark settlement involving the Catholic Diocese of Covington and the longtime abuse of children by Catholic priests. The Catholic Church was already dealing with a torrent of lawsuits nationwide, charging it with permitting a pattern of sexual abuse of children by priests, but the legal action in Covington would prove to be unique. Chesley once again managed to avoid the messy business of meeting clients and grinding out individual litigations by having the case declared a class action, the first ever against the Roman Catholic Church in the United States.[3]

The litigation also featured wrangling between the diocese's defense attorneys Mark Guilfoyle and Carrie Huff and the now familiar Judge Jay Bamberger. According to newspaper reports, after Bamberger made the sudden and surprising declaration that "there is no question in my mind the plaintiffs have a right to a class certification," Guilfoyle and Huff petitioned Chief Justice Joseph Lambert of the Kentucky Supreme Court to remove Bamberger because of his relationship with the plaintiffs' trial consultant, Mark Modlin. Chesley, who had hired Modlin, struck back with a vitriolic twenty-five-page denunciation of the defense attorneys. He did not deny the relationship between Bamberger and Modlin but implied that the defense attorneys' action was a ruse to goad Bamberger into an "angry verbal response" for the purpose of disqualifying him and to "smear the name of a good man." Chesley described Guilfoyle and Huff as desperate "forum shoppers," and Bamberger threatened to hold them in contempt of court after the pair tried to subpoena Bamberger's phone records.[4] The unprecedented squabble became so vociferous that it merited a feature article in the *National Law Journal*.

The whole issue was rendered moot when Bamberger suddenly retired as circuit court judge to become senior judge, an essentially itinerant position. Bamberger's decision baffled journalists and attorneys alike. Up to that point, he had fought hard to retain his position as presiding judge in the sex scandal lawsuit. But Guilfoyle and Huff were certainly justified in their concerns, as there was a growing consensus among attorneys that when going before Judge Bamberger, having Modlin on one's team was a ticket to success.

In July 2005, after mediation, the Diocese of Covington agreed to pay

$120 million to the 373 plaintiffs who composed the class. Individual awards ranged from $5,000 to $450,000, depending on the severity and length of the abuse. A separate special victims' fund was set up for those subjected to the most grievous crimes. It was the largest settlement in the nation on a per-plaintiff basis. Chesley and the other attorneys were awarded $18.5 million in fees.

Seventeen months prior to this sizable settlement, Bonar had abruptly quit the class-action team. Despite her decision to abandon that ship (as well as her former clients), Bonar believed she was entitled to a share of the attorneys' fees amounting to half of the $18.5 million. During the civil case she filed against Chesley to get her "fair share," Bonar described a scene in which Chesley had explained that the case needed to be filed in Boone County because "we have a real friendly judge there" (meaning Bamberger), before giving her a wink. Ostensibly this offended Bonar's delicate sense of legal ethics.

Unfortunately for Bonar, it was learned during the trial that she had sought to negotiate individual settlements for members of the class while she was still counsel for the class action. Worse yet, Bonar tried to delay the disbursement of funds to the victims (her former clients) by concocting a series of false complaints about the terms of the settlement. Bonar asked her friend and fellow attorney Jacqueline Sawyers to write an objection to the settlement for the purpose of delaying the disbursements, threatening to hold up the funds for years, if necessary, until Chesley paid her. Bonar supplied Sawyers with the names of those claimants who were "aggrieved" and arranged for Sawyers to speak to two journalists so that an article critical of the proposed settlement could be published just before the January 9, 2006, fairness hearing. Sawyers refused, noting that Bonar was committing a gross ethical violation by working against the interests of her former clients.

Even more shocking, Bonar then asked a perfect stranger to file a complaint about the settlement. Russell McRoberts had come to Bonar's office after selecting her name from the Yellow Pages; he needed a lawyer to write a power-of-attorney agreement for his grandmother. During their conversation, Bonar learned that McRoberts had gone to the Catholic high school in Covington and was a plaintiff in the class action against the diocese. Bonar then provided McRoberts with talking points for his complaint. During this conversation, Bonar repeatedly cautioned McRoberts, "Now remember, we are not having this conversation." Bonar told McRoberts that the lawyers representing him and the other members of the class were "not Catholic and did not understand the Catholic religion." According to McRoberts, she assured him that, as a "bar leader," she wanted to "get rid of the dirty lawyers and clean up the profession."[5] All this damning information eventually made it back to Chesley, who provided affidavits from both Sawyers and McRoberts.

The final curtain came down on this ugly drama on May 11, 2007, after a two-and-a-half-day trial in the Boone County Circuit Court that awarded Bonar zero compensation. As reported by the *Louisville Courier-Journal*, Judge McGinnis concluded that Bonar had "committed numerous ethical violations." He determined that the "building blocks" of the successful lawsuit Bonar claimed she had created consisted mainly of old newspaper articles. He also found that Bonar's declarations of concern about the too cozy relationship between Chesley and Bamberger were nothing but a smoke screen.[6]

Bonar was later investigated by the Kentucky State Police for falsely claiming to represent Robert Helming, another victim in the Covington diocese sex scandal. Helming, who was the sheriff of Boone County, denied ever meeting or speaking with Bonar. By this time, she had already been elected vice president of the KBA, which meant that she would automatically become president the following July. Bonar was again reprimanded by the KBA Board of Ethics but declined to resign from her office. Soon after becoming KBA president, Bonar intentionally misled four members of the KBA Ethics Committee into believing that their terms had expired, sending them letters thanking them for their service. Not surprisingly, all four had friendly ties to Chesley. After this ruse was uncovered, Bonar essentially pleaded nolo contendere and offered to reinstate all four.

At a special meeting held on December 14, 2007, Bonar was again formally admonished by the KBA Board of Governors. The board concluded that she had inappropriately removed the four individuals from the Ethics Committee and had not been "forthcoming" about her reasons for doing so. Bonar claimed she was trying to add "variety and diversity to the Ethics

Committee." Debra Pleatman, who was one of the four removed, was the committee's only woman.[7]

To avoid tangling with Bonar any longer than necessary, the Board of Governors let her retain the KBA presidency and extracted an agreement to "limit her authority" for the seven months remaining in her term; it also levied a $22,000 fine to cover the cost of the investigation. An editorial in the *Courier-Journal* stated, "Most any other group would have given Ms. Bonar the boot."[8] Bonar declined to attend the 2010 KBA Convention to receive a plaque thanking her for her service as president.

Bonar is certainly not alone among Kentucky's legal rogues' gallery. An Associated Press article detailed the most grotesque example of deceit. After graduating from law school, Eric Conn opened a law office in a trailer in his hometown of Stanville, Kentucky, population 206. From those humble beginnings, Conn built a legal empire via a racket that obtained Social Security disability and supplemental security income benefits for the undeserving. Conn's neon-yellow billboards, topped by life-size cutouts of himself, sprang up along the highways of eastern Kentucky. The parking lot of his office complex, which now consisted of five adjoining trailers, featured a nineteen-foot replica of Abraham Lincoln. He even hired young women known as "Conn's Hotties" to cavort provocatively in Daisy Dukes shorts at festivals and other public events with his name and toll-free number printed on their yellow tank tops. He hired a former Miss Kentucky USA as his director of public relations.[9]

Eventually, these antics caught the attention of Tom Coburn, a Republican senator from Oklahoma. His investigation resulted in a 161-page document titled *How Some Legal, Medical, and Judicial Professionals Abused Social Security Disability Programs for the Country's Most Vulnerable: A Case Study of the Conn Law Firm*. This report, published in 2011, detailed how Judge David Daugherty rubber-stamped thousands of federal disability claims based on phony medical evidence supplied by various physicians and psychologists who were paid up to $450 by Conn. The judge received $10,000 per month for his role in the scheme. Conn pleaded guilty to fraud in March 2017 and agreed to reimburse the Social Security Administration $46.5 million.[10] Given Conn's guilty plea, the KBA finally suspended his license to practice law, after he had been stealing the public's money right under its nose for years.

Although it is unfair to paint Kentucky's entire legal community with the same brush that stained the reputations of Bonar, Bamberger, and Conn, it is likewise true that they could not have attained positions of wealth and prestige had it not been for the corruption that too often infects the profession. Sadly, these ethical breaches take place within a self-policed profession that has exhibited little interest in reform. It is up to the KBA to sharpen its ethical standards and minimize future embarrassments.

9

The Deal

ON THE MORNING OF May 9, 2001, Chesley, Gallion, Helmers, Cunningham, and David Shaffer, a Louisville attorney hired to represent AHP, all drove in separate cars to the Boone County courthouse to inform Judge Bamberger of the details of the AHP settlement. The lawn leading up to the four gigantic pillars at the courthouse entrance still bore wisps of the heavy river fog that had snarled traffic and delayed their arrival, but as the sun rose higher, the sky cleared. In contrast, the mental fogginess obscuring Bamberger's judgment lasted throughout the day.

In the hearing room, the five attorneys rose to their feet when Bamberger entered, then fell back into the leather swivel chairs at the tables in front of the judge's mahogany-paneled dais. Chesley did most of the talking. Despite his penchant for very expensive suits (he was particularly fond of Brioni), Chesley often had a rumpled appearance because of his tendency to slouch. When Chesley rose to speak, he carefully smoothed his jacket and straightened his silk tie. With the solemnity that characterized his courtroom dramatics, Chesley handed Bamberger an order decertifying the class and dismissing the action, which he had already prepared for the judge's signature. The decertification and dismissal meant that no other plaintiffs would be able to join the *Guard* action and that the claims of the 431 had been satisfied and permanently settled. Since the request to dismiss was coming only a few days after approval of the settlement at AHP's corporate office, not a single plaintiff was present, making it very likely that none of the 431 had been informed of the settlement. This fact alone was a gross impropriety, as Rule 23 of the Kentucky Rules of Civil Procedure specifically requires attorneys to notify their clients in plain written language prior to a dismissal hearing.

Realizing that something might be amiss, Bamberger asked, "If the class is decertified, what will be the recourse for other persons from Kentucky who fit the definition of the class but are not among the 431 *Guard* plaintiffs?" Using a slow, deliberate cadence, Chesley tried to divert Bamberger's attention from this critical question, giving the decidedly incongruent answer that although the *Guard* settlement was only for the 431 claimants, it was still a class action. "The good news for you, your honor, is there is no other case pending, the good news for these folks is that any remaining victims could seek redress through other venues."[1]

Chesley's verbal contortions were designed to convince Bamberger that *Guard* was both fish and fowl and was later described by trial commissioner William Graham as "chimeric doublespeak."[2] *Guard* could be settled either as 431 aggregated claims or as a class action, but not both. The purpose of the decertification of the class action was to deny any other Kentuckian injured by fen-phen the opportunity to join *Guard*. Chesley's insistence that these individuals could make claims elsewhere was essentially untrue, as they had previously opted out of the national settlement.

The pieces were falling into place for the eventual swindle. The number of claimants would be limited to the 431 who had contingency contracts with GCM, leaving all other Kentucky opt-outs out in the cold. However, if the *Guard* plaintiffs were "still a class," the 431 contingency contracts (giving GCM 30 to 33 percent) could be disregarded. This left the door wide open for the award of attorneys' fees in any portion of the $200 million that Bamberger agreed was fair.

Chesley went on to reassure Bamberger with another bizarre statement, telling the judge that some people in West Virginia had declined to make claims because of religious beliefs. He was apparently hoping to convince Bamberger that the remaining diet drugs users who had not joined *Guard* or the national settlement preferred to be healed by prayer rather than by medicine.

According to the Kentucky Supreme Court's Report of the Trial Commissioner in *KBA v. Chesley,* not all that transpired during this "astonishing hearing" was recorded; instead, it was conducted "in camera," or in private. In this case, this meant deliberately switching off the video and audio recording system in the courtroom. This incomplete record was the last time any of the meetings between Bamberger and GCM or Chesley were documented. Accordingly, it is not certain whether Bamberger was told of the settlement amount at that time. The KBA's brief stated that Bamberger was not provided with a copy of the side letter signed by GCM.[3]

Chesley's aura of self-confidence and authority apparently awed Bamberger. The trial commissioner's report in Chesley's later disbarment proceeding described the lawyer's responses to Bamberger's questions as "nonsensical" and stated that the judge had been "bamboozled." Indeed, Bamberger later testified that he had never even read the settlement agreement with AHP.

Bamberger's untoward deference to Chesley was largely due to his lack of experience with class-action lawsuits. Class-action law is very complex, and a classic treatise on the subject, *Newberg on Class Actions,* runs to ten volumes of fine print. In contrast, the Kentucky procedural rules used by Bamberger run less than two pages, and they allow judges considerable discretion. This worked to Chesley's advantage, since Bamberger invariably deferred to the celebrated Prince of Torts.

It is unknown whether Shaffer, who had been hired to represent the interests of AHP, objected to Chesley's assertion that, after *Guard* was decertified, other opt-outs could still pursue settlements. In addition, given the emptiness of the courtroom, Shaffer must have inferred that none of the plaintiffs had been informed of the meeting or even that *Guard* had been settled. Did AHP approve of tactics that were so clearly wrong? Did it know in advance what Chesley intended to say at this largely secret hearing? Ten years later, in a brief on behalf of Chesley, his attorneys would state that Shaffer had argued that day that it was appropriate to decertify *Guard,* despite the fact that no notice of the certification or decertification had ever been sent to members of the class. Not providing notice to clients of either occurrence is clearly contrary to Rule 1.4 of the American Bar Association's Rules of Professional Conduct, which requires attorneys to keep clients "reasonably informed" about the status of their case. Apparently, AHP's legal representative made no objection to this impropriety.

On May 16, Judge Bamberger decertified the *Guard* class "with prejudice," meaning that none of the 431 plaintiffs could ever seek additional recompense from AHP. Again, this left the opt-outs who had not signed contracts with GCM with nothing. Bamberger also signed an order prepared by Gallion asserting that the "allocations were legal and fair." How Bamberger came to this conclusion is a mystery, as he had not been provided with any document listing how much each claimant was to receive. Such knowledge is essential to conduct what is known as a fairness hearing, which is required to allow claimants to appeal to the judge if they believe the settlement is unsatisfactory. In keeping with the Wild West nature of the prior proceedings, not one of the 431 claimants was present at the May 16 meeting. Despite the obvious irregularities, it was deemed a fairness hearing.

With the decertification behind them, GCM's next task was to obtain signed settlement agreements from at least 95 percent of the *Guard* plaintiffs. Once this was accomplished, GCM would be free to divvy up the $200 million. Helmers was assigned to oversee the gathering of the signed agreements. During his testimony at GCM's criminal trial, Helmers described the outrageous tactics used to obtain these signatures. He was joined by Rebecca Phipps, Sandy Rios, and Walter Overstreet, who worked for Mills, Gallion, and Cunningham, respectively.

Before the four set out to fulfill AHP's proviso, Gallion gave Helmers a lesson in how the deals were to be brokered. Gallion and Helmers met with a client who, according to the matrix, was supposed to receive $5 million. Gallion offered the man $1 million and informed him that the 33 percent contingency fee would be deducted from that amount, per their agreement. Gallion told the man that AHP had designated $1 million, and not a penny more, specifically for him. The man took his $666,666, and Helmers took the hint: he was to offer the claimants the smallest amounts possible. Helmers claimed he met personally with 10 percent of the plaintiffs, while Phipps, Rios, and Overstreet handled the rest. Plaintiffs were not provided with copies of their signed releases, and they later insisted they had been told that doing so would violate the confidentiality agreement with AHP.

A few examples of these lowball offers are illustrative: Jacquelyn Murphy of Louisville received only $78,954 of the $120,833 settlement she was entitled to, based on the matrix calculation, for her purported heart valve damage. Steve Taylor of Jenkins, Kentucky, whose wife had died of heart failure ostensibly caused by fen-phen, should have received $3.15 million based on Helmers's matrix. Instead, Taylor was informed that only $1 million had been set aside for him. When he complained about the amount, Helmers offered another $500,000, and after a final round of negotiations, Taylor's hard-won signature was obtained for $1.6 million—still only slightly more than half of what he should have received. To avoid claimants comparing notes in the law office lobbies or during chance encounters in the elevator, Helmers, Overstreet, and Phipps met with them off premises. Shopping malls were one of the most common places to inform claimants of their "windfalls."

When Dylan Roberts of Lexington asked to see a copy of the settlement agreement with AHP (which all the plaintiffs were not only entitled to but also required to receive), someone at Mills's office told him that these documents were confidential. Also at Mills's office, Andi Peace was warned not to discuss the settlement with anyone, not even her own family. On her way back to Corbin, Peace became so sick from anxiety that she had to pull off the road. As reported by the *Louisville Courier-Journal,* when Mills was later asked about sweetening the pot should a client balk at the initial offer, he responded, "If it took a little more to make them happy, we agreed to it." When asked how much each plaintiff deserved to be compensated, Mills replied, "Whatever he agreed to take."[4]

The modus operandi used by Helmers and the other members of his settlement negotiation team was not to inform the 431 claimants about the $200 million settlement amount and not to share accurate information about the amounts of the legal fees being deducted or who received those fees. Both omissions were in violation of Rule 23 of the Federal Rules of Civil Procedure for Class Actions. They also represented that the dollar amounts offered had been specifically calculated and approved by AHP for each of the 431 plaintiffs—this was a complete falsehood. In addition, all the claimants were allegedly informed that if they divulged their settlement terms or amounts to anyone, they faced a fine or even jail time. Some of the claimants professed to be truly frightened by this warning, but it is hard to believe that most of the 431 were that gullible. After all, these folks had been canny enough to opt out of the national settlement. Many were probably more than happy to go along with the legal charade, as a large portion of them likely had no symptoms and no heart damage whatsoever.

Margie Berry insisted that she was "too afraid to comment to investigators," claiming to be "scared to death." Berry later stated that she had been told if she informed anyone, even her own family, about her settlement, she "could go to jail." Gerry Jones believed she would be fined if she disclosed the amount of her settlement or even that she had received one. She was told to be careful what she said because "the phones might be bugged." Beverly Little claimed she had been threatened with a $500,000 fine for a single disclosure, an amount triple her settlement offer.[5] In a later interview, Mills said the ingestion of fen-phen "made people crazy."[6]

Within a few weeks, Helmers, Phipps, Overstreet, and Rios had obtained all but 8 of the 431 signatures, well ahead of the September 1 deadline. Phipps obtained the signatures from most of Mills's clients, Gallion's legal assistant Rios handled Gallion's three clients and a portion of Cunningham's, and Overstreet handled the balance of Cunningham's. Helmers obtained the signatures for the thirty largest settlements. None of the agreements stated the settlement amounts received; rather, they stated that each claimant had accepted an unspecified, agreed-upon amount. The claimants generally received their checks within six months.

Once all the settlement documents were signed, the amount disbursed to claimants totaled a mere $45 million, which represented just 22 percent of the $200 million. Although this dollar amount was more than what mediator Weinstein believed was warranted, it was still far short of the $131 million that should have been distributed had Helmers offered the 67 to 70 percent stipulated by the aggregated contingency agreements. GCM would later make the spurious argument that after the 431 plaintiffs had been paid, the balance was GCM's to keep. During the criminal trial, Gallion explained that the extra funds kept by GCM were a bargain, considering the tremendous risk they had assumed in signing the side letter agreement. He reasoned that, just as in the case of a home owner's insurance policy, if the house does not burn down or is not whisked away by a tornado, the premium paid belongs to the insurance company.

Before his involvement with the *Guard* negotiations, Helmers's salary had been $50,000 a year. Soon thereafter, in the summer of 2001, he was awarded a bonus of $3 million plus a new car.[7] Gallion paid Helmers's bonus directly from the settlement proceeds, thus circumventing the established fee-sharing agreements with his partners.

After numerous amendments, final judicial approval of the national settlement occurred on January 3, 2002, less than eight months after *Guard* was decertified. The settlement amounts for the 650,000 claimants in the $5 billion national settlement averaged $77,000. The average payout for the *Guard* claimants was $104,408. In the clear majority of instances, the *Guard* payouts were far less than Helmers's matrix calculations; however, even though they were shortchanged by $95 million, the claimants invariably received more than they would have in the national settlement. Many *Guard* claimants with preexisting heart conditions who would have been awarded nothing in the national settlement received settlements in excess of $1 million. Other claimants, such as Pamela Clift (who received $228,000), Kathy Hutchenson ($38,600), and Connie Mason ($27,268), would have been refunded only the cost of the drugs. Those claimants who had not taken fen-phen or Redux for more than sixty-one days were disqualified from the national settlement altogether; others who could prove they had taken the drugs received only $30 for every month they took fen-phen or $60 per month for Redux, up to a maximum of $500. In contrast, every *Guard* claimant received a minimum of $25,000, even those who had no proof they had taken fen-phen or Redux at all.

Of the eight claimants for whom Helmers's team had failed to obtain signatures, two had died and two were missing and could not be found; only four had refused to sign. On orders from Chesley, Helmers hand-delivered all the signed releases to AHP headquarters in New York City on June 19, 2001, and AHP transferred $150 million to Cunningham's escrow account. On the same day, both Gallion and Cunningham had approximately $42 million transferred to their personal accounts. Mills received $9 million, and Chesley received a check for precisely $12,941,638.46. Over the course of the summer, settlement checks were mailed to the plaintiffs, typically with the words "Final Settlement" stamped on each. The checks were prepared by Overstreet under the direction of Helmers.

In November, AHP parted with the remaining $50.45 million. At that time, the personal accounts of the attorneys were as follows: Gallion, $54 million; Cunningham, $48 million; and Mills, $17 million. Modlin received $2.05 million from Gallion. By this time, Chesley had received two additional checks for $1,777,741.70 each, bringing his total to $16,497,121.87, as later confirmed by KBA accountant Vicki Hamm. Later, the KBA Board of Governors would conclude that, assuming Chesley was reasonably conversant in fifth-grade math, he should have known that the nearly $16.5 million was several million ($3,555,438.41, to be exact) more than the 21 percent of attorneys' fees to which he was legitimately entitled. But for Chesley, there was much more to come. This left a balance of $20 million, the distribution of which is discussed later.

Several individuals in the Lexington legal community believe that GCM's idea to ignore their client contingency arrangements and keep the lion's share of the $200 million settlement likely originated in a bizarre out-of-state conspiracy that tangentially involved Gallion and Cunningham. The Mississippi fen-phen action known as *Stevens* was settled in November 2000, and AHP set aside $215 million to compensate up to 3,000 plaintiffs. Each plaintiff was to be awarded $72,000 and would net $48,000 after paying 33 percent for attorneys' fees, as set out in their contracts with Beasley Allen. However, Beasley Allen provided its clients with only $29,500 each, keeping the $42,500 balance for itself. The catch was that the AHP settlement was contingent on Beasley Allen obtaining signed settlement statements from at least 95 percent of the 3,000 eligible claimants. When it came up approximately fifty-three signatures short, one of the *Stevens* attorneys who knew Cunningham asked for his help. Likely for a fee, Cunningham provided the names of fifty-three *Guard* plaintiffs with the weakest claims—some of them may not have taken the diet drugs at all. Since Cunningham could not represent clients in both *Guard* and *Stevens,* he recruited Lexington attorney Brent Austin to nominally represent the fifty-three. Austin, who frequently played tennis with Gallion, was believed to be just the man for the job.

Austin somehow obtained the necessary signatures from these fifty-three individuals, despite their later contention that Austin "never provided them with any documents or meaningful information about the transfer of their cases."[8] (The Kentuckians who received $29,500 in their mailboxes should have been delighted by this windfall, but they later became angry when they learned they should have received $48,000. There is no indication that receipt of this money from the *Stevens* settlement disqualified them from participating in the *Guard* settlement.) From this sordid process, GCM learned that by keeping clients in the dark about the size of the settlement pie, the clients could be made happy with tiny slices. GCM would employ the same recipe to augment their own fortunes.

Gallion and Cunningham should have paid heed to the rest of the story. Robert Arledge of Beasley Allen was later sentenced to six years in prison, not for shorting his clients but for knowingly submitting fraudulent claims. Federal officials believed that 20 percent of the Mississippi plaintiffs had not taken the diet drugs at all.

Gallion and Mills were members of partnerships, but they had no compunction about keeping their partners, like their clients, completely in the dark. Typically, in a law partnership, a portion of the total earnings is pooled and then shared among all the partners in accordance with a written agreement. In addition to its strictly legal aspects, a partnership implies an ethical obligation of trust and loyalty. But Gallion and Mills lied to their partners and claimed that the entire settlement totaled only $40 million. Based on the partnerships' 10 percent profit-sharing agreements, this deception was intended to bilk their partners out of millions. Gallion and Mills were also concerned that if their partners knew the truth, one of them might insist on taking the ethical path and honoring their client contingency agreements to the letter.

Not surprisingly, the actual *Guard* totals could not be kept secret indefinitely. Closed-door conversations, telltale smirks, and ubiquitous office gossip eventually led to news of the trio's ill-gotten good fortune. Informal interoffice communications were frequent, and new friendships had formed among the paralegals. Rebecca Phipps had inspired Sandy Rios to become a vegetarian. Rios was also fond of Mills; they were both fans of Elvis Presley and would share their mutual admiration for the King when Mills was drunk.[9]

At Gallion, Baker, and Bray, Mike Baker was the primary victim of Gallion's deceit since, by that time, Pam Bray was working only part time. Eventually, strands of office gossip wound their way to Baker. His suspicions grew once he learned that Helmers had received a $3 million bonus along with a new car. Baker was also curious about where Gallion got the money to pay for his new Porsche. Baker confronted Helmers, who refused to divulge the total amount of the settlement, so Baker fired him. Unbowed, Helmers purchased a boat, took his kids out of school, and toured the world for ten months, visiting seventeen countries on six continents.[10] Undaunted, Baker continued to pursue his internal investigation and, after slipping into Gallion's office to read his email, confirmed that the settlement was $200 million.[11]

Mills's partner David Stuart had similar suspicions, and he soon learned the truth from Baker. By that time, the relationship between Mills and Stuart had already grown sour. Mills had needed someone experienced in insurance law, but because of his shameless TV ads and sketchy reputation, no Kentucky lawyer with the necessary qualifications was interested in partnering with him. Out of desperation, Mills had hired Stuart, who was eager to leave his home state of Arkansas, where he had worked for a major insurance carrier. What both men had hoped would be a mutually beneficial partnership soon deteriorated. Stuart developed a personal antipathy toward Mills, which he made little effort to conceal, and Mills was loath to pay millions of dollars to a person for whom the feeling was mutual.

Having been duped by their partners, Baker and Stuart were both incensed and, in January 2002, filed separate civil lawsuits against Gallion and Mills, respectively. They also filed complaints with the Kentucky Bar Association.

At roughly the same time, Tracy Curtis, a client of Cunningham's, began asking questions about the settlement and requested documentation that the amount she received had been designated by AHP specifically for her. After several rounds of certified letters back and forth, and claims by Cunningham's office that her straightforward queries were "unclear," Curtis finally had enough, and she too complained to the KBA, which launched an investigation. On February 11, 2002, the Inquiry Commission of the Kentucky Bar Association requested subpoenas for GCM's bank records and other documents related to the distribution of the settlement proceeds. However, the attorneys were one step ahead of the investigation.

On that same afternoon, five wire transfers from the accounts of Gallion and Cunningham totaling $59 million were made to a bank in Florida. They knew the KBA would be granted the authority to subpoena their banking records just as soon as a preliminary hearing could be convened. The KBA's subpoena powers were far more limited when dealing with out-of-state banks.

However, this subterfuge proved to be ill considered, as it set the stage for a later indictment for federal wire fraud. A crime since 1872, wire fraud is an action intended to deprive someone of their rightful property using any form of interstate telecommunication—a definition so broad that it includes the telegraph as well as the Internet. Accordingly, GCM had opened the door to an FBI investigation and eventual prosecution by US attorneys in federal court. From that point forward, GCM's scheme would slowly unravel.

Gallion and Cunningham also tried to cheat Mills. According to Rebecca Phipps, Mills learned about the actual amount of the settlement not from Gallion but from David Stuart. Stuart's letter informing Mills that he was being sued for withholding the information that the settlement totaled $200 million was a double shock for Mills, as Gallion had told him the settlement was for $150 million.

As revealed in the trial transcripts, Gallion had been invited to attend Mills's February 6, 2002, birthday party. Gallion arrived just as the guests were bringing in the cake, and he joined in the singing of "Happy Birthday." When Mills spotted Gallion, he shouted out that Gallion was a "thief." A flummoxed Gallion attempted to soothe Mills, who was well into his cups. The last thing Gallion wanted was for a drunken Mills to spill the beans in front of the gathered guests. To his credit, Mills insisted that more of the settlement funds should be shared with the claimants, to which Gallion assented.[12] Mills then demanded that Gallion leave. It turned out that Phipps had convinced Gallion to attend Mills's party, and Gallion had the distinct sense that Phipps had orchestrated the confrontation, as indeed she had, for reasons that will be explained later.

Mills's high dudgeon left Gallion shaken, as he rightly feared that Mills, in another drunken rampage, would vent his spleen in the presence of someone familiar with the KBA investigation. Within a month of his birthday party, Mills was hospitalized for medical conditions brought on by alcoholism, but he resumed drinking soon after his release.

After leaving the party, Gallion phoned Chesley and informed him what had just transpired. Chesley immediately grasped the gravity of the situation, and together they hatched an outrageous plan designed to keep them ahead of the cascade of potentially catastrophic developments. They needed to get some of the purloined $95 million into the hands of the 431 claimants as soon as possible.

Before 5:00 p.m. on the day of Mills's party, Gallion and Cunningham had invited Judge Bamberger to an impromptu meeting. By the time they arrived at the Boone County courthouse, it was largely empty, and their hastened strides echoed down the vacant hallways leading to an unoccupied jury deliberation room. The three were soon joined by Chesley and Modlin, the latter having had been driven to the courthouse by Chesley to ensure his crucial presence. Although Modlin remembered being Chesley's passenger, he would later testify that he had no other recollection of this or any other *Guard*-related meetings with Bamberger. Modlin blamed his lack of recall on the pain medication he was taking as a consequence of his golfing accident twenty years earlier. In direct contravention of the rules of legal procedure, the meeting was ex parte, meaning that only one side (party) was represented. But that was far from the only outrage that occurred in the empty jury room.

The group was now acutely aware that tens of millions of dollars of unearned settlement funds controlled by the four attorneys would be impossible to justify. As the moon rose above the courthouse, they cobbled together a scheme that was jaw-dropping in its audacity. Rather than simply bow to reality and distribute the remaining $95 million to their clients, they instead chose to pitch the proverbial sop to Cerberus. The sop would consist of a second distribution to the claimants in the still outlandishly inadequate amount of $28 million. Convincing Bamberger to approve the second distribution would be simple, but the remainder of the plan would require a mastery of brazenness and humbug.

After they were all seated, Chesley, sitting to Bamberger's left, handed him a copy of a multipage decision by the US District Court of New York in the 1972 case *City of Detroit v. Grinnell Corporation.* Grinnell, a distributor of fire and police safety equipment, had been accused of price fixing; the company was also rumored to be linked to organized crime. Grinnell immediately agreed to settle the class action for $10 million. From that total, the attorney who represented Detroit billed the city for the contracted fee of 25 percent, which amounted to $2.5 million. When several of the municipalities involved in the class action balked at this huge amount, given that very little effort had been required on the part of the attorney, the judge lowered the attorney's fee to $1.5 million. Thus, this precedent established that the court could establish attorneys' fees in class actions, in this case, adjusting the amount downward.

After confusing Bamberger with a misleading explanation of *Grinnell,* Chesley was ready to discuss how it applied to *Guard.* He reminded Bamberger that *Guard* had previously been certified as a class action apart from the national settlement. Chesley, speaking in measured tones, noted that GCM had risked all their accumulated and future assets in the pursuit of justice for the victims of AHP's recklessness. Because Bamberger was thoroughly unfamiliar with *Grinnell,* he had no basis to question Chesley's claim that the precedent established by that case gave the judge complete discretion to determine the amount of attorneys' fees.

But before pressing Bamberger to rule on that amount, Gallion and Cunningham used the opportunity to inform the judge of their impoverishment, claiming they were still trying to scrape up the $5.5 million in expenses they had personally paid to bring the settlement to fruition. Had this been a proper hearing, Bamberger would have demanded a full accounting of those expenses. But when he asked for financial records, Gallion and Cunningham argued that obtaining them would be too difficult after so much time had passed. Bamberger eventually relented and approved reimbursement for the undocumented expenses. Bamberger later admitted that he "regretted not asking for the list of expenses they represented at $5.5 million."[13]

After this $5.5 million "gift" from Bamberger, Gallion then had the temerity to suggest attorneys' fees amounting to 49 percent of the $200 million—certainly a distorted application of the *Grinnell* doctrine. Gallion argued that this enormous portion of the claimants' money was fair compensation, considering the risks the attorneys had shouldered and the generous settlements they had won for their clients. Bamberger declared that such a portion was fair, since it was less than 50 percent of the settlement. It must have been difficult for the others in the room to contain their smirks and sidelong glances. The final piece of the scheme had just snapped into place.

Bamberger should have been aware that once a class action has been decertified, the judge has no authority to approve attorneys' fees. After decertification, fees must be based on the percentages contained in the contingency agreements. But Bamberger never even inquired about these contingency agreements, which any first-year law student would have known existed. During his criminal trial, Gallion testified that "no lawyer who is licensed in Kentucky who has ever represented a plaintiff in an action would not know that you must have a written contract with a client to pursue a claim. It's just, it's just beyond my belief that he would not have known."[14]

Despite his obligation to ensure that all claimants were informed of all hearings, Judge Bamberger communicated with only one claimant—Lisa Swiger—and he later had difficulty recalling her name. Some months after distribution of the settlement funds, Gallion brought this noisome client to Bamberger, looking for assistance in making her go away. As he testified later, Bamberger quickly determined that Swiger was mentally incompetent, based not only on her demeanor but also on the knowledge that she had already purchased five Dodge Durangos with her settlement checks.[15] Even so, she continued to pester Gallion for more money, and Bamberger ruled that she was to receive an additional $500,000, to be meted out in monthly installments. Much to the vexation of Gallion, this would not be his final contact with Swiger. Despite this additional $500,000, she remained thoroughly unsatisfied. Swiger was so fixated on obtaining a larger settlement that she might have sought assistance from another attorney (possibly Angela Ford; see chapter 12). In any case, Swiger's tale of woe was one that led to big trouble for GCM.

The judicial order the attorneys drafted for Bamberger's signature used the deceptive language "remaining funds" to describe the allowance for attorneys' fees. The document also gave the attorneys the discretion to distribute funds to individual claimants. In rough numbers, Bamberger's inattention allowed the attorneys to collect legal fees of $99 million (49.5 percent), plus $5.5 million in undocumented expenses for Gallion and Cunningham and $2.5 million in documented expenses for Mills. The claimants received a total of $73 million—$45 million from the first distribution and $28 million from the second (still $67 million short). This still left $20 million of undesignated settlement funds.

Bamberger would later testify that he provided Chesley with a copy of his order establishing these exorbitant attorneys' fees. According to a later Judicial Conduct Commission report, that order contained many factual inaccuracies, and Chesley claimed he did not read it. Since the order essentially provided Chesley with 21 percent of $99 million, and given his key role in concocting the *Grinnell* scheme, it is likely that Chesley drafted the document himself. Despite his dominant presence at the February 6 meeting, Chesley would later testify under oath that he could not recall being in attendance. Bamberger, also under oath, confirmed that Chesley had indeed been present, and he clearly described the room, the participants, details of the conversations, and even the seating arrangements. Even the heavily medicated Modlin remembered being driven to the courthouse by Chesley.[16]

At the same meeting, Chesley cited another obscurity known as the cy pres doctrine (from the French, meaning "as close as possible")—like *Grinnell*, a legal standard totally unfamiliar to Bamberger. Cy pres is a rule requiring that the intent of a benefactor be followed as nearly as possible when a strict adherence to instructions is impossible, impractical, or illegal. For example, if a person set up a trust to care for a beloved pet, when the pet dies, a judge may approve the donation of the residual trust funds to the local humane society. Chesley's suggested application of cy pres to any portion of the *Guard* settlement proceeds was a contortion of this doctrine. Any residual amount could have been resolved simply by issuing 431 additional disbursement checks.

Chesley explained that in another class action he had been involved in, a large amount of money had been disposed of through the cy pres doctrine. He was referring to the Agent Orange settlement, in which $45 million went into a cy pres fund. What Chesley failed to mention is that the class in the Agent Orange suit contained as many as 1.5 million members, making it impractical to track down 1.5 million people to deliver a $30 check to each one. Bamberger would later describe Chesley as "leading the charge" in the cy pres effort, having come prepared with a two-page description of the doctrine. But this was unnecessary because, as far as Bamberger was concerned, if Chesley said it was the right thing to do, how could it be wrong? Bamberger recalled that Chesley either strongly implied or explicitly stated that the claimants had already been fairly compensated and were not entitled to any more money from the settlement, yet another betrayal of Chesley's duty to his clients. These residual funds were handled in such an irresponsible manner that it would have disastrous consequences for Judge Bamberger.

After Bamberger's February 6 approval of the second distribution (as well as everything else requested), the claimants were told the happy news: GCM had managed to obtain the release of additional funds from AHP's tightfisted grip. A cover letter stated, "We are pleased that we have been able to accomplish this for you . . . as this is highly unusual." These second payments amounted to slightly less than half of the first. Despite Chesley's claim that his only role was negotiating the settlement, according to a report in the *Louisville Courier-Journal*, a forensic analysis confirmed that one of Chesley's associates, Fay Stilz, edited the draft of Helmers's letter accompanying the second distribution checks. Although Stilz denied that Chesley was involved, it is highly doubtful that she would have acted without Chesley's approval. A later Judicial Commission report noted that Stilz had been an employee of Chesley's for her entire career, earning more than $500,000 a year. The Judicial Commission also determined that Chesley had been fully involved in the second distribution; he had assigned the task to Helmers, who was back from his world tour. Once again, the plaintiffs were not informed of the total settlement amount, and again, they were warned not to share information. The two distributions to the claimants totaled $73 million out $200 million.

But before this newfound wealth was handed out to the claimants, GCM came up with a new fee-splitting agreement to appease Mills, who was still miffed about not being told the actual settlement amount. In this handwritten document, Mills was to be reimbursed $200,000 for expenses and would receive 50 percent of the $7.5 million contingency fund after its release. In a sworn deposition, Mills stated that the notes from this meeting were torn up or burned.

On April 1, 2002, Chesley received a final check for $4 million. This round amount contrasted with the other three checks, which had been derived from percentages and calculated to the penny. Also notable was the fact that this check was drawn on a different bank from outside of Kentucky. In *KBA v. Chesley,* the trial commissioner concluded that Chesley's final $4 million check represented a predetermined agreement with GCM to pay Chesley for obtaining Bamberger's approval of the 49 percent attorneys' fees based on *Grinnell,* as well as teeing up the idea of creating a cy pres trust to soak up the undesignated residual.

At this point, the money had been apportioned as follows: Gallion received $30 million, Cunningham $21 million, Mills $24 million, Chesley $20.5 million, Lawrence $10 million, Helmers $3 million, Modlin $2 million, Stuart (Mills's former partner) $3 million, Baker (Gallion's former partner) an unknown amount, and various other incidental expenses, leaving an unclaimed balance of $20 million. Because they had already received more than the 49 percent in fees allowed by Bamberger, GCM were unable to allocate this residual among themselves.

Chesley's $20.5 million was well beyond the $12.8 million (21 percent of $61 million) he was legitimately entitled to (interestingly, his $20,597,121 was nearly identical to 21 percent of the total fee approved by Bamberger). Chesley would argue during GCM's trial that he had failed to fully grasp the extent of the trio's greed and recklessness and that he had been unaware they had already taken their contingency fees on top of the 49 percent approved by Bamberger. The trial commissioner in *KBA v. Chesley* later concluded that Chesley had been aware of the contractual agreements with the *Guard* class and purposely withheld that information.

David Helmers personally handled about thirty-five plaintiffs during the second round of distributions and provided management oversight for the rest of them. They were again told that the amount of each award had been specifically designated by AHP. They were also told that, after this generous second distribution, the amount remaining was exceedingly small. As a result of this deception, the claimants agreed that the balance should be donated to a charitable trust called the Fund for Healthy Living (FHL). The *Guard* claimants were informed that the FHL's mission was the promotion of healthy dietary practices in Kentucky.

Mildred Abbott, the person named in *Abbott et al. v. Chesley et al.*, which was filed in the Fayette County Circuit Court in December 2004, had been told there was "some money left, but not enough to go around." Eleanor Berry had been led to believe that "the small amount of money left over was maybe $25." Cindy Armstrong had been told the "left over funds amounted to a pittance, less than $100."[17] In reality, the amount to be set aside in the trust was hardly a pittance: it was $20 million!

Did GCM act purely out of greed? How were they able to rationalize misleading and shortchanging their clients? Although a number of people had been harmed by the diet drugs, some irreparably so, many others had suffered no adverse consequences. Did GCM believe that their clients had already received much more than they deserved? The *Guard* plaintiffs had certainly ended up with much more than they would have received in the national settlement. Hadn't they already received enough?

The medical evidence was contradictory. In contrast to Dr. Heidi Connolly's alarming report just one year earlier, which had led to the diet drugs being pulled from the market, the September 10, 1998, issue of the *New England Journal of Medicine* published a study by Dr. Hershel Jick on the long-term effects of fen-phen and Redux. That study involved more than 20,000 subjects divided into control and experimental groups that were carefully matched by age, sex, and weight. Jick found that the incidence of heart valve disorders in persons who had taken either fen-phen or Redux for less than four months was 7.1 per 10,000; it was 35 per 10,000 for those who had taken either drug for four months or longer. Among an average mix of former users of fen-phen of any duration, Jick found only 11 individuals with diet drug–related damage out of a sample of 8,000. For those who took either drug for more than four months, the chance of acquiring heart valve damage was 0.0035 percent. Among those who joined the national settlement, 0.007 percent experienced some kind of heart valve disease. In absolute numbers, this difference was 2,275 versus 4,550 of the 650,000 claimants, both relatively tiny percentages. If the 0.0035 percentage is applied to the 250,000 Kentuckians who took either drug, that yields a projection of 875 for the entire state, assuming all 250,000 took the drugs for four months or more, which is unlikely. When the 0.0035 percentage is applied to the 431 *Guard* plaintiffs, less than 2 would be expected to have heart valve damage from taking the diet drugs. Although many of the 40 in Helmers's matrix were categorized as having heart valve abnormalities, many of these conditions could have existed before the drugs were ingested.[18]

Even more incisively, according to an October 1999 article in the *New York Times,* a study by Boston's Beth Israel Deaconess Medical Center "failed to show a correlation between Fen-phen and severe heart damage." The study consisted of 226 patients, roughly ten times larger than the Mayo Clinic study that first linked fen-phen to heart damage. The lead researcher, Dr. Andrew J. Burger, concluded: "The bad valve disease suggested by the Mayo group has not been found. . . . Maybe there is less of an association between Fen-phen and valve disease than we thought previously."[19] According to the London-based Social Issues Research Center, the Mayo study was an example of "panic incited by bad science."[20] Fortunately for GCM, Chesley, and hundreds of other tort attorneys, this information came two years after the demise of the diet drugs and the billions in damage claims against AHP.

If Jick and Burger are correct, it is highly likely that the majority of the damage claims by the *Guard* plaintiffs were without basis. It is telling that, of the thirty-eight former clients whose circumstances were described in a later civil lawsuit, not one claimed to have heart valve issues.

GCM and Chesley wanted to settle *Guard* as soon as possible because they suspected that if patients had not already experienced valve leakage, it was virtually certain that they never would. As Gallion later testified, reports were beginning to come in from physicians that those few persons diagnosed with heart valve regurgitation or murmurs as a consequence of taking fen-phen were showing dramatic improvement. It was becoming apparent that, after patients stopped taking fen-phen, whatever plaque may have accumulated on their heart valves would gradually be flushed away.

How is one to reconcile these two completely irreconcilable versions of whether these diet medications actually caused long-term heart valve damage? Were the tens of thousands of plaintiffs falsely influenced by the advertising blitzes of trial attorneys casting about for clients? Was Pam Ruff reading too much into the sonograms in Fargo? Were the Mayo Clinic and Dr. Connolly swept up in a self-deceiving confirmation bias? Or were Drs. Jick and Burger the purveyors of bad science?

Indeed, the conflation of fact and falsehood in scientific research is more common than might be assumed. A 2013 article in *Science* magazine described a contemporary meta-analysis of published neuroscience studies. The author concluded that such research often "suffers from a dearth of statistical power," which has resulted in "a dramatic increase in the likelihood that statistically significant findings are spurious."[21]

The question of the extent of the deleterious side effects of fen-phen and Redux remains open.

10

Judge Not

AT ITS 2002 ANNUAL CONVENTION, the Kentucky Bar Association bestowed the distinction of "Outstanding Judge of the Year" on Judge Jay Bamberger. The KBA was not alone in this gaffe. The previous year, the Kentucky Trial Attorneys Association had named Bamberger its "Judge of the Year." Both organizations would soon regret these honors.

Prior to the 2002 awards dinner, the cavernous ballroom was filled with the raucous laughter of hundreds of lawyers, most of them dressed in the power ensemble of the day—dark suit, white button-down shirt, and solid red tie. Ironically, the theme of the event was "Raising the Bar." With the exception of perhaps two people in the packed room, all were oblivious to the fact that their honoree was an accessory in one of the largest heists in US history.

Sitting conspicuously at Bamberger's table during the KBA dinner and nodding in assent to the many accolades Bamberger received that evening was Gallion. By this time, the lawyer and judge had bonded. On at least one occasion, when someone from Gallion's office had called him at his new home in Florida, Bamberger had answered the phone. As reported in the *Louisville Courier-Journal,* on the evening of his KBA award, Bamberger slept at Gallion's home in Lexington. Throughout his testimony at the criminal trial, Bamberger referred to Gallion as "Bill."

Bamberger had grown up in the tiny burg of Latonia, Kentucky. Like Gallion, he had a modest upbringing; he worked in the family butcher shop to help pay for college. Bamberger was employed for several years as a social worker before deciding to become an attorney. After graduating from the University of Kentucky School of Law, Bamberger served for a few years as a public defender. After a brief stint as the city attorney in Warsaw, Kentucky, Bamberger became the assistant commonwealth's attorney for Boone and Gallatin Counties. He was elected district judge in 1981, and in 1982 he won the much more prestigious position of circuit judge, serving the counties of Boone and Kenton in northern Kentucky. There he presided over criminal cases involving felonies, civil actions for more than $5,000, and various other disputes.

Before the wheels fell off the *Guard* settlement, Bamberger was well liked by many in the legal community. One reason for his popularity among judges was his very large caseload and his willingness to take on complex finance and banking cases. This relieved his judicial colleagues of many headaches. Bamberger often agreed to add to his caseload rather than take the more prudent path of referring cases to other judges. His selfless desire to help may have been a carryover from his days as a social worker. While the average caseload of a circuit judge was around 950, Bamberger was managing nearly 1,800 cases.[1]

Other, less virtuous qualities earned his popularity among attorneys. Many of them took advantage of Bamberger's self-imposed overscheduling and thoughtfully wrote and presented him with judicial orders, ready for his signature, before they had even argued their cases. Bamberger would later testify that he hardly ever wrote his own orders. Although this practice is not uncommon, there is some evidence that Bamberger did not even bother to read some of those orders. By his own admission, he did not read the settlement document for *Guard*. His willingness to simply sign, unread, the orders prepared by the attorneys who appeared in his courtroom may explain why the KBA named him "Outstanding Judge of the Year." Bamberger admitted that, during the *Guard* settlement discussions, he asked GCM to tender an order.

The February 8, 2002, judicial order establishing attorneys' fees and allowing application of the cy pres doctrine for any "excess funds" was not signed until February 15. In keeping with his desultory attention to detail,

Bamberger did not file the order until June 6. This interval would have given the judge ample time to conduct his own research into the applicability of *Grinnell* and the cy pres doctrine, but he did not. Once the order was entered, Bamberger instructed the circuit court clerk to provide copies of all future orders only to the plaintiffs' attorneys and to seal all future orders entered in the fen-phen case. Thus, neither the *Guard* claimants nor AHP received copies of this or subsequent orders, in direct violation of procedural rules. It seems that, after February 8, all vestiges of Bamberger's integrity faded away.

On June 27, 2002, Gallion, Cunningham, Modlin, and Taye Robinson, an expert on structured settlement investments, met with Bamberger to discuss the final disposition of the remaining undisbursed settlement funds now sequestered in a Vanguard investment account. After they all took their seats in his private chambers, Bamberger recalled that Gallion, who had requested the meeting, did most of the talking. He informed Bamberger, "There are excess funds we need to speak about" and then nonchalantly added, "It's a lot . . . $20 million." Gallion then asked that the $20 million be set aside in a trust fund for charitable purposes, under the cy pres doctrine. But rather than laughing Gallion out of his chambers, a credulous Bamberger asked, "Do the claimants know about it?" With a broad smile and all the charm he could muster, Gallion affirmed that they had all been informed and averred, "They're thrilled, they think it's great."[2] As proof, Gallion cited the signed consent agreements obtained during the second settlement fund distribution. However, he did not mention that the claimants had signed these consents as a condition of receiving their second disbursement checks and had therefore been coerced. Nor did he mention that the claimants had been grossly misinformed, being assured that the leftover funds amounted to only a "pittance." Gallion's assertion essentially meant that all the claimants were willing to forgo an average of $45,000 each for some vague charitable purpose. Nonetheless, Bamberger went along with Gallion's fiction and ordered the creation of the Fund for Healthy Living using the remaining $20 million.

Later, when Helmers's notes were subpoenaed, it was discovered that he had written and circled the words "$50 million to charity" in the margin of his copy of the settlement document. At trial, Helmers could not recall why he had written this note, but the fact that it was written during the 2001 settlement mediations indicates that the cy pres scheme had been a topic of discussion long before the February 2002 meeting with Bamberger.

Gallion volunteered to draft the judicial order for the overburdened judge. The order Bamberger signed that day provided for the creation of the trust and specified that 30 percent of any distribution from the trust could be used for administration, including legal fees. Gallion was careful to insert language to the effect that the settlement funds could be used to reimburse $5.5 million of GCM's undocumented expenses, and the document specified that this $5.5 million was to be taken out of the 51 percent of the settlement fund designated for the claimants. As a special bonus, Bamberger also released the $7.5 million reserve set aside for any future contingencies, per the side letter. But rather than ordering that the money be distributed to the claimants, which would have been proper, Bamberger essentially gave the $7.5 million to GCM. As revealed earlier, half of the $7.5 million went to Mills to compensate him for being kept out of the loop as to the total settlement amount.

Beginning with $20 million in assets, the Kentucky Fund for Healthy Living was incorporated on January 23, 2003, as a nonprofit organization. Lexington attorney Whitney Wallingford was hired as FHL's general counsel. Members of the board of directors, as determined by Bamberger, were Modlin (president), Gallion, and Cunningham. For their willingness to take on the burden of sitting through monthly board meetings—usually held in the judge's office, where lunch was served—Bamberger authorized the payment of "management fees": Modlin received $6,500 a month, and Gallion and Cunningham were each paid $5,000 a month. All three were also given a $350 monthly expense allowance. To further salve Mills's hurt feelings, he was added to the board later in January.

After observing how carefully the funds were being managed, Bamberger gave up all oversight of FHL a mere week before his surprise decision to step down as circuit court judge and take a much-reduced caseload as senior judge. This allowed Bamberger to accept Modlin's offer of a seat on the FHL board without having to obtain the approval of his successor on the

Boone County circuit court. To lend Bamberger's elevation to the board the veil of propriety, Wallingford found a legal rationale to justify the appointment. He cited an administrative ruling in *Shake v. The Kentucky Ethics Commission,* an obscure case that vacated a prior advisory opinion stating that a judge could not serve on the board of a "mediation service." In fact, *Shake* was irrelevant, since FHL was in no way a mediation service, and Wallingford ignored the fact that it is unethical for a judge to set aside a considerable amount of other people's money and then take a portion for his private gain. Nonetheless, this provided the fig leaf Bamberger needed.

In a move that was equal parts stupidity and cupidity, Bamberger joined the FHL board and began receiving his own $5,000 monthly stipend. Bamberger's ultimate disrobement and disbarment by the Judicial Conduct Commission (JCC) would be for "fraud, deceit and misrepresentations," but taking a seat on the FHL board, though perhaps not technically a violation of the KBA's Rules of Professional Conduct, was rightly regarded as unethical and his worst disgrace. While on the witness stand during GCM's criminal trial, Bamberger gave the contorted explanation that, after much consideration, he had concluded that it would be proper to accept the board position because the claimants had been delighted to let FHL take off with $20 million of their money. The JCC's report used the word "inexcusable" to describe Bamberger's acceptance of a position on the FHL board.

The August 2010 edition of *True Crime Report,* an online publication that details the most outrageous crimes and criminals in the United States, contained a feature by Chris Parker titled "Top Five White Collar Villains." Parker's list included Blackwater Worldwide, which used federal funds meant for Hurricane Katrina relief to hire strippers, and Trevor Cook, a televangelist who bilked an estimated 900 elderly investors out of $190 million. But the number-one *True Crime Report* villain was Bamberger.

At about the time Bamberger joined the FHL board, Rebecca Phipps requested a seat on the board herself. In a letter to Bamberger dated May 2, 2003, Phipps argued that she deserved a place on the board because she had worked tirelessly to obtain most of the agreements for the two distributions that allowed FHL to be created in the first place. Phipps also argued that, as the person most familiar with the claimants, she would be in the best posi-

tion to convey their sentiments to the board.[3] This was accurate but insufficient of overcome Bamberger's elitism. It was perfectly fine for Phipps to do
the dirty work, but as a lowly legal assistant, she was judged unqualified to
enjoy the fruits of her own labor, and Bamberger denied her request. Phipps
would later answer the judge's insult with injury.

11

Bad Times, Good Times

AS HIS DRINKING TOOK ON epic proportions, Mills's relationship with caution grew more remote, and becoming an instant multimillionaire only accelerated this process. As a consequence, Mills became entangled in a legal mess related to the *Guard* settlement—a mess between friends.

The relationship between Cindy Sawyer and Melbourne Mills began when he represented her in a 1991 breast implant lawsuit. Following the successful outcome of that case, Sawyer recommended that her friends with worrisome implants hire Mills too. Sawyer was so proficient at recruiting clients that Mills asked her to join his staff as a legal assistant. Soon Sawyer and her husband were on such friendly terms with Mills that they frequently vacationed together. Despite the steady diminution of his once lucrative workers' compensation business, Mills never stinted on his own pleasure and arranged exotic getaways for the trio, even when he struggled to make payroll. Cindy Sawyer was exceptionally attractive and had lived in Hollywood briefly during her unsuccessful pursuit of an acting career. Her good looks were apparently derived from her mother, whom Mills had once dated.

Based on Mills's promise of a big bonus if she helped him land a class action with a big payday, Sawyer spent a considerable amount of effort on that task. After her initial suggestion of a lawsuit involving the dietary supplement Saint-John's-wort resulted in a dead end, Sawyer brought fen-phen to his attention. According to Sawyer, it was at her urging that, beginning in September 1997, Mills launched the television ad campaign that led to 6,500-

plus phone calls from potential plaintiffs. Eventually, 311 people signed contingency contracts with Mills, accounting for the majority of the 431 *Guard* plaintiffs. In her mind, Sawyer had played an essential role in the subsequent award that raised Mills from near penury to wealth. Mills would later insist that his decision to sue AHP on behalf of fen-phen users had been inspired by a 1997 article in *Time* magazine.

After receiving more than $20 million from the *Guard* settlement, Mills handed out $100,000 bonuses to six paralegals and $800,000 to Rebecca Phipps. Part-time employees, including Sawyer, received bonuses of only $1,300 each. Sawyer believed she had been cheated, and both she and her husband appealed to Mills for more cash. During a morning meeting, Sawyer reminded Mills of his earlier promise, as well as her essential role in bringing the fen-phen bonanza to his attention. Sawyer suggested that a bonus of $1 million plus $45,000 for a new car would be fair. Mills, filled with Old Crow–induced magnanimity, agreed. Aware of Mills's tendency to forget his promises, Sawyer recorded the conversation.

Mills soon sought to change the terms of the payout: rather than the agreed-upon lump sum, he proposed installments of $10,000 per month, ostensibly to keep the agreement secret from the other part-time staff. To ease Sawyer's qualms, Mills asked an attorney to draw up an agreement, and although Mills never signed it, he did pay Sawyer a total of $165,000 over several months. Then in February 2002, for reasons that are unclear, Mills terminated Sawyer's employment and refused to honor the remainder of his commitment. An incensed Sawyer sued, leading to a four-day trial.

During a light moment in the courtroom, Mills made a curious attempt to weaken Sawyer's claim of an enforceable agreement. Because her secret recording had been made at 10:00 in the morning, Mills assured the jury that he would have been drunk long before that time. Although the spectators erupted in laughter, the jury was apparently unamused and awarded Sawyer $900,000.

Mills's attorney immediately petitioned the court for a judgment notwithstanding verdict, which allows a judge to nullify a jury verdict. Judge James Ishmael granted the petition and reluctantly ruled that an oral agreement (Mills had never signed the written document) was not enforceable.

Ishmael based this opinion on the 1677 Statute of Frauds. This act of English common law has been adopted by all fifty states in some version to avoid phony oral contracts. In his written opinion, however, Ishmael stated, "Honoring the oral agreement would be the moral and right thing for [Mills] to do." Since neither Ishmael nor the defense had asserted this well-established legal concept until after the verdict, the trial had been nothing but a great waste of time for the jury.[1]

In contrast to Mills's misfortunes, for a brief interval, life was sweet for Bill Gallion. He already owned a 5,000-square-foot home beside a golf course in Lexington. He also rewarded himself with a 5,029-square-foot home on Sanibel Island in Florida (where he established his legal residence), as well as a château in France. In addition to his first black Porsche, Gallion purchased three more—one in yellow, one in red, and one in stainless steel—along with a BMW and a Jaguar.

Gallion's self-indulgence was not limited to material possessions. He also had an appreciation for pleasures of the flesh. One evening, Gallion and a friend dropped into a Lexington strip club known as Three Tree House and ordered lap dances. As lap-dance connoisseurs, both men were dissatisfied with the services rendered and refused to pay. The club's bouncers were not sympathetic and tossed the two out the door, resulting in bruises to both their bodies and their pride. Gallion subsequently filed a lawsuit for damages, which he later dropped after an undisclosed settlement.[2] The salacious incident further enshrined Gallion's boorish reputation in the Lexington legal community.

Cunningham was also enjoying the good life. The touchstone of success in the bluegrass region of central Kentucky is owning a horse farm. But, as the joke goes, to have a $5 million Thoroughbred operation, you need to start with $10 million. Many horse farms are displays of vanity, and Cunningham's $8.6 million purchase of a 135-acre farm in Scott County was no exception. Enormous letters spelling out the name "Cunningham" were sculpted into the greenery of a hillside, and his initials graced an ornate gateway with limestone pillars.

Cunningham and Gallion loved to spend time at Lexington's Keeneland racetrack, where the most prestigious Thoroughbred auction in the world is held each autumn. Inside the one-story, windowless brown brick building are rows of padded chairs forming a semicircle around the sales ring, featuring the auctioneer's dais. Each September the gavel falls on the dais's oaken rail, conveying title to Thoroughbred yearlings to the highest bidders. Every buyer harbors the fantasy that his or her purchase is destined for greatness. And Keeneland has sold its share of champions, including nineteen winners of the Kentucky Derby, eighty-eight Breeders' Cup winners, and eleven Eclipse Award Horses of the Year.

It was at the Keeneland pavilion that Gallion and Cunningham began to spend some of their fortunes on horseflesh to fill their newly established business partnership: Midnight Cry Stables, named after a Baptist hymn. As part of this objective, they entered into a gentlemen's agreement with respected horse expert Kenny McPeek to procure a few of the more promising Thoroughbreds. At the 2005 Keeneland sale, McPeek took notice of a colt sired by the pedigreed Smart Strike that was expected to bring at least $250,000 at the auction block. However, when a radiograph revealed an abnormality in its ankle bone, interest in the yearling evaporated. McPeek snapped up the Thoroughbred with the worrisome ankle for the bargain-basement price of $57,000. Gallion and Cunningham named the horse Curlin after Cunningham's great-great-grandfather Charles Curlin, a slave with the dubious distinction of fighting on the side of the Confederacy during the Civil War.

After being trained by Helen Pitts, Curlin won his first event—a seven-furlong race for three-year-olds at Florida's Gulf Stream Park—by an astonishing 12¾ lengths. Having witnessed this magnificent performance, a broker immediately contacted wine billionaire Jess Jackson, who paid $3.5 million to acquire an 80 percent share of Curlin. Jackson claimed he had no idea that the remaining 20 percent was co-owned by the now notorious pair of lawyers.

Jackson was the sole owner of the fabulously successful Kendall-Jackson winery, which produced more than 5 million cases of wine annually. He was determined to cut a wide swath in Kentucky horse country, just as he had done in California wine country. He snapped up 1,100 acres of prime bluegrass countryside for $32 million and filled its fence-lined pastures with more than 200 Thoroughbreds valued at $75 million. Unfortunately, the brokers he had entrusted with the task of buying these horses misrepresented the amounts paid by nearly $5 million and kept the difference for themselves. Having previously worked as a police investigator, Jackson sniffed out the kickback scheme and managed to get his money back from some of the top names in the Thoroughbred consignment business.

In contrast, Jackson's acquisition of majority ownership of Curlin was practically a steal. Author Jim Squires describes Curlin as "an intimidating presence, a gleaming red, chiseled example of what a precision regimen of feed, proper exercise and pharmaceuticals can do to an already beautifully conformed athlete." Squires's reference to pharmaceuticals came from the conviction that Curlin bore all the telltale signs of having been administered the steroid Winstrol. The use of steroids was not illegal as long as the horse was free of all traces of the drug for some time before the race. However, after the 2008 congressional hearings into the use of steroids by racehorses, Jackson ordered the discontinuation of Winstrol for Curlin.[3]

The victories that Curlin chalked up were incredible. After winning both the Rebel Stakes and the Arkansas Derby at Oakland Park, Curlin entered the 2007 Kentucky Derby, a mere three months after his maiden race at Gulf Stream. Having never raced as a juvenile, Curlin was at a distinct disadvantage, but he still managed to place third. The Derby loss was forgotten two weeks later when Curlin made an all-out drive in the final furlong to win the Preakness, tying the track record. In the winner's circle photo, a grinning Gallion and Cunningham can be seen grasping the silver trophy behind the intimidating physical presence of Jackson.

Curlin went on to further glory. He placed first in eleven out of sixteen lifetime races, racking up winnings of more than $10 million. In 2008 Curlin won the Dubai World Cup by more than seven lengths and became the first horse to win one of the legs of the Triple Crown, a Breeders' Cup race, and the Dubai Cup. Curlin was named the American Horse of the Year for 2008 and 2009.

With their abundant newfound wealth, Cunningham and Gallion also acquired the ultimate status symbol for most Kentuckians. In exchange for scholarship gifts of $313,060 each, they were granted courtside season tickets for University of Kentucky basketball games at Rupp Arena for life.

Cunningham's most notorious expenditure initially seemed to be based on selfless virtue, but it turned out to be anything but. The new law school at Florida A&M was struggling to attain full accreditation by the American Bar Association. The historically black college, located in Tallahassee, had inaugurated its first law school in 1949 in response to the University of Florida's refusal to admit black applicants. By the 1960s, though, African Americans had gained the right to attend that law school, and Florida State University (formerly the Florida State College for Women) also had a fully integrated law school. Florida A&M's law school was no longer needed, and it graduated its final class in 1968. In the ensuing decades, the university lobbied to reestablish a law school on its campus, and these persistent pleas eventually won the approval of the Florida state legislature. The stated mission of the new law school, which opened in 2003 with provisional accreditation, was to serve historically underrepresented communities. The ABA had scheduled a review to grant full accreditation status in 2005.

The timing could not have been worse. In 2002 Cunningham pledged to donate $1 million to help the law school establish its educational credentials. As part of a matching grant, the school was awarded an additional $750,000 of public funds. The anticipated investment income from the $1.75 million was dedicated to the creation and maintenance of the Cunningham chair, which was to be occupied by a distinguished legal scholar who would also be a member of the teaching faculty. The hope was that this endowment would fund the Cunningham chair in perpetuity. The Florida A&M public-relations department showered accolades on Cunningham to entice other wealthy donors to do the same. However, it neglected to inform the public that in exchange for his $1 million, Cunningham insisted that he himself be hired to fill the Cunningham chair, at an annual salary of $100,000 plus benefits. Because Cunningham did not wish to subject himself to the tedium of actually teaching, he and the law school came to an agreement whereby Cunningham would take on various other responsibilities, such as fund-raising, organizing a series of lectures, obtaining summer internships for law students, assisting in the creation of a specialty in agricultural law, and organizing what was to be known as the Cunningham Summer Academy.

From August 2003 through April 2005, Cunningham received $193,243 from the law school. However, when questioned by administrators, the maintenance staff could recall seeing Cunningham on campus only once, and the teaching staff was unaware of any work that Cunningham had performed. An anonymous tip about a "ghost professor" led to an investigation by the state's inspector general. When university maintenance personnel unlocked Cunningham's office and swung open the door, dust motes swirled on the floor. A computer sitting on an empty desk had never even been connected. But astonishingly, Cunningham was standing in the room. Apparently, after being warned of the impending investigation, he had grabbed the next flight to Tallahassee, arriving just moments before the inspector. The startled Cunningham was still holding his travel bag.[4]

As detailed in the *Orlando Sentinel,* the ensuing publicity prompted Governor Jeb Bush to comment that "this arrangement stinks." Percy Luney Jr., the dean of the law school, was summarily fired.[5] As reported by the *ABA Journal,* the scandal did little to impress the ABA accreditation team. The report it issued in January 2006 was highly critical of the university, not only for the Cunningham fiasco but for other problems as well. It found no fewer than forty-one other employees on the payroll who did virtually no work, and some of them lived out of state. Other employees had been caught exchanging cash for grades, changing Fs to As.[6] The law school also faced a host of lawsuits filed by its students for failing to conform to its own written standards.[7]

In fairness, not all of Gallion's and Cunningham's expenditures were self-indulgent. Cunningham converted an empty metal building into an 11,600-square-foot gymnasium for disadvantaged youth. Unfortunately, the property was several miles outside of Lexington off a crooked, lightly traveled highway, making it difficult for young people from Lexington's inner city to get there. For his part, Gallion created the Gallion Family Foundation with $3.9 million in assets, and the foundation contributed $122,474 over three years (roughly 1 percent of its assets per year), with the largest donation being $25,000 to Habitat for Humanity.

While Gallion and Cunningham were enjoying their moments in the sun, Mills continued to live under a cloud. Dave Stuart, his former law partner, was unstinting in his determination to recover his fair share of the fen-phen settlement income. Stuart had obtained an enforceable order for Chesley to provide an out-of-state deposition. Prior to the scheduled deposition, Stuart and Mills met to negotiate a settlement. At Chesley's behest, Rebecca Phipps was also in attendance. Numbers were exchanged until the two were only $500,000 apart. Stuart was demanding $3 million, but at that point, Mills dug in his heels and refused to budge, oblivious to the fact that Stuart had everyone, including Chesley, over a barrel. At this juncture, Phipps slipped out of the room and phoned Chesley, telling him that the negotiations were at an impasse. Aware of his own vulnerability should this dispute end up in a courtroom, Chesley wired Mills the extra $500,000. Mills and Stuart then settled for $3 million. Chesley later cajoled Gallion and Cunningham into reimbursing him for half of the $500,000 he had paid to keep Stuart quiet.

Mills's behavior was not reformed by the fen-phen escapade. In 2002 he applied for renewal of his professional liability insurance from the Continental Insurance Company. Question 3 of the application asked whether there were any issues that "may reasonably be expected to be a claim to the firm that had not been reported," and question 4 asked whether the applicant was the "subject of any disciplinary complaint or proceeding." Mills checked the "no" box in both cases. Mills's policy was approved for up to $5 million in insurance coverage. This came not a minute too soon, as GCM were now fending off both the KBA and their unhappy former clients. By the time Continental realized it had been deceived, it had already paid $233,674 for Mills's legal representation. Continental then sued Mills to rescind the coverage and recover the $233,674. Both orders were granted by summary judgment.

Like Mills, Gallion had to deal with his former partner. Mike Baker was about to take Gallion to court for attempting to jilt Baker out of his rightful partnership fee. Before that happened, the two reached a settlement for an undisclosed amount. Soon thereafter, Baker moved to South Carolina.

With all these allegations and all that money flying about, rumors of the KBA investigation, the settlements with Baker and Stuart, and the possibility of criminal charges spread through Lexington's legal community. Soon, GCM's faces would begin to appear in Kentucky newspapers with growing frequency because of yet another human foil.

12

The Alligator

WHILE GCM AND CHESLEY were looking over their shoulders, trying to stay a few steps ahead of the KBA investigators, they were ambushed by a five-foot-two virago in heels: Angela Ford, a Lexington attorney in solo practice. One of eight children, Ford described herself as painfully shy and a middling student in high school. After enrolling at the University of Louisville for her undergraduate studies, Ford emerged from her cocoon of self-consciousness to become the first female student government president, as well as the student representative on the prestigious Kentucky Council for Higher Education. In 1982, while on the council, Ford led an effort opposing a proposal to allow state universities to increase the maximum student activity fee from $20 per semester to $100. Ford's activism caught the attention of Humana CEO David Jones, who was also serving on the council at the time. Jones described Ford as "tiny but with a big brain and a big heart, and a lot of moxie."[1]

Soon after graduating from the Chase School of Law at Northern Kentucky University, Ford was appointed by Governor Brereton Jones to serve as the first female general counsel of the Kentucky Cabinet for Human Resources; she was also the first general counsel younger than thirty. At that time, the cabinet's responsibilities encompassed an enormous range of duties, including overseeing local health departments, behavioral health services, billions of dollars in Medicaid reimbursements to hospitals and physicians, and Kentucky's network of county social workers. It was in this last capacity that she was tossed a blistering hot potato when four state-employed social workers were indicted by a grand jury in Wayne County for complicity in the murder of twenty-two-month-old Daniel Thomas Reynolds, who had been beaten to death by his stepfather. The county attorney charged that the four had failed to notice obvious signs of abuse during a home visit four days before the murder.[2] Ford was in the unenviable position of walking the political tightrope of defending the actions of the cabinet while empathizing with the public outrage toward the cabinet's employees. Although the social workers were eventually acquitted, the case was a baptism by fire for the young Ford.

Ford next worked for Landrum Shouse, an established Lexington law firm that also happened to employ Pierce Hamblin, who mediated the AHP settlement negotiations. Ford eventually hung up her own shingle, and on display at her Lexington office is an enormous stuffed head of a Florida alligator. It was presented to Ford by her cocounsel in a lawsuit as a token of his admiration for her tenacity. As a sole practitioner, Ford handled a variety of cases, one of which led her to lock horns with Chesley. While Chesley was arguing for the creation of a class action against the Catholic Diocese of Covington, Ford convinced her eighteen clients to opt out of this class action and won them a combined settlement of $4.4 million.[3] Chesley was not amused, and this marked the beginning of the bitter animosity between them.

In an astonishing coincidence, just as this feud was starting to simmer, a woman dropped into Ford's office with a provocative question: can a lawyer give away settlement money without the client's consent? The woman (possibly Lisa Swiger or Tracy Curtis) was a *Guard* claimant who was unhappy with her settlement and had recently been asked to agree to use the remaining settlement funds for the creation of a charity—the Kentucky Fund for Healthy Living. Ford's interest was piqued. As soon as she began to investigate, she immediately noticed red flags. FHL had been created in a flurry of motions with an undisclosed portion of the $200 million long after *Guard* had been settled. In addition, the attorneys who had created FHL were paying themselves fees in undisclosed amounts. Ford would eventually use this information as the basis for a civil lawsuit on behalf of the *Guard* claimants. But as soon as GCM got wind of Ford's contacts with large numbers of their former clients, they took steps to quash her plan to turn the *Guard* claimants against them. Accordingly, they sought the assistance of Bamberger, but that effort would be badly bungled.

Shortly after stepping down as circuit judge, Bamberger became embroiled in controversy during a malpractice trial in Pike County, where he was assigned to preside as senior judge. Pike County lies in the heart of Appalachia in the far-eastern corner of Kentucky. Before the trial even began, the attorneys for the plaintiffs accused Bamberger of improper communications with his friend Mark Modlin. Not surprisingly, Modlin had been hired by the defense as a trial consultant. The accusation was based on a November 9, 2004, communication from Modlin to Bamberger that had been found in a fax machine in the Pike County courthouse. The gross impropriety of such communications between a trial consultant and the presiding judge was bad enough, but the content of the fax was even more shocking. It contained a draft of a judicial restraining order and a message from Modlin asking Bamberger to preemptively block Ford from filing a lawsuit against GCM over the formation and funding of FHL. The ostensible basis for the restraining order was to prevent Ford from interfering in the client-attorney relationship between GCM and the *Guard* claimants. The order also charged that Ford was soliciting plaintiffs for a lawsuit against GCM to seize the $20 million used to fund FHL.

By this time, GCM was aware that Ford had spent the better part of 2004 rounding up as many of the 431 *Guard* claimants as she could in an attempt to recover the purloined settlement funds. Unfortunately for GCM, Modlin's fax, which had been intended for Bamberger's eyes only, soon found its way into Ford's hands. Later, Modlin would implausibly tell a reporter that he "didn't have a clue" why a document asking Bamberger to sign a restraining order against Ford would have been sent from his own fax machine.[4]

Having the remarkable good fortune of obtaining GCM's battle plan in advance, Ford filed suit on November 16, 2004, not only against GCM but also against Chesley. The lawsuit accused the four of stealing millions from their former clients. Because the circuit court docket in Fayette County was too overcrowded to take on new lawsuits, and because Ford was under the gun to beat GCM to the courthouse before they could obtain Bamberger's approval of a restraining order against her, Ford filed suit in neighboring Woodford County.[5] *Abbott v. Stanley Chesley, William Gallion, Shirley Cunningham, Melbourne Mills and the Kentucky Fund for Healthy Living* was later refiled in Fayette and ultimately transferred to Boone County, where it would be heard by Bamberger's successor, Judge William Wehr.[6]

The discovery of the fax in the Pike County courthouse affirmed the growing suspicions about the odd and improper relationship between Bamberger and Modlin. Bamberger recused himself from the Pike County case. By this time, Bamberger must have realized that he was in trouble for ordering the creation of the Fund for Healthy Living using the $20 million of *Guard* settlement funds that rightfully belonged to the claimants

When the *Abbott* case was filed on November 16, 2004, Ford had managed to sign on virtually all of the 431 *Guard* claimants. According to the KBA's Rules of Professional Conduct, although ads for legal services intended for the general public are acceptable, lawyers are prohibited from directly or through another person soliciting professional employment when a significant motive for doing so is monetary gain. How Ford was able to avoid violating this rule is an interesting question. Gallion would later assert that Ford had indeed improperly solicited the *Abbott* plaintiffs. Mills believed that Helmers had given Ford the list of names of the *Guard* plaintiffs in exchange for not naming him as a defendant in *Abbott*, which indeed he was not. Mary Mead McKenzie, Cunningham's attorney during the *Abbott* civil lawsuit, testified at the criminal trial, "I do recall that in a complaint that was filed by Ms. Ford at one point also had David Helmers listed as a defendant, but that was later withdrawn."[7] What was not in doubt was the potential of an enormous payday for Ford if the $20 million could be recovered. In the looming legal battle, no quarter would be asked or given.

Despite Ford's success in garnering so many *Abbott* plaintiffs, GCM initially shrugged off this threat. By long-standing custom and legal etiquette in Kentucky, attorneys did not sue other attorneys. GCM's insouciance was reinforced when Bob Sanders, Wallingford's replacement as FHL counsel, commented to a reporter from the *Kentucky Post* that Ford was a bad lawyer and was in way over her head. According to one of the attorneys on the GCM defense team, when the "Bad Lawyer" headline hit the *Post,* Ford was furious. She became even more determined not to relinquish her alligator-like grip on GCM and Chesley until they were all brought down.

The *Post's* headline likely left GCM with a false sense of security. Their erroneous self-assurance led them to completely misread the peril of the situation. When a legal colleague ran into Gallion and Cunningham on the street and strongly advised them to hire a criminal attorney, they both laughed out loud. So strong was the mutual contempt between the two camps that mediation was apparently never attempted. Perhaps if GCM had been willing to negotiate a settlement with Ford, they would have been able to sidestep the calamity awaiting them.

Beginning in January 2005 and throughout the year, the media coverage of *Abbott* began in earnest for both the *Lexington Herald-Leader* and the *Louisville Courier-Journal.* Investigative reporter Andrew Wolfson wrote numerous articles for the *Courier-Journal* covering the saga of GCM. In an interview with Wolfson, Gallion described the *Abbott* lawsuit as resulting from a "cottage industry of lawyers who attacked class action settlements" and stated that the nondisclosure clause of the settlement agreement was essentially a "gag order" that prevented GCM from sharing information with their clients.[8]

Meanwhile, the KBA investigation of GCM was proceeding. Gallion and Cunningham had hired Whitney Wallingford, the legal counsel for FHL, to prepare their responses to the KBA inquiries. Mills was represented for this same purpose by attorney William E. Johnson. Mills and Johnson were old friends who had first met back in the 1970s when they both worked for the Kentucky Legislative Research Commission. Although the KBA had yet to announce an investigation of Chesley, he likely knew it was only a matter of time before it turned its attention to him as well. Accordingly, GCM and Chesley decided to meet and plan a coordinated defense strategy. Both Wallingford and Johnson were in attendance, as was Rebecca Phipps. At Chesley's insistence, they all agreed to use Johnson as their common counsel, thus firing Wallingford. Following this decision, Johnson and his four clients discussed how they might create "reverse PR" troubles for Ford because of her presumed solicitation of the *Guard* plaintiffs for *Abbott*. To whatever extent reverse PR was attempted, it had little effect.

Of all the attorneys in Kentucky, William E. Johnson carried the most gravitas and credibility. Raised in Pendleton County, he had once considered a career as a professional baseball player but opted for the law after being inspired by Erle Stanley Gardner's Perry Mason novels. Like Mason, Johnson became renowned as a skilled defense lawyer. In one remarkable stretch in his fifty-year legal practice, he went eleven years without losing a single case. Johnson was also considered a lawyer's lawyer. He frequently took on the thankless task of defending fellow attorneys before the KBA Disciplinary Board when other attorneys were unwilling to do so and risk jeopardizing their standing in the KBA. Johnson's regal bearing, courtly manner, and mellifluous voice radiated integrity to judges and juries alike. It is uncertain whether Johnson knew, before agreeing to represent GCM and Chesley, that the KBA had already subpoenaed their banking records. In the end, Johnson's charge of keeping the quartet out of trouble with the KBA would prove to be a fool's errand.

After being fired, Wallingford handed off his defense counsel duties to Johnson, but in doing so, he dropped the baton. Wallingford had prepared a report for the KBA detailing how the settlement proceeds had been distributed to the *Guard* claimants up to that time. As determined in *KBA v. Chesley*, Wallingford's chart of payments inaccurately and grossly inflated the aggregate amount paid to the 431 claimants: instead of the actual $73 million paid out, Wallingford reported $116 million. According to a report by the trial commissioner, Wallingford had submitted the report for Chesley to review, and Chesley did not correct the glaring inaccuracy. Chesley admitted that he told Wallingford to go ahead and file the report, which he did. Even though Chesley had convinced GCM to use Johnson as their common counsel, in a move that was vintage Chesley, he secretly engaged Louisville attorney Scott Cox to handle his own separate defense.

As reported by the *Courier-Journal* during GCM's trial, Wallingford was contrite about the miscalculations and testified that the FHL board had done a "great job managing the fund and were diligent, energetic and prepared." When asked whether Mills was as energetic as the others, Wallingford replied, "I don't think anyone would describe Mel Mills as energetic," at which the defendants and spectators "broke into laughter."[9]

Despite Wallingford's assurances, FHL was largely a sham. In May 2003 members of the FHL board voted to treat themselves to a retreat at Pebble Beach, California, even though the board did not approve a single grant until September 2004.[10] During GCM's trial, Bamberger testified how the four members of the board earned their combined monthly stipend of $20,000. He recalled that FHL gave money to an organization in northern Kentucky that helped handicapped children, known as BAWAC. Had he read the grant application, he would have known that BAWAC serves adults. He also had a vague memory of providing funds to a drug-treatment program in eastern Kentucky. Neither of these causes was related to FHL's ostensible mission of addressing the deleterious health consequences of obesity.

GCM's plan to resurrect their image with the KBA by using Johnson as a cat's-paw did not have the desired effect. On August 24, 2006, the KBA temporarily suspended the licenses to practice law of all three. Johnson, speaking on their behalf, acknowledged that his clients had not done a good job of accounting but argued that the suspension of their licenses was severe. Notwithstanding Johnson's quixotic defense, by that time, it was obvious that GCM's troubles went far beyond bad bookkeeping. GCM would not be alone in their misery.

As he had predicted, GCM's accomplice Stan Chesley would also suffer his day of reckoning. He was named as a defendant in the *Abbott* lawsuit, and in late April 2006 he became aware that a KBA inquiry commission was investigating his role in *Guard*. Soon thereafter, in an effort to elude both potential catastrophes, Chesley traveled to Washington, DC, and paid a visit to his old friend and AHP's chief *Guard* negotiator Jack Vardaman. Chesley was carrying an envelope containing a handwritten document, but this time, the Chesley magic would fail.

Although Chesley described their relationship as long and mutually respectful, Vardaman had sought to distance himself from Chesley after the *Guard* settlement. When asked at trial his opinion of Chesley's legal abilities, Vardaman almost begrudgingly described him as able. For a legal legend like Chesley, this was faint praise indeed. Their apparent bond of congeniality had cooled by the time of Chesley's DC visit. In fact, Vardaman was absent when Chesley arrived, so he left the envelope with Vardaman's receptionist.

Yet there remained telltale evidence of some kind of an understanding between the two. During the criminal trial, Vardaman testified that he remembered Gallion as the lead negotiator, despite Chesley's reputation as the king of all mediators.[11] Why would Vardaman wish to minimize Chesley's role in the settlement negotiations? Most telling, Chesley seemingly believed that Vardaman's interests were so intertwined with his own that he could casually drop off, for Vardaman's endorsement, a document filled with a contorted version of the facts. The document read:

> *The case [Guard] was settled as a class action.* Decertification was not relevant to the collateral issues of attorneys' fees or administration of settlement proceeds and process. AHP intended and, in fact, treated the settlement, for all purposes, as a settlement of a class action, and of all existing and contingent Kentucky claims, *not for some 431 or so individuals.* AHP expected that the settlement would be treated as a fluid recovery because of the contingencies and indemnities for which plaintiffs' attorneys undertook responsibility and subrogation issues that were unresolved, such as Medicaid liens. *AHP expected that funds would be available for these future claims and unresolved contingencies* [emphasis added].

Apparently, Chesley's intention was to provide Vardaman with advantageous talking points for future depositions. This all speaks to the possibility that Vardaman had been conniving with Chesley from the beginning. It is also telling that Chesley intended the document for Vardaman's eyes only, writing it out by hand. Whether due to virtue or cold feet, Vardaman placed Chesley's proposed statement in his files unheeded and would later testify that *Guard* had been settled as an aggregate of 431 claimants and not as a class action. It is also worth noting that, by this time, both the national and Kentucky lawsuits had been settled, so there was no reason for Vardaman to stick out his neck to come to Chesley's rescue.

At this point, it is worth probing how the settlement reached the stratospheric heights of $200 million. Chesley would later testify that Vardaman's body language gave him a sense of how high he was willing to go. In contradiction, a later report by the KBA contained Chesley's statement that the *Guard* settlement mediations had been merely for show. This strongly implies that Chesley and AHP had come to an agreement sometime before the formal settlement discussions were convened in Pierce Hamblin's Lexington law office on April 30 and May 1, 2001. This explanation also fits the theory that the final $50 million Chesley obtained on the second day of negotiations represented a giveaway to pump up the total settlement to $200 million.

Even more revealing was the testimony of Cunningham's attorney, Mary McKenzie, who worked closely with Chesley in crafting Cunningham's defense. Quite reasonably, McKenzie suggested arranging for a representative from AHP to testify on Cunningham's behalf. Chesley nixed that idea and told McKenzie that AHP could not tell the truth.

While Chesley was just beginning to feel the heat from the KBA, Bamberger was toast. After joining the FHL board of directors, he became aware that his friends were being investigated by the KBA and the FBI. By this time, he had already "earned" $48,150 from his $5,350 per month stipend and expense allowance. In the hopes of mollifying the KBA, Bamberger resigned from the FHL board and returned all the money he had received. But it was too little too late. On December 27, 2005, the Kentucky Judicial Conduct Commission served notice that Bamberger was being investigated for alleged misconduct in *Guard*. The Kentucky Constitution authorizes the JCC to investigate and impose sanctions on judges and other court officials who engage in misconduct or wrongdoing. In preparation for the hearing before the commission, Chesley coached Bamberger for what was certain to be a painful ordeal. Chesley also accompanied Bamberger to the hearing, where he attempted to justify Bamberger's application of the cy pres doctrine to the *Guard* settlement, as well as the establishment of FHL as a receptacle for the $20 million of cy pres funds. Chesley's skills as a virtuoso of dissembling failed to impress the commission.

The order of public reprimand issued by the JCC on February 24, 2006, was scathing. It was particularly incensed by Bamberger's personal relationship with Modlin. The JCC wrote that Bamberger's actions "shocked the conscience of the court." Rather than wait for his formal removal from the bench, Bamberger resigned as senior judge on February 27, 2006.[12] He had lost both his job and his reputation.

Not surprisingly, Chesley expressed a contrary view to reporters. He claimed that Bamberger's friendship with the *Guard* lawyers had no impact on the case. Chesley went on to praise the work of GCM and said they had won an amazing settlement for their clients. Chesley would later repudiate all these statements of support for both Bamberger and GCM.

Bamberger's ultimate demise came five years later with his disbarment. On the morning of October 27, 2011, Bamberger walked into the hearing room of the KBA in Frankfort. His wan smile was met by the grim countenances of his soon-to-be-former colleagues. The man applauded as the KBA's 2002 Judge of the Year had now been accused of egregiously violating his ethical obligations. His transgressions had sullied the reputations of both the bar and the bench. With its knives of retribution sharpened, the KBA prepared to excise Bamberger from the practice of law.

At the hearing, Bamberger was questioned about his many informal, off-the-record meetings with Chesley and the GCM legal team. Contrary to basic rules of procedure, these meetings had been conducted without the presence of opposing counsel, clients, or cameras to record the proceedings. It was impossible for Bamberger to defend his agreement to award attorneys' fees amounting to 49 percent of the settlement, an act made worse by the fact that the 431 claimants had been kept in the dark about these key developments. Nor could he adequately explain his rationale for accepting payment to serve on the FHL board. The KBA concluded that Bamberger had "entered numerous orders containing false statements of fact, conducting secret proceedings, sealing the court record, failing to review *any* documentation of the allocation of settlement funds, and personally benefiting from the fraud."[13]

Bamberger was also grilled about his relationship with Modlin. It was evident that, on numerous occasions, Modlin had exploited his relationship with Bamberger to curry favor for the legal teams that had engaged him as a trial consultant. Even more appalling, while serving as senior judge at one such trial in Pike County, Bamberger had failed to disclose to district court judge Charles T. Moore that he and Modlin were partners in Panoply, a venture that owned, among other properties, a $412,000 house in Bonita Springs, Florida.

There was very little Bamberger could say to excuse his behavior. The KBA Board of Governors ordered that its former Judge of the Year be "hereby permanently disbarred from the Kentucky Bar Association" and further ordered that Bamberger "may never apply for reinstatement."[14]

Judicial corruption in Kentucky did not begin and end with Bamberger. In Kentucky, judges are elected, not appointed. This makes them more likely to be influenced by the contributors who help keep them in office. An all too common example of the corruption engendered by this system was circuit court judge Cletus Maricle, who was convicted in 2014 of racketeering as part of an extensive vote-buying scheme. This was the same Judge Maricle who indirectly helped Chesley become *Guard* cocounsel when he amiably decertified *Feltner v. AHP* as a class action in Leslie County, Kentucky.

According to the *Lexington Herald-Leader,* approximately 160 complaints against members of the judiciary are filed each year with the JCC. They are not handled with the same alacrity and thoroughness as Bamberger experienced. The JCC employs only one part-time staff member, making Kentucky's the most poorly staffed judicial investigative body in the region. The general laxness of the JCC in its watchdog capacity extends throughout the Kentucky court system.[15]

The Administrative Office of the Courts is notorious for giving its staff exclusive rights to purchase property classified as "surplus" at bargain-basement prices. For instance, former Kentucky Supreme Court justice Will T. Scott snapped up a Crown Victoria automobile for $2,300. While still on the bench, Scott received a contribution from Eric Conn in the felonious amount of $10,000. When the contribution was revealed, Scott returned the money.[16] The Democratic Party establishment worked out a deal with then state attorney general Jack Conway that allowed Conn to plead guilty to a misdemeanor and pay a $5,600 fine, netting him $4,400 of his intended contribution.

The ethical concerns emanating from the Kentucky Supreme Court are not limited to these relatively modest transactions. According to an investigative report by the *Lexington Herald-Leader,* between 1998 and 2008, more than half of the $800 million spent to construct courthouses went to no-bid contracts. Many of these contracts were awarded to Codell Construction; owner James Codell IV is the son of James Codell III, a former secretary of the Kentucky Transportation Cabinet. Among Codell's $61,000 in campaign contributions was $3,500 to the wife of then Kentucky Supreme Court chief justice Joseph E. Lambert. Construction bonding was handled by another Kentucky firm, Ross Sinclaire & Associates, which at one time employed Lambert's son. Another employee of Ross Sinclaire was state senator Johnny Ray Turner, who had earlier pleaded guilty in a voter fraud case. It was estimated that during the ten-year period, Ross Sinclaire earned $6 million in courthouse projects alone.[17]

In the meantime, the FBI investigation of GCM inched forward. To present the full picture of this federal investigation, it is helpful to backtrack a few years. The FBI inquiry began in February 2002. It is possible that the FBI was tipped off by the KBA after Gallion and Cunningham transferred tens of millions of dollars into out-of-state financial institutions to make it more difficult for the KBA to subpoena their banking records.

The FBI's responsibilities cover a vast range of criminal activities. These include "white-collar crimes," a term coined in 1939 by sociologist Edwin Sutherland to denote "deceit for financial gain by a person of respectability in the course of his occupation."[18] "Deceit" can be a vague term, and not all deceit for financial gain violates federal law. The federal government's authority to prosecute deceit was made clear by a law that dates back nearly one and a half centuries: the Wire Fraud Act of 1872. Because GCM used the Internet to transfer the funds, it became a matter for investigation by the FBI.

For several years, the investigation essentially simmered on the back burner as the FBI waited to see whether the matter could be settled civilly rather than criminally. Had GCM successfully negotiated a monetary settlement with Angela Ford and their erstwhile *Guard* clients without going to trial, the criminal charges might have been obviated. Since no such mediation took place, on March 8, 2006, Judge Wehr issued a partial summary judgment against GCM in the amount of $42 million in *Abbott*.

Just one week later, federal prosecutors, under the supervision of assistant US attorney Linda Voorhees, impaneled a federal grand jury, seeking criminal indictments against GCM for violating the Wire Fraud Act. Every Thursday, the grand jury gathered at the federal courthouse in Covington for Voorhees's presentation of the government's evidence. Indictment requires the agreement of at least twelve of the twenty-three grand jury members. Despite Voorhees's best efforts, weeks went by without attaining the twelve votes needed.

Given Voorhees's seeming inability to obtain an indictment, the FBI stepped up its efforts by interviewing all the legal assistants and other office staff who worked for GCM. On June 8, 2006, fifteen weeks to the day that the grand jury was first impaneled, FBI agents met with the person who would prove to be their dream informant: Rebecca Phipps—a woman with a trove of information and a bone to pick.

Rebecca Phipps had started working in the Versailles, Kentucky, law office of Melbourne Mills in 1996. Previously, she had been a claims adjuster for Allstate Insurance, in which capacity she had met Bill Gallion, thus beginning their sometimes contentious relationship. Although Phipps had no formal education as a legal assistant, her work ethic and uncanny organizational skills soon made her Mills's most trusted associate.

In 1997 Mills began advertising for fen-phen plaintiffs on television, on the radio, and in print. Within months, Phipps and the staff had fielded more than 6,000 phone calls from former diet drug users seeking to claim damages. Phipps mailed follow-up letters to each one, along with contingency agreements bearing Phipps's signature. More than 2,500 signed agreements were returned.

It was at this juncture that Gallion paid a visit to Mills's office with a proposition: they should join forces in pursuit of a lawsuit against AHP, with Mills handling client management and Gallion handling the litigation. Mills, with coaching from Phipps, eventually came to an agreement with Gallion.[19]

Of the 2,500 potential clients, the majority either lost interest or sought compensation through the national settlement. The 311 who remained became the core client group, accounting for more than 70 percent of the *Guard* plaintiffs. Foremost among Phipps's involvement with the *Guard* settlement was her essential role in negotiating with hundreds of the claimants. She was instructed to start the settlement offers at $15,000, less Mills's 30 percent contingency fee. To GCM's surprise, so many of the claimants grabbed at this modest amount that they raised the minimum to $25,000. Nevertheless, at the end of this first round of distributions, only $45 million had been paid out of the $200 million settlement. As far as Mills was concerned, Phipps was effective and loyal, but others in the office found her to be meddlesome. Sandy Rios testified that Phipps was unpleasant to the other workers, who suspected that she snooped in their desks.[20]

Phipps's eventual disillusionment likely stemmed from three incidents. The first occurred on a Saturday morning when Mills called Phipps at home and asked her to come to the office. She found him slumped on the floor with his back against the wall. Mills had just learned that *Guard* had been settled for $200 million, not the $150 million Gallion had told him. To add injury to insult, he had learned this shocking news from his law partner David Stuart, who was suing Mills for not honoring their fee-sharing agreement. Mills was shocked that Stuart had discovered the actual amount of the settlement long before he did, and Phipps agreed that her boss had been betrayed by Gallion.[21] (This stunning news was the prelude to the birthday party confrontation between Gallion and Mills, described in chapter 9.)

Subsequently, Gallion instructed Phipps to destroy the *Guard* documents, which added to her suspicion that something untoward was brewing. In the downtown Lexington office space shared by GCM, Phipps was maintaining the thousands of pages of correspondence and other documents related to *Guard,* including those belonging to Gallion. As discussed later, thanks to Phipps, Mills's documents would find their way to a different location.

The third and most galling incident occurred after Phipps, who recorded the minutes of FHL board meetings, asked for a seat on the board. She was most familiar with the wishes of the *Guard* claimants, and more than anyone else, she had been responsible for obtaining the funds that now constituted the assets of FHL. As already described, Bamberger rebuffed Phipps's request in a condescending letter and informed her that she was no longer welcome at FHL board meetings.

By that time, in large part because she had been asked to destroy Gallion's files, Phipps realized that she had been pulled into a nefarious conspiracy that was likely to result in criminal charges. Her negotiations with hundreds of the claimants meant that her fingerprints were all over the scheme. She had received combined bonuses of $1.4 million from GCM, but Phipps's only loyalty was to herself. Whether Phipps contacted the FBI or agents called her is not known, but she knew she had to come clean.

The FBI's initial face-to-face questioning of Phipps occurred on June 8, 2007. The interview was conducted by Mary Trotman, an eighteen-year FBI veteran who was heading up the GCM investigation, and E. J. Walbourn, an assistant attorney for the US Department of Justice. As in all federal criminal cases, the two branches work in tandem: the FBI gathers criminal evidence, and the Department of Justice uses that evidence at trial.

During the meeting, Phipps produced a thick stack of notes as well as a large scroll of paper fastened with a rubber band. When Phipps unfurled the paper, Trotman's and Walbourn's jaws dropped. The sheet contained a detailed chronology of everyone and everything involved in the *Guard* settlement from its initiation in Mills's office in 1997 to the current date. Phipps had created the document to help her get her own thoughts in order, but it was precisely the break the FBI needed. The timeline included when and how she had been instructed to make lowball offers and destroy documents. So clear and convincing was this evidence that the grand jury delivered an indictment six days later.

Phipps's cooperation with the FBI and the government prosecutors did not end there. Knowing that she could be deemed an accessory to the crime, she retained the services of Burl McCoy, a Lexington criminal attorney (the same one who had advised Gallion and Cunningham to hire a criminal attorney, only to be laughed at). McCoy obtained immunity for Phipps in exchange for her testimony at trial. This is known as a Kastigar agreement, which precludes a witness from asserting Fifth Amendment privileges when providing testimony.

Phipps's cooperation extended far beyond court testimony. She took notes during the previously described meeting among Chesley, GCM, and legal counsels Wallingford and Johnson (where they agreed that Johnson would act as sole legal representative). Obviously, none of them suspected that Phipps was an FBI informant. As requested, Phipps turned her notes over to the FBI.

On another occasion, Mills asked Phipps to represent him during a telephone board meeting of FHL. Prior to the meeting, Trotman fitted Phipps with a wire. Once the meeting went into executive session, Phipps, as a non–board member, was not entitled to participate. However, unknown to the others, she remained on the line and secretly recorded their conversation. Clearly believing that Phipps had exited the conference call, Gallion and Cunningham voiced their concern that Mills would inform the FBI that he had been deceived about the size of the settlement.

Much later, when Mills's defense attorney James Shuffett learned that Phipps had provided information about meetings where defense tactics were discussed, he immediately cried foul, asserting that the FBI and the federal prosecutors had intentionally accessed privileged client-attorney information, which is protected by the Sixth Amendment. The government successfully countered that it had used a "taint team" of federal attorneys who were not involved in the prosecution of GCM to scrub any information from the tapes that could be considered privileged. The defense team likened this explanation to hiring a fox to count the chickens. McCoy, who had kept Phipps out of harm's way through a grant of immunity, assured reporters that Phipps was cooperating with the government and "hasn't been charged."[22]

Phipps had secured a safe harbor, but GCM had not.

13

The Crucible

IGNORING THE IMPENDING PERIL, GCM continued to enjoy their wealth, rather than flee. Gallion and Cunningham counted their winnings from the racetrack; Curlin had just come in second at the Belmont, losing by a nose to the filly Rags to Riches. Mills moved into Barrister's Hall, a downtown Lexington office building owned by Gallion and Cunningham. From there, Mills continued to handle product liability cases, most prominently a lawsuit involving Baycol, a drug to treat high cholesterol manufactured by Bayer.

GCM first became aware of the FBI investigation in May 2007, just a few weeks prior to their indictments. According to Mills, he and Phipps had secretly stored documents related to *Guard* in a cave at Herrington Lake, a recreational area about forty-five minutes from Lexington. Whether Mills's intention was to keep sensitive information out of the hands of Angela Ford and the KBA or simply to protect the documents from destruction is an open question. While Mills was vacationing in Europe, he learned that the FBI had raided his office as well as the subterranean hideaway, seizing 448 boxes of documents all told. Clearly, Phipps had led the FBI there, and the jig was up.[1] On June 14, 2007, GCM were informed that a grand jury that had been meeting since March had recommended that all three be indicted on federal wire fraud charges.

A defense team was recruited, consisting of Stephen Dobson of Tallahassee, Florida, and David Davidson of Covington for Cunningham; Hale Almond of Macon, Georgia, and Robert Lotz of Covington for Gallion; and

James Shuffett of Lexington for Mills. This crew of relative strangers would soon find themselves in a multiple-week struggle with not only the KBA, the FBI, the US Department of Justice, and the media but also the legal establishment of Kentucky.

On August 10 GCM were stunned with more bad news when US District Court judge William Bertelsman denied bail and sent all three to the Boone County jail. Ironically, this surprise decision came about because of the federal Speedy Trial Act, which requires the prosecution to schedule a trial within 120 days of an indictment. The act is intended to keep the accused from languishing in jail for months on end before going to trial. For GCM, the act had precisely the opposite effect.

The FBI and federal prosecutors had had five years to prepare their evidence. By contrast, the GCM defense team was expected to copy and review the more than 200,000 documents gathered by the prosecution, as well as devise an effective strategy for the defense, within the 120-day window. GCM and their team of lawyers knew this was not possible, so they filed a motion for an extension. Prosecutor Voorhees agreed that the defense should be granted a delay and stated, "We don't want the case to be overturned on appeal." Judge Bertelsman worried about how a delay would look to the public: "In my opinion, not only are these three men on trial, the whole legal profession is on trial." Bertelsman agreed to grant the motion for an extension, but only on the exceedingly harsh condition that the three lawyers remain behind bars. The judge gave the defendants fifteen minutes to discuss his terms. Given the Hobson's choice of going to trial unprepared or living in decidedly unpleasant surroundings until they were fully ready to proceed, GCM reluctantly chose the latter.[2]

The Boone County jail is a grim affair, a sprawling one-story structure of rust-colored brick with narrow plate-glass windows just below the roofline. The facility sits on an expanse of closely clipped grass, barren of trees or bushes. On the off chance an inmate managed to slip away, there would be no place to hide. The isolated jail is located just beyond the outskirts of the tiny town of Burlington, far from any bus stop. This means that families without access to a car are unable to visit their inmate relatives, and the public parking lot is as empty as the landscape, even during Saturday visiting hours.

Although some of the occupants are drunk drivers and deadbeat dads behind on child support, many others are homeless alcoholics, meth addicts, mentally ill, street thugs, and prostitutes. It was a most unusual place for three multimillionaires whose triumphs and foibles had occupied the pages of the *Northern Kentucky Tribune* and the *Cincinnati Enquirer* for the past six months. Every day they could bemoan the terrible irony that, despite their great wealth, their purchases of such luxuries as chips and soda at the jail commissary were financed by contributions from family and friends and limited to only $250 per month.

The dreariness of their stay in the Boone County jail was punctuated with one bright spot for Gallion and Cunningham when Curlin won the Dubai Cup, the richest horse race in the world! The duo shared a single cell phone, listening while a waitress they knew from better days called in the race results.

With the indictments of GCM, the FBI augmented the resources devoted to the investigation, and the methods used to ferret out information favorable to the prosecution became even more intensive. Sandy Rios recalled being questioned by FBI agent Mary Trotman over the phone when an unfamiliar male voice unexpectedly broke into the conversation. According to Rios, "The man on the phone interjected and said, 'Are you sure?' Or something to that effect. Made me feel like I wasn't answering the way he wanted me to answer." Rios also testified that the man "twisted her words."[3]

Meanwhile, the KBA Board of Governors met to consider the disbarments of Gallion and Cunningham. KBA attorney Linda Gosnell used the occasion to disparage the pair, describing their behavior as unbridled greed. Gosnell reviewed twenty-two counts of misconduct, ranging from deceiving clients about settlement amounts to failing to adequately supervise David Helmers. Before the KBA Board of Governors came to a decision, Gallion and Cunningham voluntarily relinquished their licenses to practice law. (On October 23, 2008, the Kentucky Supreme Court made their voluntary actions permanent, disbarring both for life.) On a brighter note for GCM, after ten months behind bars, the defense team's preparations were complete, and the trial opened on May 12, 2008.

The Crucible

The clear, brisk morning began with a fifteen-mile van ride from the jail to the federal courthouse in Covington. Just before reaching downtown Covington, the prisoners were afforded a magnificent view of the gleaming steel and glass skyscrapers of Cincinnati, directly across the Ohio River. Throughout GCM's long confinement, Chesley had been free to stroll the Cincinnati streets at will and live in luxury. Chesley's vaunted reputation and overreach had helped land them in their awful predicament, and soon the figurative knives Chesley had used to butter them up would be stuck in their backs.

The van turned onto Fifth Street and, just before reaching the courthouse, passed two blocks of nineteenth-century Italianate houses. In cheerful shades of cyan and vermilion, these pleasant-looking structures held law offices and retail boutiques. In marked contrast, the imposing federal courthouse scowled down from the opposite side of the street. Still wearing handcuffs and shackles, GCM shuffled inside, where they were allowed to shuck their olive uniforms, cinched at the waist with elastic bands (belts were forbidden, lest someone try to hang himself), and change into business suits, neckties, and street shoes.

In the courtroom, lined with heavy cornices and wainscoting, the many spectators had already taken their seats. A faint, pleasant scent of wood oil from the polished walnut paneling hung in the air. Presiding over the trial was Judge William O. Bertelsman, a graduate of Chesley's alma mater, the University of Cincinnati School of Law. Bertelsman had served as a captain in the US Army from 1963 to 1964. Then, after several years in private practice, President Carter had appointed him to serve on the federal bench for eastern Kentucky in 1979. Bertelsman had a reputation for running the train on time, and he had little patience for attorneys who tried to plow the same ground more than once. Considering the months of adverse publicity, the defense team was facing a gale-force headwind.

The first day was taken up with the process of voir dire (a French term meaning "to speak the truth"). From the fifty-person jury pool, the prosecution and defense lawyers winnowed out those deemed to be prejudicial to either side, followed by the random selection of twelve jurors and two alternates.

The second day began with the defense protesting Angela Ford's presence in the courtroom. Having been appointed a "victims' advocate," Ford would be in attendance for the entire trial and would be privy to all exhibits, giving her a distinct advantage in the still unsettled *Abbott* civil suit. Hale Almond, of Macon, Georgia, argued for the defense that Ford could not serve as both an advocate and a witness: "Under the Victims' Rights Statute, there is very great ambiguity as to what the obligations and duties and rights of the advocate are. But the one thing I think the statute makes clear is, the rights of the victims and the victims' advocate does not trump the rights of the defendants to a fair trial. And that's what we're speaking of here when we have, in essence, a person that will be a witness remain in the courtroom and be allowed to hear testimony as it goes on."[4] To the consternation of the prosecution team, led by federal prosecutor Linda Voorhees (with assistance from E. J. Walbourn and Wade Napier), the defense prevailed.

Following this skirmish, Bertelsman called in the jury. The remainder of the day was devoted to opening remarks. In her address to the jury, Voorhees accused all three lawyers of exhibiting unbridled greed and engaging in an illegal conspiracy. Standing before them with an enigmatic smile that conveyed both shock and disdain, Voorhees informed the jury that Gallion, Cunningham, and Mills were dangerous men who had stolen $45 million—the biggest crime she had ever prosecuted. By doing so, GCM had betrayed their own clients, whose interests they were legally and ethically bound to honor. Voorhees described how the defendants had contorted the language in the settlement agreement and fooled Bamberger into awarding 49 percent of the settlement as attorneys' fees, eventually leading to the creation of the phony Fund for Healthy Living and the demise of Bamberger's judicial career. Voorhees emphasized how GCM had willfully withheld the total value of the settlement from their clients, as well as other essential information, as a means of hiding their criminality.

Leading the defense for Gallion, and taking a prominent role throughout the trial, was Hale Almond of Macon, Georgia. Almond had graduated from the Citadel and afterward served on active duty in Vietnam. He was a graduate of the Law School of Mercer University in Macon. As Almond rose from the table to face the jury, he attempted to lighten the mood after Voorhees's vitriol. A grinning Almond acknowledged that his seersucker suit lent him an uncanny resemblance to the TV lawyer Matlock (played by Andy Griffith). In a straightforward argument delivered with a candied southern cadence, Almond informed the jury that retention of the $45 million was simply the consequence of a misreading of the settlement agreement's side letter. Overwhelmed by the intensity of the mediation and the intricacies of the multipage settlement document, his client, William Gallion, had understandably failed to notice that an inadvertently misplaced word had radically changed the meaning of the side letter. For added effect, Almond spelled out the offending word: "n-o-r." Absent this single syllable, GCM would have been justified in keeping the $45 million Voorhees had just described as stolen. As far as the establishment of FHL was concerned, Almond deftly explained that no one had twisted Bamberger's arm when he agreed to allow its creation. Why should they second-guess Bamberger, who had been honored by the KBA as Outstanding Judge of the Year not so long ago?

Almond also preemptively refuted several other allegations he assumed Voorhees would make. The length of his opening remarks irritated Judge Bertelsman, who cut Almond short, telling him that such arguments were more appropriate as summary statements at the end of the trial. Bertelsman was insistent that the trial conclude within twenty-seven days, with each side limited to sixty-seven and a half hours of testimony. These hours were meticulously tracked down to the minute, with time starting to run as soon as an attorney began to speak.

Stephen Dobson, representing Cunningham, was decidedly briefer. He explained to the jury that if there was a conspiracy, Cunningham had not been involved, as witnessed by the fact that he had initially been excluded from the settlement mediation. During the cy pres discussions and the establishment of FHL, Cunningham had merely been an onlooker.

James Shuffett for Mills was even more to the point, informing the jury that throughout many of these supposedly nefarious activities, Mills was not present. He did not attend, nor was he invited to, the settlement mediation or the various sessions with Bamberger when attorneys' fees were determined and FHL was created.

On day three, the judge was informed that a variety of documents in

Chesley's possession had finally been delivered, as requested by the defense. Though the documents had arrived, Chesley himself had not. The defense had hoped to use Chesley as an expert witness to share his knowledge of class-action law. When planning their defense strategy, GCM had assumed that Chesley would support their version of the facts, as he had in his *Abbott* deposition. Although Chesley had been happy to stand with GCM to fend off Ford in the *Abbott* suit, this trial was not about money. Now people were fighting to stay out of jail, and Chesley was worried that he might soon be a defendant himself. Chesley had the power to make or break either side; this gave him enormous leverage, which he applied with all his might.

Just prior to the commencement of the trial, GCM's defense team was dealt a major setback when it became aware that Chesley would not voluntarily testify as an expert witness. Chesley's attorney, Scott Cox, told a *Courier-Journal* reporter that his client had chosen not to appear because "his role [in *Guard*] was so limited." The article hinted that even if subpoenaed, Chesley would refuse to testify. Angela Ford made the obvious observation that Chesley wanted to "distance himself" from GCM.[5] This left the defense with no other option than to subpoena Chesley as a factual witness, but it was highly likely that he intended to assert his Fifth Amendment privilege and refuse to testify.

Once Chesley was on the witness stand, Almond was prepared to turn the tables and portray him as the sole mastermind behind the events that transpired after the *Guard* settlement. Almond was ready to pepper Chesley with questions and force him to assert his Fifth Amendment rights ad nauseam before the jury. However, after obtaining a subpoena to compel Chesley to at least take the stand, the defense was shocked to learn that Chesley's name was not on the list of unindicted coconspirators. Of all the other people involved, one would have expected Chesley to be at the top of that list. He also continued to make one excuse after another to delay his court appearance. The defense team smelled another rat.

With that backdrop, the issue of not notifying the *Guard* claimants of the total settlement amount was addressed. Voorhees had called David Helmers to the stand, and during his cross-examination of Helmers, Almond attempted to introduce a letter from Judge Bechtle, who had presided over the national settlement. Knowing full well what the letter contained, Voorhees tried to block its introduction into evidence, claiming that it was hearsay. After wrangling over related precedents, Bertelsman overruled her. The letter, addressed to Chesley, requested that the amount of the *Guard* settlement not be shared, as it would interfere with the ongoing deliberations in Philadelphia, where Chesley was the most prominent member of the Plaintiffs Management Committee for the national settlement. In fact, similar pleas not to reveal settlement amounts had already been honored in New Jersey, New York, Pennsylvania, Washington, Illinois, and Texas. To comply with the judge's request, the letter of notice of the *Guard* settlement had been left in draft form on Helmers's computer, seriously undercutting one of Voorhees's major contentions. But the familiarity with which Bechtle addressed Chesley (calling him Stan), along with the fact that the letter was not sent to Bamberger, indicates a cozy relationship between them. Even more distressing, the request to delay notifying GCM's clients of this critical information was contrary to the rules of ethical procedure.

Judge Bertelsman made the prosecution's task an even steeper climb when he informed the jury that ethical violations, even if they occurred, should not be determinants of guilt or innocence. This directive referred to the jury's knowledge that GCM's licenses to practice law had been suspended and ultimately revoked for various violations of the KBA's Rules of Professional Conduct.

Another strong point that Almond hammered home was that the settlement for the 431 *Guard* plaintiffs had been granted by Bamberger "with prejudice," meaning that it was absolutely final. Crucially, his order also referred to any unknown claimants, for whom the settlement was "without prejudice," meaning that such individuals did have access to further legal recourse. The importance of Bamberger's reference to "unknown claimants" was his tacit acknowledgment of the existence of others who might seek compensation apart from *Guard*. (However, because the statute of limitations had expired by then, Bamberger's recognition of the right to sue by any other potential plaintiffs meant nothing.)

As reported by the Associated Press, the trial took a rather bizarre twist when jurors informed Judge Bertelsman that people were following them and attempting to eavesdrop on their conversations during breaks and lunch periods. Bertelsman warned everyone in the courtroom, "If someone is doing this, they will find themselves in real trouble."[6] The spying ceased.

Another complication occurred when Almond suffered an unspecified illness and missed two weeks of the proceedings. Had he not recovered sufficiently to return to the courtroom, a mistrial would have been a distinct possibility. The trial also had to be adjourned early on May 28 when Mills was taken to the hospital with complaints of dizziness, possibly the result of fatigue, as the incessant noise in the jail made sleeping difficult. Mills claimed that he slept through much of the trial.

The most dramatic portion of Rebecca Phipps's testimony was her description of how Gallion had asked her to destroy evidence: "On January 31st of the year 2002, I was working a little bit late at the office, not very. And I looked up, and Bill Gallion was moving some furniture into another office, a little office space there in the Class Action Associates. And I went across to say hello to him, and he came out of his office, and he met me halfway. And we had some chit-chat. And then he told me that we needed to get rid of the documents." Phipps understood this to mean the *Guard* files, but she did not destroy the files as instructed. She continued: "I went back to my office. Then I had a wooden file cabinet with a key, and I'd already put a lot of the Fen-phen documents in that file cabinet, but I scooped up some others that I thought were significant, and I put them in the file cabinet also. I locked the file cabinet and hid the key under my Post-it note holder there in my office."[7] Missing from her testimony was any mention of the trove of documents that, according to Mills, Phipps had helped secrete in a cave at Herrington Lake.

The remainder of the trial was marked by the testimony of dozens of witnesses, both minor and major. Those whose testimony was most anticipated were Bamberger, Gallion, and Chesley. However, an unscheduled witness would prove to be the most influential in the trial's outcome.

On the stand, Bamberger rationalized his actions, stating that he had done "nothing to dishonor the bench" and that, with regard to *Guard*, "I believe and continue to believe . . . there was a fair distribution of the settlement proceeds," referring to the diversion of $20 million to establish FHL. "The claimants had already been compensated more than their injuries justified . . . to give them more would have been unjust." Bamberger also insisted that he had no idea GCM had already taken their one-third contingency fees prior to his award of 49 percent for attorneys' fees. Had he been aware of the double-dipping scheme, "it would have changed life dramatically for everybody." Bamberger lamented spending the night at Gallion's home on the evening he received his Outstanding Judge of the Year award by the KBA, noting that the honor "seems kind of strange now in light of what has happened to me."[8]

Bamberger also made an unconvincing attempt to justify his improperly close relationship with Modlin, claiming that it was not unusual for judges to be on friendly terms with attorneys and expert witnesses. While that much was true, being co-owners of a Florida investment property and accepting what appeared to be a payoff in the form of a seat on the FHL board went well beyond a friendly acquaintance. Although Judge Bertelsman had instructed the jury not to consider ethical violations when determining criminality, GCM's association with such a fallen character did nothing to improve their image with the jury.

On June 11, 2008, William Gallion appeared in the courtroom dressed in a natty gray suit and yellow tie. Mills had also been scheduled to testify, but he later withdrew, making Gallion the sole defendant who spoke at the trial. It was clear from the beginning that Gallion had taken full advantage of the knowledge obtained from his former wife's medical school textbooks. Early in his testimony, he clearly and with considerable detail explained the mechanics of heart valve damage for the apparent purpose of demonstrating his competency to the jury and to dispel the notion that he was a mere ambulance chaser. During his three days on the stand, Gallion also made a point of dismissing the testimony of Phipps and strongly denied asking her to destroy documents. Gallion tried to portray her as unstable and went on to assert, "I hate to criticize anyone, but Rebecca Phipps believed she was a lawyer. She always wanted to step over the line and act like she had the knowledge and authority to make decisions."[9]

Regarding the settlement itself, Gallion stuck to the rationale that it was unique because it was a settlement not between AHP and the 431 claimants but between AHP and GCM. According to Gallion, GCM took $200 million to indemnify AHP from any and all future claims in Kentucky within the twelve-month statute of limitations. Gallion insisted that every claimant had been more than fairly compensated, relative to the awards in the national settlement, and all 431 had signed agreements to this effect. Gallion explained, "This is an indemnification like an insurance policy, and it's as if the settling attorneys took a premium, like Lloyds of London, they took a premium, to cover all of these contingencies. When the contingencies didn't happen, the hurricane didn't strike, the insurance company keeps the premium."[10]

Under Gallion's contract theory, any funds remaining after the expiration of the statute of limitations, including the $7.5 million reserve for legal expenses, were GCM's to keep. Since Judge Weinstein had initially valued a fair settlement for the 431 at between $30 million and $50 million, Gallion made the startling assertion that GCM properly could have retained as much as $170 million of the settlement. As reported in the *Courier-Journal,* Gallion pointed out that "clients who may have gotten nothing in the national case, collected as much as $1.4 million."[11] He also presented another excuse by claiming that he had never read the side letter and that the signature on the settlement agreement was Helmers's, not his. Since Chesley's signature was also absent, it was apparent that neither wanted to leave his fingerprints on a document he might later have reason to disavow.

Almond used Gallion's testimony to bolster an important pillar for the defense: every one of the 431 claimants had received a generous settlement. Based on prior testimony from Rios, Overstreet, and Helmers, it was clear that the overwhelming majority of the claimants were very happy with their awards at the time. Compared with the Kentuckians who had joined the national settlement, the *Guard* claimants had every reason to be content.

Gallion went on to make the explosive assertion that Angela Ford, who was present in the courtroom throughout the trial, had breached ethical boundaries by recruiting the *Abbott* plaintiffs through improper means and then putting the idea in their heads that they had been wronged. According to Gallion, Ford had contacted the 431 *Guard* claimants in alphabetical order, and the fact that more than 400 of them joined *Abbott* was an indication that she had used overt and irregular means to recruit her clients. While attorneys are free to advertise their services to the general public, contacting potential plaintiffs personally is considered to be solicitation, which is contrary to ABA standards of conduct.

Most happily for the defense, during Gallion's testimony, Judge Bertelsman decided he had heard quite enough about individual settlements versus class action and informed the jury that *Guard* had been settled as a class action and "that issue is behind us."[12] Arguably, the issue of whether *Guard* had been settled as a class action was the most crucial aspect of the trial and should have been left for the jury to decide. But the fact that Bertelsman made any ruling favorable to the defendants was noteworthy.

After being thrown in the Boone County jail, Cunningham had filed a lawsuit charging that Bertelsman was "wholly incapable of serving as a judge." In a fifty-three-page affidavit laden with invectives, Cunningham claimed that the judge was attempting to use bail as a means of improperly wringing restitution from GCM. The document noted that Bertelsman had repeated twenty-two times that "the amount of restitution is going to have to be secured before anyone [GCM] is going to be released."[13] Although Cunningham's charges obviously did not result in the judge's removal, they may have paradoxically compelled Bertelsman to take greater pains to maintain at least the appearance of impartiality. In contrast, Mills's impression was that Bertelsman had "done everything we asked him to do" and had largely ruled in favor of the defense throughout the trial.[14]

Meanwhile, Chesley's testimony was still to come. Government prosecutors were so eager to put GCM away that in late May 2008, just prior to his scheduled date to testify per subpoena, Chesley was granted full immunity as a state's witness. This stunning news was potentially cataclysmic for the defense. To use one of Lyndon Johnson's earthy metaphors, their erstwhile partner who had once been "in their tent pissing out, was now outside pissing in."

Chesley's testimony began on the twenty-fourth day of the trial and continued for two and a half days. Gone was the man who "held court" in the presence of others. The bluff and bluster he had so successfully used in past decades to cow the elite legal representatives of major corporations into ruinous settlements were nowhere to seen in Bertelsman's courtroom.

Instead, he adopted the persona of a humble, courtly gentleman on the verge of dotage. Throughout his testimony, Chesley fumbled through documents and often had difficulty finding his place. His frequently responded, "I don't know what you're reading from" or "Help me by showing me what you're reading from." Even in his humility, Chesley was conspicuous.

Whenever he disagreed with a statement made by one of the examining attorneys, he was overly solicitous rather than condescending. Chesley's many statements of contrition included, "I'm sorry for being so long, but I'm just trying to explain," and "I'm sorry. I don't mean to be rude and I want to be polite." This was in stark contrast to his superciliousness toward Ford during his *Abbott* deposition, when he berated her for screaming at him, or his abrasiveness toward AHP attorney Helen Madonick, who had been brought to tears during the *Guard* mediation.

Thanks to Chesley's newfound mental fog and prosecutorial immunity, he claimed no memory of virtually everything of importance that happened subsequent to hammering out the *Guard* settlement with Vardaman. This included the crucial February 6, 2002, meeting with Judge Bamberger, at which attorneys' fees of 49 percent were awarded. By contrast, Bamberger's memory had been crystal clear when he testified earlier about Chesley's lead role in the events of that day. And in her opening statement, Voorhees had told the jury that "Gallion, Cunningham, and Chesley met Judge Bamberger after hours on February 6, 2002." Since neither Gallion, Cunningham, nor Bamberger would have volunteered the details of this bizarre and undocumented meeting, the source had to be Chesley. This he denied. Chesley's memory lapses flew in the face of the testimony of numerous persons who had been present at these crucial meetings and who clearly recalled the key role Chesley played in each.

Using his newly minted amnesia, Chesley also denied having much knowledge about the side letter that was part of the overall agreement. This stood in direct contrast to his own statements to FBI agent Mary Trotman. According to her notes of the interview, Chesley believed the settlement amount would be increased if GCM agreed to take on the extra risk outlined in the side letter.

Chesley testified that the fees taken by GCM were "too much" and that, after the first round of "front-ended, fluid distributions," any residual settlement funds should have been placed in an interest-bearing account for later distribution to the claimants.[15] Needless to say, this was not what Chesley had asserted during the clandestine gathering in the Boone County courthouse on February 6, 2002, when he planted the notions of *Grinnell* and cy pres in Bamberger's head.

When Almond asked Chesley whether he believed GCM's contingency contracts with their *Guard* clients were valid, Chesley answered: "There would be no reason that I would have any interest in their contingency fee agreements. But more importantly, since it was a class action, my experience in class actions, going all the way back 30 years ago to Beverly Hills, the contingency fee contracts have no validity." This was just what Almond wanted to hear, as it lent credence to the defense's argument that the fees received by GCM were not improper or too high. Chesley must have realized he had inadvertently thrown GCM a life preserver, so in practically the same breath, he pivoted 180 degrees and stated, "You're putting words in my mouth. I didn't express it has no validity. I said it is up to the determination of the court" whether it has validity. All three lawyers on trial stared at Chesley with grim faces as he testified against them.[16]

During his cross-examination of Chesley, Almond was relentless. He asked Chesley how many hours he had devoted to his work on *Guard* and whether his $20 million fee was justifiable. A briefly defiant Chesley declared, "I saw Tiger Woods yesterday. Tiger Woods did not get paid on an hourly basis." Chesley's self-comparison to the golf superstar likely did not endear himself to the jury. When asked how his $20 million fee had been calculated, Chesley replied that he "did not do math."[17] Later, in *KBA v. Chesley*, the Kentucky Supreme Court would drily conclude that $20 million did indeed exceed the "fee customarily charged in the locality for similar services."[18]

Almond also questioned Chesley about his immunity deal: did the attorneys who negotiated the deal inform the prosecutors that Chesley was intending to invoke his Fifth Amendment privileges? Almond was likely probing whether Chesley's legal team had coerced the immunity deal from the prosecution. Chesley was not about to volunteer this information, and his tedious circumlocution made it seem as if he were confused by the simple question. As Chesley spoke in circles, Almond yawned and looked at the ceiling. Exasperated by Chesley's obfuscation, Almond asked the judge to direct the witness to answer with a simple "yes" or "no" and restated the question: "Did your attorneys inform the prosecution of your intent to refuse to testify under the Fifth Amendment prior to your immunity arrangement?" When, despite Bertelsman's directive, Chesley continued to find it impossible to utter either of the requested single-syllable words, Almond had no choice but to give up and move on.[19]

Chesley did manage to emerge from his cognitive fog at one point to bemoan his abuse as a "media poster child" and mastermind of a theft perpetrated exclusively by GCM. Paradoxically, Chesley had always been willing to use the media to intimidate his adversaries throughout his career, and in fact, he was an expert at it.

Almond scored points when he noted that Chesley had managed to delay his testimony until he was granted immunity. After Chesley arranged to be excused from testifying on the scheduled date of May 13, it took more than a month to reschedule his court appearance. Curiously, after being engaged in such pressing business for so many weeks, Chesley managed to find time to take the stand a mere five days after being granted full immunity. Almond strongly implied that during this extended period of unavailability, Chesley and his legal team were busily working to strike the immunity deal. Presumably, Chesley had been granted immunity after convincing Voorhees that his testimony would ensure the convictions of GCM. Chesley's extremely broad immunity agreement stated that, "in exchange for [his] agreement to provide truthful testimony in the trial U.S. v. Gallion, the United States agree[d] that it [would] not prosecute [him] for any criminal conduct [he] may have committed or any violations of statutes of the United States or Kentucky."

When pressed by Almond, Chesley contended that he had always intended to tell the truth. Almond retorted that this claim would have been more believable had his testimony taken place without being granted immunity. Chesley once again rose to Almond's bait and snapped, "Sir, I received a letter of immunity with the government by virtue of what was worked out with my counsel so that I would be able to come in here and tell the truth, which I've done up to today and continue to and will continue until we finish this discussion."[20]

At the conclusion of day twenty-five of the trial, which Chesley spent on the witness stand, court adjourned a few minutes early so that Judge Bertelsman could attend a meeting in Lexington. While the jury was preparing to leave the courtroom, Almond declared, within the earshot of the prosecutors and the jury, that Chesley had lied on behalf of the government in exchange for immunity. Angry words were exchanged, and it was later reported to Bertelsman that the two sides had nearly come to blows.

Given Chesley's immunity deal and his appearance as a witness for the prosecution, he clearly could not testify as an expert witness for the defense. Under this highly unusual circumstance, Bertelsman granted the defense attorneys' request to call another expert witness, even though they had not provided a summary of the witness's intended testimony, as required under the federal rules of criminal procedure.

The expert witness Almond selected was Richard L. Robbins, a 1980 graduate of Harvard Law School. His receding hair line, mustache, and wire-rim glasses lent him an aura of bookish competence. While at Harvard, Robbins had been a member of the prestigious Harvard Law Review, a student-run organization that publishes works of legal analysis. Only the upper 8 percent of each class is invited to join the Review. Robbins was on a first-name basis with John Roberts, the Review's editor at that time, who would go on to become the chief justice of the US Supreme Court.

Robbins's career boasted a string of successes and honors. He joined the illustrious Atlanta-based firm of Sutherland, Asbill, and Brennan in 1981 and become one of its 500-plus partners after only five years. *Atlanta* magazine named Robbins the city's "Super Lawyer" for four consecutive years. In Georgia's first class action, Robbins successfully defended Merrill Lynch in a $100 million lawsuit that spanned three years. By the time of his involvement in GCM's trial, Robbins had been lead counsel or cocounsel for thousands of cases, many of them class actions. When a panicked Almond called Robbins, asking him to recommend a last-minute expert witness, Robbins did one better and offered himself at $500 per hour, below his customary rate. Robbins would prove to be worth every penny.

Professor Edward Brewer, on the faculty of Chase Law School in Covington, had already testified in support of the prosecution's contention that

GCM had an obligation to notify all the *Guard* claimants of the size of the settlement. In stark contrast, Robbins dismissed Brewer as "reckless and wrong" and assured the jury that notifying the claimants was the responsibility of the judge, not the attorneys. Robbins further stated that it would have been foolish for GCM to tell the claimants about the $200 million, which might have set off a stampede of greed. Brewer had foolishly testified that class-action law was so simple that "a third grader could understand it," for which Robbins mercilessly ridiculed him.

With regard to Vardaman's earlier testimony that *Guard* had been settled individually and not as a class, Robbins declared, "Vardaman knows better than that." Robbins also testified that *Guard* had been decertified as a class, and "you don't decertify something that does not exist." In other words, *Guard* had been a class action from beginning to end.

Robbins also addressed one of the thornier problems with the settlement agreement: the fact that the side letter "had been poorly written." Robbins had to shake his head in disbelief that a prestigious law firm like Williams and Connolly had prepared such an ambiguous document for a settlement of such magnitude. Even if Vardaman was not complicit in a scheme to help Chesley grab a $20.6 million payday, at the very least, Vardaman had opened the door for subterfuge with the opaque language of the *Guard* settlement agreement. Gallion, an experienced attorney, described the agreement as "having been written in Chinese."

Robbins also testified, "There was nothing sinister about the creation of FHL, as GCM could have been justified in keeping the $20 million had they wanted to." In his opinion, it would not have been improper for a judge to award attorneys' fees for the balance of the settlement after Judge Weinstein's assessment of the value of the 431 claims had been satisfied.[21]

Because Robbins's last-minute testimony had not been preceded by a written summary, the prosecution was left flat-footed. On cross-examination, Robbins stood his ground, fending off questions about notice to claimants and the size of settlement awards. Somewhat puzzling, many of the prosecution's questions pertained to the performance of Bamberger. Of particular significance, no attempt was made to sully Robbins's professional credentials as an expert witness.

Robbins later provided a written affidavit that stated, "While [the defendants' actions] were clearly innovative . . . they are not indicative of any intent to defraud or other wrongful motive." It went on to state, "it would be difficult to establish that there had been any intent to violate class action law." Robbins also noted that GCM had justifiably "relied heavily on the advice of Chesley and the court orders of Bamberger" in the distribution of the settlement funds. With regard to FHL and cy pres, Robbins wrote that "there was nothing improper." And most critically, the dispute over client fees "was a civil matter rather than a criminal matter." This document could not have been more helpful for GCM's defense if Gallion had composed it himself.

At the end of twenty-six days of testimony and the submission of more than 5,000 pages of documents, both the prosecution and the defense rested. However, before making their closing statements, the defense attorneys asked Judge Bertelsman to issue a summary judgment of not guilty, based on an issue of law that had not been raised during the trial. They contended that because of the government's foot-dragging, the five-year statute of limitations had expired, exempting GCM from prosecution. The indictments of GCM had been issued on June 14, 2007, more than five years after any of the three had received any direct payments from the *Guard* settlement, but less than five years since any of them had received a monthly fee from FHL. Almond argued that because the creation of FHL had been approved by a judge (Bamberger), any actions related to FHL should not be considered part of an alleged conspiracy to commit wire fraud.

This argument caught Judge Bertelsman by surprise, and at first, it seemed that Almond had introduced a deus ex machina. Voorhees, however, foiled the defense by retrieving a document that referenced the transfer of a portion of the $7.5 million contingency fund in September 2002. This evidence of the ongoing conspiracy meant that the indictments fell within the statute of limitations by a mere three months.

In Almond's closing argument, he declared that GCM had obtained a remarkable outcome for the *Guard* plaintiffs and had proved themselves to be extremely competent and good attorneys. Almond pointed the finger directly at Chesley, declaring that GCM had merely followed his lead. Then, to save himself, Chesley had lied about his former colleagues.

Many considered the closing remarks by Cunningham's lead attorney, Stephen Dobson, a tour de force. He carefully detailed the highly unusual nature of the *Guard* settlement and pointed out that, with the exception of Chesley, everyone involved was plowing new ground. He concluded by telling the jury, "Mr. Chesley, he's keeping his $20 million and he is walking away with immunity."[22]

Mills's attorney, James Shuffett, closed by arguing that the second distribution to the claimants had been a direct consequence of Mills's indignation at his birthday party and that Mills had not been present during the meeting with Bamberger later that evening. Shuffett insisted that since most of the clients were originally Mills's, he had not been overpaid. He also pointed out that Mills had been kept in the dark about the size of the settlement, and after he learned the truth, Mills had insisted that the claimants' settlements be increased, which is exactly what happened.

Although it was widely believed that Shuffett used stories related to Mills's alcoholism to support his lack of complicity in the scheme, Shuffett actually said very little during the proceedings, which was his style. In fact, Shuffett brought up Mills's drinking only twice during the trial—once with Phipps and again with Gallion—but obviously to great effect. At one point, Judge Bertelsman asked Shuffett, "Are you going to ask for an alcoholism defense instruction?" And the lawyer replied, "I think the evidence justifies that instruction."[23]

Voorhees based her closing statement on an awkward attempt to garner empathy for the 431 *Guard* claimants. She portrayed GCM as heartless villains who had deprived their clients of the monetary resources they needed to restore their broken lives. Then Voorhees lowered her voice to a murmur and said, they're "individuals, they're human beings, they deserve respect."[24] Nodding in assent were several of the *Guard-Abbott* claimants who had been bused in by Ford. Voorhees's use of this argument shows that she failed to grasp how convincingly the defense had demonstrated that the so-called victims had been more than adequately compensated. She also argued that GCM's former clients had been subjected to a campaign of intimidation, being threatened with jail time if they revealed their settlement amounts to anyone—even their own spouses. But this assertion stretched the bounds of credulity, and besides, the settlement agreement with AHP did in fact contain strong and broad prohibitions against breaching confidentiality.

Now it was time for the jury to decide. The twelve jurors—eight men and four women—filed into the deliberation room, where they would spend fifty-two hours in a concerted effort to reach a verdict. After the first day of deliberations, the jury requested a flip chart, tape, and calculator, as well as the video record of Chesley's testimony. It was assumed that the jurors wanted to compare his trial testimony to his preimmunity deposition. Time dragged on interminably, and on the fourth day, the jurors sent Judge Bertelsman a question: was it legal for GCM to take additional fees after their contractual contingency fees had already been paid? This was a shock to the prosecution, as the essence of its argument was that GCM had stolen the claimants' settlement by illegally taking two massive slices from the same loaf. A puzzled Bertelsman called a conference with the attorneys for both sides and exclaimed, "I don't know what they are thinking." Rather than answer the jurors' question directly, Bertelsman referred them back to his original written instructions. With this, the defense team took heart. The strategy of adding even more complexity and doubt to an already byzantine series of events, and portraying Chesley as the chief instigator, was having the intended effect. Conversely, the prosecutors were growing apprehensive. If the jury was unsure of the answer to this question, it represented a massive failure on their part.

On July 2, after six days of deliberation, the jury informed Judge Bertelsman that it had reached a verdict. The defendants and their legal teams, friends, and enemies, along with a dozen or more reporters, filled the hushed courtroom. All rose as Bertelsman took his seat. The jury foreman handed the judge the decision, and a rictus of disappointment fell over his face. It was only a partial verdict. Mills was found not guilty, but the jury could not reach a unanimous verdict for either Gallion or Cunningham. Apparently, the jury believed that Mills had not helped organize the conspiracy, and that he was a witless alcoholic as well.

On the afternoon of July 2, 2008, Melbourne Mills walked out of the Boone County jail and into the bright sunshine. For the first time in eleven months, he was outside the jail and not wearing shackles. As the seventy-seven-year-old Mills walked arm and arm with his future wife Darlene La, who was several decades his junior, he chortled to a band of reporters, "This is the greatest country in the world with the greatest court system." Apparently unaware that he faced imminent disbarment, Mills added, "I'm looking forward to getting back in it." For her part, La was so overcome with emotion that she had difficulty speaking to reporters. She finally said, "I knew all the time he wasn't guilty. I think he just got caught up in a bad deal."[25] Mills had been La's attorney in her lawsuit against American Home Products, but her support and affection were apparently unfazed by the fact that GCM had shortchanged her in her settlement with AHP. As Mills would later explain, La's settlement had to be low to avoid the appearance of favoritism.

After Mills's acquittal, Ford huffed to reporters that he was "not so drunk that he couldn't make it to the bank," and she grumbled that the prosecution had "more than enough evidence to convict."[26] Shuffett, however, had been correct: there was no reason for Mills to testify.

Back in the courtroom, a frustrated Judge Bertelsman hammered his gavel, sending Gallion and Cunningham back to jail and the jurors back to their deliberations. The following afternoon, with still no verdict, he asked the jury to deliberate one more day, making eight days in total. Beyond such time, any verdict would likely be driven more by exhaustion than reason.

Following Bertelsman's exhortation, the prosecution offered to accept a mistrial. Gallion and Cunningham declined the offer. In Bertelsman's memory, no defendants had ever turned down such an offer, but Almond and the others had a gut feeling that the prosecution was on the ropes. Cunningham, speaking through Dobson, took the extremely unusual step of offering to accept a verdict of nine jurors rather than a unanimous decision. The prosecution, knowing that the defense had confused many of the jurors, declined.

The following day, the foreman notified Bertelsman that the deadlock could not be broken. The judge declared a mistrial, thanked the jurors, and sent them home, this time without the admonition not to discuss the trial or their deliberations. When the prosecution announced its intention to launch a second trial, the defense attorneys immediately asked Bertelsman to release Gallion and Cunningham from the Boone County jail, where they had languished for the last eleven months. Bertelsman refused. He likely disagreed with the verdict, telling those present that, "after the trial the evidence is even stronger in my mind," and he thought Gallion and Cunningham had too much incentive to flee.[27]

After the trial, jury foreman Donald Rainone gave low marks to the government prosecutors. He told reporters that the prosecution "just didn't have a strong case" and heaped criticism on its lack of preparedness. The error in granting Chesley immunity was evident when Rainone added, "There's a lot of people that had their hands in this ... there's a lot of people that should have been on trial that weren't." Rainone refused to name Chesley, saying he didn't want to get sued. However, he was not reticent in his praise of the defense, noting, "If I were in trouble, I would hire Mr. Almond."[28]

Almond had run circles around the prosecution and demonstrated a keen understanding of the jury. Among his more potent arguments was that GCM's so-called victims had already been more than amply compensated—by some calculations, getting more than thirty times what they would have received from the national settlement. In contrast to the skillful defense, the prosecution blundered badly by granting immunity to Chesley. His extravagantly courteous manner was obviously for show, and his enigmatic answers to direct questions likely struck many jurors as willful evasion. Nor did they believe Chesley when he claimed to have no memory of key events. So when Chesley switched sides, that allowed the defense to substitute Robbins as its expert witness. Fortunately, Robbins proved to be vastly more credible than Chesley, and his opinions dovetailed perfectly with the defense team's arguments.

In the end, the prosecution snatched defeat from the jaws of victory. University of Kentucky law professor Bill Fortune, an expert on legal ethics, remains baffled as to why Chesley was granted immunity. Professor Fortune uses the story of the *Guard* settlement as a morality play of sorts, warning students of the perils of disregarding established codes of ethical conduct.

In granting immunity to Chesley, Voorhees had promised her bosses in the Department of Justice the moon, but those promises were only moonshine. For all of Voorhees's missteps, though, she did one thing right. By refusing Cunningham's offer to accept a less-than-unanimous verdict, she saved the day—the jury vote had been two to convict and ten to acquit.

14

The Second Bite

DESPITE MISSING VICTORY by only a hairbreadth, the legal teams of Gallion and Cunningham were not sanguine about their prospects in a second trial. When prosecutors have another opportunity to convict after a mistrial, the defense is at a disadvantage. Although Gallion had appeared credible when portraying the settlement funds retained by GCM as a hedge against additional claims, and although his insurance premium argument had nearly succeeded, the government was now fully aware of that game plan and would be better prepared to counter it.

To complicate matters for the defense, seven counts of wire fraud had been added to the first, as well as the theft of $95 million ($200 million less $60 million of legitimate attorneys' fees and $45 million from the first distribution to the claimants). The additional wire fraud charges came about when a forensic analysis of their banking records by the FBI revealed that tens of millions had been transferred between banks on eight separate occasions to avoid detection by the KBA and Angela Ford, as well as to create FHL. Each transfer earned another charge of federal wire fraud, and these additional charges raised the maximum sentences from twenty to thirty years. The defense teams for Gallion and Cunningham had run the gauntlet on the first round, but it would be more difficult to perform the same feat while shouldering these extra burdens.

Voorhees and her team were anxious to erase the humiliating image of Mills walking away and to refute the criticism heaped on them by the jury foreman. It was a near certainty that attorneys throughout Kentucky were gossiping with bemusement at how badly the prosecution had missed its shot at virtually point-blank range. They were now resolved to use any means necessary to ensure that after the next verdict, Mills's two accomplices would be perp-walked to jail.

Soon after declaring a mistrial, Judge Bertelsman announced that he would no longer preside over criminal trials.[1] After managing eight contentious attorneys over the course of nearly thirty weeks, from bail hearing through trial, Bertelsman had had enough. His replacement was Judge Danny Reeves. Reeves had a tendency toward peevishness and did not suffer fools gladly—albeit fools in the broadest sense of the term. According to Mills, he was known among the legal community as "Maximum Reeves" for his harsh sentencing. This change of judges would prove devastating for the defense.

In his first action, Reeves denied a motion by Gallion and Cunningham for a delay to prepare for the additional charges, citing the provisions of the Speedy Trial Act. After agreeing to start the trial within seventy days, Reeves provided the one bright spot for the defendants when, on July 17, 2008, Gallion's bond was dropped to $2.5 million and Cunningham's to $1.25 million. However, even these much-reduced amounts would be difficult to find. Seven years of very high living, mountains of legal bills, the freezing of their cash assets, and the loss in *Abbott* had severely depleted their once prodigious bank accounts. Even the effort to raise bail by transferring the proceeds from the sale of their jointly owned Thoroughbred stock to Cunningham's wife, Pat, and Gallion's new girlfriend, Mellissa Green, had been stymied. Eventually, Cunningham managed to scrape together his bond money by the end of August, and Gallion did the same sometime thereafter. The two were able to leave the Boone County jail after nearly a year of incarceration, but with certain limitations set by Reeves, including GPS-monitored home incarceration and restrictions on telephone and computer usage.[2]

Reeves also moved the second trial to Frankfort, the state capital, eighty miles from Covington. The jurisdiction of the US District Court for the Eastern District of Kentucky covers a large swath of the Bluegrass State, with courthouses in Ashland, Covington, Pikeville, London, Frankfort, and

Lexington. Thus, the trial could have been held in any of these locations, depending on the wishes of the assigned judge. Reeves's rationale for moving the trial to Frankfort was that it would be easier to seat a jury untainted by publicity. But that rationale seemed thin, as Frankfort is a mere forty-minute drive time from Lexington, the home of both Gallion and Cunningham. Both major newspapers for the region, the *Lexington Herald-Leader* and the *Louisville Courier-Journal,* had covered the story in a manner that was unrelentingly negative for GCM. Accordingly, it would have been difficult to seat twelve jurors anywhere who hadn't already been influenced against the defense.[3]

By the time the second trial opened, the front pages of every prominent newspaper in the region featured the faces of Gallion and Cunningham. The public reacted to stories of their lavish spending with a mixture of amusement and scorn. But it was in the legal community where attitudes had grown most toxic. Prior to the second trial, a March 2007 article in the *New York Times* noted that "legal experts said the fraud might be one of the biggest and most brazen in legal history."[4] Even worse than being labeled liars and thieves, Gallion and Cunningham had committed the sacrilege of despoiling the temple of justice. The leadership and membership of the KBA seemed to be driven by a nearly universal impulse to redeem the profession by destroying the pair. As Linda Gosnell, chief counsel for the KBA, told reporters at a hearing to suspend the law licenses of GCM, "This is a case of absolute, unbridled greed."[5]

Indeed, the second trial would be much different from the first. Before it even got under way, Voorhees argued that Robbins should not be allowed to provide expert testimony. Despite his exceptional qualifications, Voorhees maintained that Robbins had not written or spoken professionally on any of the relevant issues. She cited Rule 403 of the Federal Rules of Evidence, which allows courts to exclude evidence that poses "risk of unfair prejudice, confusion of issues, misleading the jury or waste of time." Despite the fact that Robbins's testimony in the first trial did not precisely meet any of these tests, Reeves granted the motion to exclude him. This was a startling turn of events, considering that the prosecution had not challenged Robbins's credentials in the first trial.

Naturally, both defense teams strongly objected. They requested and received what is termed a Daubert hearing to argue that Robbins was qualified to provide expert testimony based on experience alone. Federal law gives the presiding judge carte blanche authority to interpret the law and determine how it should be applied, so the defense was only wasting its time. After its arguments were concluded, Reeves immediately handed down his ruling. He had been holding the multipage decision in his hands while the defense attorneys were pleading their case. Reeves ruled that Robbins was not qualified to testify.

In contrast, Howard M. Erichson, professor of law at Fordham University, was welcomed as an expert witness for the prosecution. A graduate of the New York University School of Law, Erichson had spent his career as an academic and had little experience in the actual practice of law. During his testimony, Erichson scoffed at the defense's contract theory argument and maintained that the fees taken by Gallion and Cunningham had essentially been stolen.

Another critical difference between the first and second trials was the explosive testimony of KBA attorney Linda Gosnell. Under Judge Bertelsman, her role in the first trial had been restricted to "custodian of the record." Gosnell's testimony had been limited to confirming that various documents from the KBA's disbarment hearings for Gallion and Cunningham had been properly filed and safeguarded. Since the records themselves contained the testimony of witnesses who were unavailable to be cross-examined by the defense, their introduction would have violated the defendants' Sixth Amendment right to confront witnesses against them. Further, it was argued in a later appeal that allegations contained in disbarment decisions are inadmissible in a criminal trial.

Despite these concerns, Reeves allowed Gosnell to testify at length about the details of the KBA's investigation, and in fact, she came to the witness stand fully prepared to do just that. Gosnell used an overhead screen to display each of the twenty-two counts of misconduct the KBA had filed against Gallion and Cunningham and read them aloud to the jury. These charges ran the gamut from deceiving clients about settlement amounts to failing to adequately supervise David Helmers. The fact the Gosnell came prepared with a PowerPoint presentation meant that she already knew Reeves would allow her free rein, regardless of its impropriety.

The jury listened to Gosnell's testimony for hours, and as the time passed, the defendants' chances of acquittal grew fainter. After relentless objections from the defense teams, Reeves agreed to provide the jurors with copies of the exhibits introduced during Gosnell's testimony with the charges and findings redacted. He also instructed the jury "that the violation of an ethical rule is not evidence or proof that a defendant committed the criminal acts alleged in the indictment." But Reeves's instructions were issued days after Gosnell's testimony, and as the saying goes, "You can't unring a bell"—that is, once the jurors had heard her testimony, it was impossible to erase it from their minds. In this case, the proverbial bell had been allowed to peal for an entire morning.

Reeves loosed the most fatal volley of all when he informed the jury that *Guard* had been an aggregate settlement—in other words, a settlement for only the 431 individual plaintiffs, rather than the potentially much larger class of all persons in Kentucky who had taken the diet drugs. This was in stark contrast to Judge Bertelsman, who had informed the jury in the first trial that *Guard* had been settled as a class action. *Guard's* settlement as a class action was at the heart of the defense argument, as it laid out the entire rationale for legal fees that exceeded those prescribed in the client contracts. Reeves's instructions made a verdict of guilty essentially a foregone conclusion, since any fees beyond the percentages specified in the contracts would necessarily be considered stolen. Somewhat paradoxically, this conclusion was valid even though the so-called stolen fees had been approved by Bamberger, the presiding judge.

Mindful of Reeves's snappish defensiveness, Hale Almond tried to tread lightly when he expressed the opinion that Reeves was taking an improper approach here. He pointed out that the judge had not yet heard all the evidence from the defendants' side and had apparently made up his mind before the conclusion of the case—something he had cautioned the jury not to do. Reeves rebuffed Almond and informed him that, based on the testimony up to that point, he had already been able to reach legal conclusions about certain issues. Federal judges are allowed enormous discretion, and Reeves did not hesitate to use all his prerogatives.

Chesley appeared at the second trial as well, but this time, a much different witness took the stand. His answers were short and matter-of-fact, and he did not equivocate about the impropriety of how the settlement funds had been distributed. According to *Forbes* magazine, when the defense probed his faulty memory of that critical meeting in June 2002 with GCM and Bamberger, Chesley acidly replied, "Bamberger is a liar who knowingly signed false orders."[6] Naturally, Chesley was still protected from prosecution by the immunity negotiated during the first trial. In a ghost from lawsuits past, Chesley's old nemesis Barbara Bonar tried unsuccessfully to get the KBA to "suspend Mr. Chesley's law license when he testified under a grant of immunity at Gallion's and Cunningham's trial."[7]

In April, the warmth of spring turns the rolling hills in the heart of bluegrass country green. On most days, the sun shines brightly through the narrow windows of the federal courthouse, but on the morning of April 3, 2009, the day of their verdicts, a leaden sky and a cold, damp wind greeted Gallion and Cunningham. In the crowded courtroom, Judge Reeves asked for the single piece of folded paper that was the final product of months of testimony, mountains of documents, reams of newsprint and barrels of ink, two judges, two juries, and hundreds of thousands of dollars in attorneys' fees. This time, the jury of seven women and five men had taken only two days of deliberation to reach its final conclusion.

As Gallion and Cunningham turned to face the jury, Judge Reeves read aloud "guilty" for each count against each man. While the prosecution team beamed with relief, the defense lawyers consoled Gallion and Cunningham, who slumped back in their seats as they contemplated decades behind prison walls. As their family members ran from the courtroom in tears, many former clients in the audience congratulated themselves and hugged one another. They were happy to know that the two lawyers would soon be carted off to prison and pleased at the prospect of receiving additional settlement payments.

Reporters outside the courthouse interviewed the victims, who were eager to tell their tales of pain and destitution. Among the most eager to speak to the press was Connie Centers, who wanted the public to know that "we are sick people and don't have long to live, all they're [Gallion and Cunningham] going to is jail."[8] According to the medical records shared at the trial, an echocardiogram on July 17, 2006, revealed that Centers had significant heart valve regurgitation and an enlarged heart. Subsequently, when she underwent a heart valve replacement, the damaged valve showed the telltale markers of rheumatic fever, which Centers had contracted as a child. It was apparent that the disease rather than diet drugs had caused her condition. In fact, Centers had already been diagnosed with heart disease when she started taking fen-phen, and she was on the diet drug for only three months. After the surgery, Centers reported that she never felt better in her life, yet she later managed to obtain disability benefits. Had Centers joined the national settlement, she would have received nothing, given her history of rheumatic fever. Even without a prior history, Centers would have been awarded only $128,000 from the national settlement. Contrary to her claims of poverty after the second round of *Guard* settlement disbursements, Centers received a total of $1.6 million.[9]

On the morning of August 18, 2009, the air was hot and heavy when Gallion and Cunningham returned to Reeves's courtroom for sentencing. They were now in shackles, and their jail uniforms were pitted with sweat stains from the oppressive humidity as well as stomach-churning anxiety. As they entered the courtroom and scanned for family, Gallion nodded to his girlfriend, Mellissa, and Cunningham acknowledged his wife, Pat, and their children. Their forced smiles were insufficient to mask their grim despair. Various other faces from better times were scattered among the spectators.

As sentencing guidelines, Reeves used a table listing the number of prior offenses across the top and amounts stolen, from least to most, down the left side of the page. Using the two variables, stair-stepped lines were printed across the table in a somewhat arbitrary manner to indicate the length of the prison sentence. Gallion and Cunningham fell into the 300-month bracket at the bottom of the page.

Before the sentence was passed, the court allowed persons invited by the defense to make pleas for leniency. For Shirley Cunningham, the first invitee was attorney William Johnson, who told the court, "This is the first time I have ever been in a courtroom during sentencing when I was not representing them as a lawyer." Johnson spoke of his high regard for Cunningham, noting that he had "known Shirley Cunningham for at least thirty years . . . he was my friend when I first met him, a friend throughout the time I have known him and he will always be my friend." He went on to say, "What I will call his people, the black community in Central Kentucky frequently looked to Shirley when they needed him." Johnson also blamed himself for not convincing the pair to agree to a civil settlement. He stated, "I have to admit I was involved, and I rue the day that I did not do more from the standpoint of pushing for a settlement of the civil action [*Abbott*] . . . and had that happened, then I don't believe we would be here today."[10]

Following Johnson was William Harman, a business associate of Cunningham's who described him as humble and honest and then contrasted him with Melbourne Mills, whom he called "despicable." Mysteriously, Harman said that Cunningham's biggest mistake had been turning the settlement negotiations over to an unnamed woman that "he would never do business with again."[11]

For Gallion, Jennifer Blakeley, director of risk management at the University of Kentucky Hospital, was called to the stand. She had worked with Gallion for nineteen years, during the time he provided legal services to the hospital. She said Gallion had "changed the culture" at the hospital by creating a safe harbor for workers to report problems without the fear of reprisal. She tearfully stated, "In my 53 years I have deeply loved and respected three men, my father . . . my husband . . . [and] lastly the third man Bill Gallion, for whom I have a love, that has made contributions in the lives of everyone he has encountered in the 19 years I worked for him."[12] Other character witnesses for Gallion were scheduled but did not appear.

Following these speakers, Angela Ford, as the victims' advocate, attempted to scrub away any patina of decency ascribed to the pair. Leading this character attack were five carefully selected *Guard* claimants. One woman who had undergone valve replacement surgery had initially been offered a settlement of only $16,000 because her injuries fell very low on the scale of damages within Helmers's matrix and her condition was likely not caused by taking diet drugs. Under these circumstances, had she sought compensation through the national settlement, she likely would have received only a $600 refund for the cost of the medications. Nevertheless, she hoped that Gallion and Cunningham spent the rest of their lives in jail.

The grievances of the next two witnesses focused almost exclusively on the years of mental anguish they had suffered from being unable to discuss their settlements with anyone, including family members. They both claimed they had been threatened with prison should they violate this covenant. However, the settlement agreements they had voluntarily signed described only a monetary penalty for disclosure, and Phipps, Overstreet, and Helmers had all denied raising the prospect of imprisonment. Further, the witnesses' claims of anger and disappointment over their settlements (which far exceeded any reasonable expectations) defied rationality. One man said that, during the drive home after receiving his first settlement check, "I couldn't concentrate to drive. At one point, I had to pull over to the side of the road. . . . I actually broke down and cried. I became physically sick."[13] It was revealing that neither of two mentioned any adverse physical effects from taking the drugs.

Next to testify was Connie Centers. She complained bitterly that Gallion's girlfriend and Cunningham's wife were well dressed, while she had to buy her clothes at Walmart. However, she did not mention that her settlement had eventually been increased from $1.6 million to $2 million.

The final tale of grief was delivered by Lisa Swiger, who had already added a touch of the bizarre by sitting through the trial wearing a surgical mask. As related earlier, after quickly going through her two settlement checks, Swiger had pestered Gallion for more money, leading him to ask Bamberger for help. Bamberger, who determined that Swiger was mentally disabled, had ordered that she receive an additional $500,000, to be doled out in monthly allotments. Despite this proviso, it was rumored that Swiger had acquired two more Dodge Durangos, in addition to the five she had already purchased, but Swiger insisted that she bought only one Durango. At the sentencing, Swiger related in considerable detail an injury sustained in an automobile accident (before joining *Guard*) that had left her with a steel plate in her head.

After Swiger, Ford rose once more to speak. To add to the spectacle, a number of front-row seats in the courtroom had been left empty to symbolize the plaintiffs who had died since joining the *Guard* action. It is uncertain whether any of those deaths were attributable to taking AHP's diet drugs, and it is very likely that they were not. Many of the plaintiffs already had heart conditions before taking the drugs, and others were in poor health because of diabetes made worse by obesity and a lack of exercise. The vast majority of the 431 had little to no discernible damage and thus did not use their settlements for medical purposes. W. L. Carter, who attended the sentencing, had told a reporter for the *New York Times* in March 2007, "I was hoping to get enough to pay the farm off, a farm that's been in my family since 1857."[14]

Ford launched into a long description of how the plaintiffs had trusted Gallion and Cunningham because of their status as attorneys, a trust they had betrayed. With this argument, Ford inadvertently revealed the subtext of the second trial: restoration of the reputation of the legal community. As observed by Judge Bertelsman, the whole legal profession had been on trial. Had the profession covered itself in glory in the pursuit of justice, or had it been a judicial show trial?

Finally, it was time for Reeves to pronounce sentence. In his preamble, the judge chastised the defendants for not displaying a shred of remorse for their misdeeds. (One likely reason is that Gallion and Cunningham believed they had already been adequately punished. Sitting in jail for a year, along with penury and disbarment, had been enough. They also believed that because of the many errors made by the trial judge, they stood a good chance of winning a retrial on appeal. Had they admitted their guilt and repented, that opportunity would have vanished.) Reeves then went out of his way to defend Chesley, saying there had been an "ugly" attempt to shift the blame to him and strongly implying that his $20 million fee was well deserved! In stark contrast, a panel of judges would later describe Chesley's actions as "shocking and reprehensible." Glowering down from his dais, Reeves scolded the pair using an analogy that was grotesquely overstated: "A lot of people did some things in World War II that claimed they were following the orders of others . . . it resulted in the Nuremberg trials."[15]

With Reeves's shockingly harsh chastisement, all hope of leniency evaporated. Gallion and Cunningham exchanged grimaced glances and prepared for the worst. Although the prosecution had argued for a multiplying factor because the conspiracy involved the coordination of five or more conspirators, Reeves settled on thirty years for Gallion and twenty-five for Cunningham. Gallion received the stiffer sentence because Reeves found that he was primarily responsible for organizing the crime. For Gallion, aged sixty-five, it was the equivalent of a life sentence.

But Reeves was not done. Each man was levied a fine of $127,450,380.05, which had been meticulously calculated based on the total fees received less the amount overpaid to some of the *Guard* claimants relative to Helmers's unused matrix. To rub salt in their wounds, Reeves also ordered that if Gallion and Cunningham were put to work while incarcerated in the federal prison system, half their wages of approximately $1 per hour would be garnished. In passing sentence, Reeves stated, the "defendants committed a very serious fraud that has affected not just the victims . . . but [also] the judicial system," confirming that the trial and the resulting punishment were as much about besmirching the legal profession as about stealing from the *Guard* claimants.[16]

The second trial's fairness was open to debate. *LawReader* concluded that allowing Gosnell to read to the jury the KBA's twenty-two allegations was "pretty poisonous material, and by itself could easily provide the basis for a new trial."[17] It is also arguable that many of Gallion's and Cunningham's actions had been influenced by a man who was not on trial: Stan Chesley. Although Chesley would not be sent to prison, he too would face a legal ordeal that would utterly destroy what little remained of his reputation.

15

Cornered

STANLEY M. CHESLEY'S DEMISE began with the November 2004 filing of the *Abbott* civil suit. Prior to that date, Chesley still inhabited the stratospheric heights of the legal profession. Then began his slow, painful descent. Chesley had gained a fortune many times over, but keeping those millions would ultimately prove far more difficult than making them. The *Abbott* lawsuit, relentlessly pursued by Angela Ford, would not be easily evaded. But Chesley would devise an audacious plan to do just that, and for many years, it worked.

Although Bill Gallion had done well in selecting Hale Almond as his criminal defense attorney, Gallion's selection of attorney Ken Feinberg for the *Abbott* civil suit was truly inspired. Feinberg was the perfect person to help a client wiggle out of a tight spot. His credentials as a mediator, litigator, and expert witness were pristine; his many accomplishments included acting as administrator of the Deep Water Horizon, 9/11, and 2003 Boston Marathon victim compensation funds. Feinberg was also employed by General Motors and Volkswagen to handle recall responses and customer compensation for faulty vehicles and false representations. So well regarded was Feinberg that a financial columnist for the *New York Times* recommended that President Donald Trump hire him to manage his assets.[1]

Based on Gallion's representation of the facts and a promised legal fee of $50,000, Feinberg prepared a seventeen-page affidavit that read in part: "There is nothing out of the ordinary in the Boone County Circuit Court approving the use of $20 million for cy pres purposes or in approving the formation of a charitable foundation, the Kentucky Fund for Healthy Living. ... In my opinion [*Guard*] was handled properly and ethically. I see nothing that credibly suggests any misconduct by the attorneys or any inappropriate action by the judge who presided over the case."[2] Gallion had intended to use Feinberg's affidavit as a key defense argument during the *Abbott* hearings, but Judge Wehr rightly refused to allow the affidavit into evidence, since a piece of paper cannot be cross-examined. Because Feinberg's affidavit was no use to him, Gallion stiffed Feinberg on his fee.

On March 8, 2006, Judge Wehr ruled in favor of the *Abbott* plaintiffs, awarding them $42 million. The calculation of the award was based on a confusing hodgepodge of figures achieved by rounding down the $64 million in overpayments, then deducting a rounded-up $20.5 million used to fund FHL, as well as a rounded-up $1.5 million for a portion of Mills's poorly documented expenses, all at an imputed interest rate of 8 percent. However, Wehr's ruling was only a partial summary judgment, meaning that it pertained only to GCM and not to Chesley. Summary judgments are possible in Kentucky when the facts are beyond dispute and the law alone is sufficient to make a judgment. In this case, Chesley's culpability was still undetermined. The contingency fee agreements did not bear his signature and thus were not explicitly between Chesley and the *Guard* plaintiffs. Chesley's omission from the judgment was not as advantageous for him as it might seem. That onus would fall on him in due time, as the fee-splitting agreements between Chesley and GCM explicitly referenced Chesley as cocounsel for all 431 plaintiffs. Despite the partial judgment, this was a remarkable victory for Ford. It was the first time a Kentucky court had directed lawyers to disgorge legal fees.

By the time of the *Abbott* decision, the mutual loathing between Ford and Chesley had deepened. During a heated exchange at his deposition, Chesley imperiously shouted at Ford, "If you will stop screaming at me, I will answer your question." Ford's war of words took a unique form: she launched a website on which she posted details of the *Abbott* lawsuit and various other documents that cast Chesley and GCM in a bad light. At least one person was an avid follower. During his testimony at the criminal trial,

Chesley stated, "I've been sued and have been all over the website by Ms. Ford for four years."[3]

While Chesley was busy devising a strategy to exclude himself from the *Abbott* decision, the Inquiry Commission of the KBA filed charges against him on December 6, 2006. He was accused of various ethical violations involving the establishment of FHL and of being GCM's coconspirator in misappropriating FHL funds. During the ensuing investigation, Chesley had no choice but to lie. According to KBA investigators, led by Linda Gosnell, Chesley's responses during depositions were "in some instances incomplete, in other instances misleading, and in some instances outright falsehoods."[4] Among the latter, the KBA found that Chesley:

1. Falsely denied having knowledge about the contingency contracts with the plaintiffs, despite being a cocounsel with complete access to these documents.
2. Falsely stated that his role in *Guard* was solely to negotiate the settlement, despite engaging in a series of meetings subsequent to the settlement, including devising defense strategies for GCM and coaching Bamberger prior to his testimony before the Judicial Conduct Commission.
3. Falsely claimed to have no memory of attending a February 6, 2002, meeting with Bamberger. During this crucial meeting, Chesley played a prominent role in the establishment of FHL, the second distribution to claimants, and the application of *Grinnell* to persuade Bamberger to allow 49 percent of the settlement to go toward attorneys' fees.
4. Falsely asserted that he was unaware that the $20,597,121 he received in legal fees far exceeded what could have been rightfully anticipated from a settlement that conformed to the contracts with the claimants.

After a lengthy investigation, a disciplinary hearing was convened at KBA headquarters in Frankfort on November 5, 2009, three weeks after Gallion and Cunningham were sent to prison. Chesley appeared with a bank of six attorneys as well as his wife, Judge Dlott. Thirty-seven witnesses gave testimony over two days. The most critical testimony was that of Chesley himself.

In an effort to explain away his acceptance of more than $7.5 million in excess legal fees, Chesley testified that he "assumed that Mr. Gallion and Mr. Cunningham would send me a check based on what the court had indicated was an appropriate amount, and I had no reason not to trust them." Chesley's verbal ploys bordered on the juvenile. While reading from the notorious "side letter," which stated, "Notwithstanding paragraph 1, the settling attorneys and settling claimants shall not be obligated to indemnify AHP for attorney's fees and expenses nor for any amount in excess of $7,500,000," he left out the word "not," which completely changed the meaning of the sentence. This deliberate omission was caught by Judge Graham, the trial commissioner. The documents Chesley filed contained deliberate deletions, including notations that certain documents had been CC'd to him, as well as the language of the fee-splitting agreements between himself and GCM. Much worse was to come.

Chesley contacted Ken Feinberg, seeking his services as an expert witness. Chesley apologized for the cheapskate Gallion and paid Feinberg $10,000 of the $50,000 fee Gallion owed him, in exchange for Feinberg's testimony. Unfortunately for Chesley, he did not ask Feinberg what he intended to say, having assumed that Feinberg would repeat the essence of his prior exculpatory affidavit. Instead, much to the shock of Chesley and his team, Feinberg repudiated the affidavit and testified that had he known all the facts, he would have "thrown his statement in the wastebasket." When Judge Graham asked whether it was "safe to say you knew nothing about the factual occurrences in this case?" Feinberg replied, "Your Honor, I'm embarrassed today that it is safe to say." Graham responded, "Holy smoke."[5] It is unknown what additional facts Feinberg was referring to that caused him to make such a declaration. As Feinberg left the stand, Chesley slumped even further into his chair and gazed at the ceiling. His four-decade legal career was about to come to an end.

Among the expert witnesses Chesley brought to the hearing, the most prestigious was Geoffrey C. Hazard of the University of Pennsylvania. As the author of sixteen books on jurisprudence, Hazard was to legal ethics what Stephen Hawking was to astrophysics. Hazard had done the simple math and testified that since Chesley's $21 million fee represented about 10 percent of the settlement, it was "well within the range of reason." Yet when the facts about the fee-splitting agreement and the 49 percent fee granted by Bamberger were pointed out, a noticeably embarrassed Hazard admitted that his statement was wrong. In his report, Graham concluded that "poor professor Hazard . . . was victimized by Chesley."[6] In his effort to hide the truth, Chesley had needlessly humiliated a well-intentioned scholar in front of his peers.

The anticlimax was the testimony from three character witnesses. One of them, Lisa Crawford, spoke of her satisfaction with both her settlement and her communications with her attorneys. Chesley essentially had nothing to do with either. Also on hand was Father Michael Graham, whose duties included fund-raising for Xavier University. Graham testified that Chesley had been supportive of the university, but "not nearly as much as I would like." The third witness, Judge Michael Brent of the US District Court of Southern Ohio, was a social friend who spoke more about Chesley's ability to raise money than his moral character. It seemed that Chesley's influence with the powerful was a mile wide but only an inch deep. His political friends in Washington, DC, did not have his back, now that it was against the wall.

In his official report, Commissioner Graham described the events concerning the *Guard* settlement and its immediate aftermath as "a tale worthy of the pen of Charles Dickens, alas this tale is not fiction." The report concluded, "Every action taken by Chesley after his February 6, 2002, meeting with Judge Bamberger was calculated to assist in the cover-up of these misdeeds by GCM. His callous subordination of the interests of his clients to his own greed is both shocking and reprehensible."[7] Graham recommended that Chesley be permanently disbarred in Kentucky. In addition, he was to return the amount he had been overpaid, calculated as $7,555,000. Because of a reciprocal agreement, should the Kentucky Supreme Court adopt Graham's disbarment recommendation, the disbarment would automatically extend to Ohio.

As a further blow to Chesley's much celebrated career, two days after the recommendation by Graham, the Ohio attorney general removed Chesley as the lead counsel in a massive class-action lawsuit against mortgage giant Fannie Mae, in which Chesley had been involved for several years.[8]

In March 2013 Chief Justice John Minton wrote for the Kentucky Supreme Court: "Therefore, we find that permanently disbarring [Chesley] is appropriate for his ethical violations." With the sure knowledge that his disbarment in Ohio would follow, Chesley "voluntarily" gave up his license to practice law in his home state. An email statement distributed by Chesley's attorney contained the hollow assertion that the "Ohio courts have never disciplined Chesley."[9]

After Feinberg's dramatic disavowal of his affidavit about the legitimacy of the actions of GCM and Chesley, this document found its way out of the figurative wastebasket and into the hands of the Kentucky Court of Appeals in 2011. There, Gallion was working to reverse the loss in *Abbott* and to compel Ford to reveal what assets she had already repossessed from GCM and still held in escrow. Since Chesley's 2009 disciplinary hearing before the KBA was not public, the court was unaware of what had transpired, including Feinberg's refutation of his affidavit, which Gallion had the audacity to introduce into evidence. Ruling that the document introduced an issue of fact that had not been considered, the appeals court reversed Wehr's summary judgment and remanded the case to Judge Wehr for a new trial. This was very bad news for Angela Ford.

Recklessly assuming that she was home free, Ford had already distributed portions of the *Abbott* award out of the escrow account before the settlement had been finalized. Ford's share of the distribution totaled an aggregate $13,277,216, per her contractual agreements with the *Abbott* plaintiffs. She used a portion of these funds to purchase Gallion's former home and some of his personal belongings at auction. Ford and Gallion's girlfriend, Mellissa Green, got into a bidding war over Gallion's laptop computer. Ford had no need for another laptop, but she was certain it contained information that could unravel the web of shell corporations hiding millions of Gallion's assets. Thanks to the *Abbott* settlement funds, Ford had way more chips than Green, and when the gavel banged "sold," Ford had won.

Meanwhile, federal judge David Reeves asked Ford to provide an accounting of all the settlement funds she was holding. This routine request sent Ford into a tailspin. She referred to the request as a "gross miscarriage of justice" and told a *Courier-Journal* reporter that Judge Reeves had "no right to know" where she was keeping the funds. With regard to the recovery of the settlement proceeds, she tartly added, "How much has the government found on its own? I think it's zero."[10] But Reeves not only had the right to ask for an accounting of the funds; because Ford had not posted a bond to protect the tens of millions she had collected, Reeves also had the responsibility. Ford's response to Reeves's directive led to a jaw-dropping irony. But to describe how this drama played out, it is first necessary to introduce yet another malefactor: Seth Johnston.

Seth Johnston was an associate attorney at the Lexington law firm of Miller Wells. Johnston's specialty was asset recovery and collections, as well as the establishment of limited liability corporations. Having sifted through all the information contained on Gallion's laptop, Ford needed help pulling in these and other assets, so she hired Miller Wells. Working together, Ford and Johnston filed more than 100 pleadings, subpoenas, and garnishments to satisfy the *Abbott* award. Johnston had become so adept at this specialty that in November 2010 he left Miller Wells to form his own law firm, Johnston Legal. One of his first clients was Angela Ford.

As described in detail by attorney John Billings, Johnston and Ford frequently discussed the need for Ford to protect her assets. With Reeves demanding an accounting of the *Abbott* assets, a sizable portion of which Ford had prematurely and improperly taken for herself, Johnston's advice became particularly appealing. Knowing that Johnston had a talent for transferring cash into offshore investments, Ford considered doing just that.

After a series of feints and delays by Ford, an exasperated Reeves finally issued a motion of accounting on June 22, 2011, noting, "If Ford fails to provide a full and complete accounting to the United States . . . the government may obtain discovery by other means." For Ford, it was now or never. In a move that was highly unlikely to be mere coincidence, five days later, on June 27, Johnston formed two Delaware-based corporations on Ford's behalf: Villa Paradiso and Solutions Ventures. Ford then opened bank accounts for both corporations at Bank of the Bluegrass, into which she deposited a total of $3.6 million. In an apparent effort to muddy the money trail, the funds then progressed on a bank crawl through Lexington that included Republic Bank, PNC, and finally BB&T. It was at BB&T where Ford's name was completely removed from the account, thus breaking the link to her.[11] Instead, the account was opened in the name of Johnston Legal, leaving her trusted collaborator Seth Johnston with signatory authority and the ability to do anything he liked with the $3.6 million. Thus, in an effort to keep the scent of the funds away from pursuing hounds, she placed $3.6 million into the jaws of a wolf.

Johnston then used Ford's money to replace the funds he had already stolen from three other clients (Harold and Kathleen Baerg and Faisal Shaw) as part of a property transaction in California. Johnston used the stolen money to purchase two bars in Fayette County and also to finance an illegal enterprise to manufacture and distribute synthetic marijuana. A man named Iqbal Khan helped Johnston set up the operation, with the assistance of seven other accomplices. After the drug scheme was uncovered by the FBI and the source of its financing was revealed, a shocked and embarrassed Ford commented to reporters, "Seth is young, extremely bright and worked as hard as any young lawyer I have ever known . . . his recent problems are all rather mystifying and a bit tragic."[12] It would also turn out to be tragic for Ford.

Obviously, Ford wanted her $3.6 million back, so she sued Johnston, as well as Shaw and the Baergs, who were represented by the aforementioned John Billings. The defense responded with a broadside stating, "The unanswerable, glaring question to Mrs. Ford's specious, false allegation that Johnston stole that money is 'Why did you voluntarily give it to him in the first place.'"[13] Sadly for Ford, in November 2017 the Kentucky Supreme Court ruled that she had no claim to the assets of Billings's clients. Even more galling, the court essentially agreed with Johnston. Because Ford had given Johnston authority over the accounts that contained Ford's $3.6 million, Johnston could not be considered a thief. Ford's money, like the synthetic marijuana operation it financed, had gone up in smoke.[14]

For his misdeeds, Johnston pleaded guilty to two counts of mail fraud, one count of wire fraud, conspiracy to obstruct justice, conspiracy to distribute a controlled substance, and tax fraud. He was sentenced to twenty years in federal prison.[15] Not surprisingly, he was also disbarred.

Ford eventually provided an accounting of the *Abbott* distributions for Reeves, but she filed a motion to vacate the order requiring her to reveal the location of the $13 million in attorneys' fees. The court granted Ford the discretion of providing the location of those funds "under seal," meaning not publicly. The accounting of the $13 million was provided on November 9, 2011. Soon thereafter, the list of recipients was shared with KBA officials. After reviewing this list, the KBA Board of Governors fired Gosnell on November 21 and removed her name from the KBA website the same day. *Law-Reader* commented that "sources close to the KBA" confirmed that Gosnell "had been fired as a result of the accounting."[16] In addition, it later reported that attorney Leslie Rosenbaum, Gosnell's husband, maintained a website that promoted his expertise in mass tort litigation, including fen-phen cases. The KBA never divulged the contents of the list of recipients or the reason behind Gosnell's abrupt dismissal. The extent of Gosnell's wrongdoing, if any, is unknown, but as the chief counsel of the KBA, she, like Caesar's wife, had to be above suspicion.

It was some consolation for Ford that on August 29, 2013, the Kentucky Supreme Court decided in favor of Ford and the *Abbott* claimants, ruling that Wehr's summary judgment was valid in full. This meant that Ford was entitled to her $13 million fee—now, ironically, $3.6 million lighter because of her bizarre scheme to keep it. The court did not base its decision on Feinberg's repudiation of his affidavit; rather, it found that the affidavit did not constitute an issue of material fact.

It is said that bad news comes in threes, and for Ford, this proved to be true. Having achieved a victory in the *Abbott* action, she found a new group of aggrieved former fen-phen users—namely, the fifty-three *Guard* plaintiffs who had been transferred to the *Stevens* lawsuit in Mississippi through a bizarre arrangement with Shirley Cunningham. Beasley Allen, the Alabama-based law firm that represented the *Stevens* plaintiffs, had been required to obtain a settlement for 4,000 claimants but had fallen short. Cunningham had provided the additional names required and referred a Kentucky attorney, Brent Austin, to be their legal counsel of record.

As described in chapter 9, the Beasley Allen attorneys attempted to cheat each of their clients out of $18,443 of their individual settlement awards, including the fifty-three Kentuckians, who were largely oblivious to the scheme. When Ford learned about it, she rounded up the fifty-three and told them they had been cheated. Then, in the summer of 2007, Ford sued both Beasley Allen and Austin in the lawsuit *Able v. Austin*. Unfortunately, with all her other legal activities, Ford missed the statute of limitations deadline by a single day. This let Austin off the hook for the entire $922,000 claim, and Ford lost $397,000 in legal fees. Even worse, Damon Willis, a Louisville attorney, rounded up sixteen of the disappointed *Able* plaintiffs and sued Ford for malpractice in *Howard v. Ford*. Ford was now reaping the whirlwind.[17]

Able v. Austin and *Howard v. Ford* were not the only lawsuits stemming from *Guard*. Because Helmers's matrix had been arbitrary to begin with, it was inevitable that some claimants would receive more settlement funds than Helmers had allotted for them. This is why the amounts Gallion and Cunningham were ordered to repay had been reduced by roughly $6.5 million. When the thirty-seven overpaid claimants learned they would not be getting any of the $42 million *Abbott* settlement, they hired Danville, Kentucky, attorney Ed Hays to sue for even more money. This lawsuit was an absurdity by any measure.

Having retrieved whatever money still controlled by GCM that she could readily identify, Ford now turned her full attention to Chesley. By this time, Gallion and Cunningham were living in ten- by fifteen-foot prison cells, and Mills was bunking with Darlene La and her children. Chesley, by contrast, was still living in a 27,000-square-foot mansion. Chesley was therefore the only person with the wherewithal to satisfy the claims of the *Abbott* plaintiffs. But Ford would not be satisfied with recovering only the $7,555,000 in excess legal fees taken by Chesley.

On August 1, 2014, Boone County circuit judge James Schrand, who had replaced the retired Judge Wehr, ruled that Chesley should be included in the judgment, which made him jointly and severally liable for the entire $42 million. Under the principle of joint and several liability, every named defendant in a civil lawsuit is equally responsible for all damages, regardless of the extent of their participation in the offending act. Generally, the person who pays the largest share is the one with the deepest pockets. In a bit of poetic justice, Chesley had acquired his wealth by using the same principle throughout his career, beginning with the Beverly Hills Supper Club fire. By Ford's accounting, Chesley owed the entire $42 million, plus the $7.5 million he had been overpaid and all the excessive legal fees received by GCM, along with interest and penalties, for a whopping total of $76 million—a sum large enough to ruin Chesley.

Chesley may have been disbarred, but he still possessed all his legal wiles. He insisted on a complete and accurate accounting of how much of the $42 million had already been seized from GCM and exactly how much each of the *Abbott* claimants was owed. Since all these numbers were still fluid, it was like asking Ford to nail Jell-O to a wall. When Schrand denied his demand, Chesley decided to hunker down on the other side of the Ohio River in Cincinnati, where his name still carried some weight. He intended to fight his battle against Ford in an Ohio courtroom. Then things got weird.

On January 6, 2015, Chesley filed a lawsuit against Ford and the *Abbott* plaintiffs, to whom he referred as "Unknown Respondents." Incredibly, this meant that he was suing his own former clients. The lawsuit contained no information about how Chesley had been wronged, but again, he demanded the names of all the *Abbott* claimants, the exact amounts each had already received, and the amounts they were still owed. Again, this was a fool's errand. The value of assets recovered from GCM was a moving target, as newfound hidden assets were still trickling in and already acquired assets were being revalued. Further, the method of allocating these funds among the *Abbott* claimants had not yet been developed. Chesley was well aware of these difficulties.

The lawsuit was assigned to Judge Robert Ruehlman, whose prior rulings as judge for the Hamilton County Court of Common Pleas had variously been described as "brazen" and "shaky" by the Ohio Court of Appeals.[18] Much to Ford's shock, on the same day Chesley filed this lawsuit, Ruehlman issued, without a hearing, a restraining order against Ford, preventing her from "taking any action in the State of Ohio to enforce the Chesley judgment." As detailed in the Ohio Supreme Court's decision in *Ford v. Ruehlman,* the order prevented Ford from representing any persons known or unknown for the purpose of enforcing *Abbott* or from seeking to ascertain Chesley's assets. Further, Chesley was not required to post any security.

Having been stymied in Ruehlman's Ohio court, Ford took a new tack. Since the issue now involved plaintiffs in both Kentucky and Ohio, that created a diversity of jurisdiction. Ford sought to go around Judge Ruehlman by having enforcement of the *Abbott* judgment against Chesley remanded to a federal court. Ford also prevailed upon a federal court judge to dissolve Chesley's lawsuit on the basis of the extraordinary length of time that had passed without a hearing.

This game of courtroom chess became even more confusing when Chesley refiled his lawsuit, this time naming only six *Abbott* claimants as defendants. Because all six lived in Ohio, there was no overlap of federal jurisdictions. This ended the diversity issue and Ford's ability to have the lawsuit heard in federal court. To Ford's disgust, on April 6, 2015, her case was remanded back to Ruehlman. Ford promptly filed a motion to dismiss Ruehlman's restraining order against her, as well as Chesley's lawsuit against the six Ohioans. Ruehlman rebuffed Ford and accused her of "coming across the river" to take Chesley's assets, stating that "Chesley has a right to defend himself." The judge once again refused to require Chesley to post bond in the amount of the judgment awarded to the *Abbott* claimants. Ruehlman stated that such an order would be "kind of cruel."[19] Apparently, Chesley was able to beguile Ruehlman, just as he had Bamberger.

On the same day, April 6, that Chesley's attorney was arguing before Ruehlman to stymie Ford's federal court end run, an elderly woman made an unanticipated appearance at the hearing. Carol Boggs was one of the six Ohio residents now being sued by Chesley, and she was incensed. When she received her first *Guard* distribution, Boggs had been informed that she was "getting less than others because of her age, since she would have less time to enjoy it." Boggs was not going to be patronized again. After receiving her notice in the mail of the scheduled hearing, she drove three hours in her thirteen-year-old car, fearful that it might break down at any moment. In the Cincinnati courtroom, Boggs wept as she recounted her financial difficulties and the struggle to keep her house. She lamented, "This ex lawyer that keep my money has really put a hardship on me. I lost my husband and had to file for bankruptcy." Boggs could not understand why she had not been paid the $160,000 still owed her or why this unknown person was suing her. The attorney representing Chesley was without empathy. He blamed Boggs's plight on Ford because she wished to move the case to federal court. According to the *Courier-Journal,* despite being assured by Judge Ruehlman that "Mr. Chesley was not trying to take her money," Boggs was "not mollified."[20]

Her skepticism was well-founded, according to a later opinion by the Ohio Supreme Court. Despite assurances by Chesley's attorneys and Judge Ruehlman that she was not at risk, "this representation was patently false." Had Chesley prevailed, it "would have had a dramatic effect on how much money Ms. Boggs and the other creditors were able to recover and when."[21] Since Chesley had already been disbarred, he was no longer bound by ethical standards, such as the one that prohibits attorneys from working against the interests of their own clients—the very same clients who had enabled Chesley to grab $21.6 million in legal fees ostensibly for sitting through two days of mediation.

An indignant Ford was also in Ruehlman's courtroom that day and petitioned the judge to subpoena Chesley's tax returns from his accountant for the purpose of learning the extent of his assets. Not surprisingly, Ruehlman ruled that her request would be contrary to his earlier restraining order against Ford. Above all, Chesley was loath for Ford to know the extent of his personal wealth. Ford obviously wanted the entire $76 million, although Chesley likely had less than Ford supposed. Regardless, Ford would have to battle Chesley for every cent.

To keep Ford out of his pockets, Chesley adopted a strategy every bit as novel as his enterprise liability invention nearly forty years earlier. Chesley transferred $59 million of his personal cash to his former law firm, Waite, Schneider, Bayless and Chesley, of which Chesley was the sole stockholder. On April 15, 2013, the stock was transferred to Thomas Rehme, a former associate attorney at WSB&C, in the form of a trust. The trust, of course, had been set up for Chesley's benefit, but with sufficient strings attached to create the illusion that it was no longer his for Ford to take. This legal hurdle made Ford's effort to value Chesley's assets and acquire the portion necessary to satisfy the *Abbott* award even more difficult. The scheme was not without its drawbacks, however. Chesley had essentially removed his cash assets from his own direct control, and he would soon be facing a creditor even more daunting than Ford and her *Abbott* claimants.

For the first time in half a century, Chesley was beginning to feel a financial pinch, and desperate times lead to desperate actions. Though Chesley had legally forsaken any interest in his former law firm, he appeared in court to represent WSB&C for the purpose of collecting a legal fee owed to the firm but that Chesley likely intended to pocket himself, since the firm no longer existed. Presiding at this trial was US District Court judge James G. Carr, who was shocked when he learned that Chesley could no longer represent WSB&C because he had been disbarred. Thus, on paper at least, Chesley had no legitimate financial interest in collecting the fee, and he had no reason to be in the courtroom other than to acquire some money he could hide from Ford. An indignant Carr wrote in his decision: "I feel tricked and complicit, albeit unwittingly so, in chicanery, duplicity and mendacity." When Carr learned that he would be unable to claw back the payment to Chesley, he commented, "However unwillingly, I helped a bandit escape."[22]

Back in Kentucky, Judge Schrand ordered Chesley to appear in his courtroom, having had more than enough of the former lawyer's cat and mouse. When Chesley failed to show, Schrand issued a bench warrant for his arrest on the charge of contempt of court. In an interview with a reporter from the USA Today Network, Chesley described the arrest warrant as "a frightening experience . . . having practiced the Bar for 53 years."[23] In response, Chesley filed a lawsuit against the Hamilton County sheriff to prohibit the sheriff from serving the arrest warrant. Incredibly, this case was also assigned to Judge Ruehlman, who ruled, not unexpectedly, that because of its unusual nature, the warrant should not be enforced. Chesley's hold over Ruehlman remains a mystery, but Ruehlman shed some light on his reasoning when he opined that the self-regulated form of attorney discipline used in Kentucky was unjust and that the *Abbott* summary judgment was unfair.

Ruehlman's rulings were soon trashed after Ford's petitions for relief were taken up by the Ohio Supreme Court. It ruled that Ruehlman "had no legal authority to inject himself into the collection of a multi-million dollar settlement in Kentucky." In what was described as a "scathing opinion," on February 26, 2015, by a vote of five to one, all of Ruehlman's orders were terminated, most importantly, the restraining order against Ford.[24] The court also scoffed at the empty assurances Ruehlman had given to the distraught Mrs. Boggs.

As all this transpired, Chesley was liquidating the assets of his now-defunct law firm, presumably to ensconce them within the trust. In a motion to the Hamilton County Probate Court, Ford attempted to block that liquidation, calling the trust controlled by Thomas Rehme a sham. However, Judge Ralph Winkler allowed the liquidation to proceed with the assistance of Hamilton County attorney Joe Deters. Deters had once moonlighted for Chesley, earning $2 million over five years. Thus the liquidation proceeded. The sell-off included twenty-nine luxury cars, including four Bentleys, six Rolls-Royces, and three Aston Martins owned by the firm. Dozens of furnishings and housewares were also auctioned, ranging from $3,050 for an oriental rug to $10 for a Panasonic microwave oven and matching toaster. The ostensible purpose of the sell-off was what is known as an ABC action (assignment for the benefit of creditors) to pay off any debts of the law firm. But according to the later testimony of Steve Horner, WSB&C's accountant, the firm had no outstanding debt.

Indeed, the trust fund was essentially Chesley's personal piggybank. As such, Chesley would direct Horner to prepare checks made out to Chesley, and Rehme would sign them. From August 2014 through February 2016, Rehme signed $5.4 million worth of such checks. However, this did not account for the massive dissipation of Chesley's wealth after the creation of the trust. As of 2011, Chesley's personal assets totaled $83 million, with a whopping net worth of $63 million between Chesley and WSB&C combined. According to a May 2018 decision by the US Court of Appeals for the Sixth Circuit, which affirmed Chesley's disbarment, Chesley's assets had fallen to $19.3 million, with a combined net worth of just over $5 million. Among the schemes used to hide money from the *Abbott* claimants was a $1 million check written to "Cory Kumler," an entity owned and operated by Chesley's wife, federal judge Susan Dlott. Chesley also transferred his interest in a car dealership to Dlott.[25]

Even more unfortunate for the *Abbott* plaintiffs, before they could get their mitts on the remaining $5 million, they had to stand in line behind a creditor with unchallengeable priority: Uncle Sam. The IRS had filed $10 million worth of liens on Chesley's Indian Hill mansion for unpaid federal taxes. Apparently, Chesley's pockets were becoming flatter by the minute.

Still undeterred, Ford sought an injunction from the US District Court of Southern Ohio to freeze all of Chesley's assets, including those held in trust by Rehme. The hearings for the injunction were held on May 26 and July 26, 2016, but before the district court made its ruling, Chesley side-stepped once again. This time, he moved the assets of the trust to Eric Goering, an "assignee" for WSB&C whom Chesley had previously used to obtain appraisals of the firm's assets. In September 2016 Chesley informed the district court that Rehme no longer had the trust assets, thus rendering the court's injunction moot.[26]

In Ford's ongoing efforts to obtain a $76 million-plus settlement from Chesley, it appears that he will run out of assets before Ford runs out of time. In 2014 the Louisville law firm of Weber and Rose sued Chesley for unpaid legal fees.[27] As of December 2015, the Hamilton County recorder's office contained a notice of federal tax liens in the combined amount of $9.5 million for his home and another condominium property. In late 2016 Chesley and his wife placed their Indian Hill mansion up for sale. Bowing to compromise, Chesley conceded that he owed "$6 million to $7 million" but "disputed the notion he owes the $76 million" sought by Ford.[28]

In another headache for Ford, since Reeves levied fines in excess of $127 million on both Gallion and Cunningham, recovery is the responsibility of the federal government. Arguably, this makes Ford's efforts redundant, thus not entitling her to attorneys' fees. For her part, Ford is unbending, noting that the "court proceeding has been going on for 11 years" and that Chesley has "chosen to fight every step of the way."[29] This theater of the absurd continues to run.

On May 24, 2017, a group of protesters gathered outside the office of the

Hamilton County sheriff to demand Chesley's immediate arrest. The group was led by Connie Centers, and a photo that appeared in the *Cincinnati Enquirer* showed her holding a sign in one hand proclaiming "Victims' Lives Matter" while holding on to her walker with the other.[30] In May 2018 Ford and the *Abbott* claimants received heartening news when the US Court of Appeals denied Chesley's appeal of a restraining order against him, after he had shuffled trust funds from Rehme to Goering. The court noted that the "settlement has been lumbering its way through federal and state courts for two decades . . . there is a fundamental public interest in ending such abuse of the judicial system."[31] However, based on Chesley's aforementioned tax difficulties, even collecting the $6 million to $7 million he acknowledges may be impossible. As of this writing, Ford still has not squeezed the first nickel from Chesley.

Epilogue

AFTER LEAVING THE FDA, Michael Weintraub, the person who set this saga in motion, received an MD from the University of Pennsylvania. He works for the Lash Group; its mission is "delivering innovative products and services that drive quality and efficiency in pharmaceutical care."

Richard Wurtman continues to study brain function, in particular, neurotransmitters' relation to Alzheimer's disease, seasonal depression, and premenstrual syndrome. It has also been reported that he is helping to market a drink that greatly enhances athletic performance but carries the unfortunate side effect of causing its users to smell like rotting fish.

After the diet drug fiasco, American Home Products changed its corporate name back to Wyeth in 2002. Having learned little from this experience, Wyeth would soon after salt medical journals with some twenty-six ghost-written scientific papers extolling the efficacy of its hormone replacement drugs Premarin and Prempro, driving sales to nearly $2 billion annually. When it was later reported that use of the drugs posed a risk of developing certain cancers, sales plummeted, and by 2008, about 8,600 lawsuits had been filed by women claiming to have suffered illness as a result of taking the drugs.[1] In 2009 Wyeth was acquired by Pfizer.

The corruption of science by Big Pharma continues as well. A stunning example is Dr. Jose Baselga. As reported by the New York Times, Baselga, "a towering figure in the cancer world" and chief medical officer at the Sloan Kettering Cancer Center, put a "positive spin" on studies conducted by the pharmaceutical giant Roche, despite their disappointing results. Since 2014, Baselga had received more than $3 million from Roche, a fact he failed to disclose to *Lancet* and the *New England Journal of Medicine,* which published the studies bearing his name.[2]

David Helmers was permanently disbarred by the KBA Board of Governors in September 2011, by a vote of eleven to five. Among the grounds for his disbarment was that, during the second settlement distribution, he provided claimants with "a letter given to him by Chesley which he knew contained misleading information." Helmers received $30,000 for this task. In *KBA v. Helmers,* the Kentucky Supreme Court affirmed his disbarment, finding that Helmers misled claimants when he told them that "their settlement award offers came straight from AHP."[3] Following his disbarment, Helmers formed The Other Side Mediation Services. His marketing material boasts, "After a dozen years litigating cases, David brings his expertise in the courtroom to help clients quickly and finally settle and move on with their lives."

On October 27, 2011, the Kentucky Supreme Court affirmed the recommendation of the Judicial Conduct Commission to permanently disbar Jay Bamberger and ordered him to pay $18,700.84 to cover the costs of his disciplinary proceedings. Because of his forced resignation as a senior judge, Bamberger fell short of the required 600 days of service and was disqualified from receiving enhanced retirement benefits. Bamberger's lost pension benefit amounts to $45,167 per year, virtually the same amount he drew as a board member of FHL and later returned. Bamberger's attenuated annual pension income is $67,000.[4]

The complicated and thankless task of distributing the assets of the Fund for Healthy Living, which had grown to $23.5 million, was assigned to Special Judge Roger Crittenden, a former Franklin County circuit court judge who retired in 2006. When addressing a group of *Guard* claimants assembled in his courtroom, Crittenden remarked, "From your perception, you don't think that justice has been done. When this whole thing is over, you won't think it's been done either."[5]

Bill Gallion resides in the federal prison in Oakdale, Louisiana. As of 2020, he was seventy-seven years old. He is scheduled to be released on January 13, 2030.

Shirley Cunningham resides in the federal prison in Montgomery, Alabama. He is scheduled to be released on August 15, 2025. Among his fellow inmates is Kevin Trudeau, the charlatan who published numerous self-help guides containing mostly fiction and few facts. His most popular book was *Weight Loss Cure: What They Don't Want You to Know.*

Erstwhile illegal drug kingpin Seth Johnston resides in the federal prison in Butler, North Carolina. He is thirty-nine and is scheduled for release on July 11, 2030.

In May 2012 the US Court of Appeals for the Sixth Circuit upheld the convictions of Gallion and Cunningham. This decision came as a surprise to Stan Billingsley, senior editor of *LawReader,* who attended the oral arguments on January 17 of that year. Billingsley thought the improper testimony by Linda Gosnell would have been enough to warrant a new trial. Among the other arguments contained in the pleading for a new trial was Richard Robbins's disqualification as an expert witness. Judge Reeves had disqualified Robbins because, unlike Professor Howard Erichson, his work had not been published. Gallion's attorney Louis Sirkin argued that "police can provide expert testimony without first having been published in an academic journal." Rule 702 of the Federal Rules of Evidence states that experience alone *may* be enough to qualify someone as an expert witness. Unfortunately for Sirkin and Gallion, the standard for the review of evidence is that it should be done in the light "most favorable to the prosecution." With regard to the disqualification of Robbins, the appellate court concluded that "may does not mean must." The petition for a new trial was denied.[6]

In May 2015 the remaining 20 percent ownership of Curlin was auctioned to Canadian John Sikura for $6 million. The money was used to partially satisfy the *Abbott* claimants. In addition to his magnificent racing record, Curlin has proved to be a champion in the breeding shed, covering hundreds of mares at $150,000 each. Incredibly, had Gallion and Cunningham retained ownership of Curlin, their original $57,000 gamble would have paid dividends at least a thousand times over—an amount rivaling the $61 million in legitimate legal fees *Guard* would have generated.

In 2016, in response to the embarrassment caused by the criminal behavior of GCM, the Kentucky Bar Association overhauled its standards of ethics, the first reform in twenty-six years in the making. In addition to new rules about contingency agreements, the revised standards require attorneys to report misconduct by any attorney or judge. According to one of its authors, University of Kentucky law professor William Fortune, "It will create an expectation that members of the bar will intercede when a lawyer is engaged in serious misconduct."[7] The result of these reforms has been less than might be expected. In July 2018 Kentucky auditor Mike Harmon released a report that noted "a pervasive lack of accountability" in Kentucky's Administrative Office of the Courts. Among the findings was the leasing of office space from the son of a supreme court justice.[8]

After his not-guilty verdict and release from jail, Melbourne Mills has kept a very low profile. As he told a reporter, "he couldn't pay . . . back . . . his former clients even if ordered to by a Judge," noting that "23.6 million may seem like a lot, but it's not."[9] However, Mills did attempt to transfer half interest in a large real estate holding to longtime girlfriend Darlene La in April 2007, in consideration of his "love and affection." This transfer assets was denied in *Mills, La and JP Morgan Chase Bank v. Abbott Claimants* on June 24, 2011. Mills and La have been married since July 25, 2008. Today, they live tucked away in a cul-de-sac of smart houses and well-kept yards in Lexington's upscale Hartland subdivision. In conspicuous contrast to neighboring houses, its landscaping is untended and weed choked. The front door bears a sticker warning, "Beware of Dog." The porch is home to a folded metal bed frame, a brimming ashtray, sundry household detritus, and a room air conditioner balanced on a window. The driveway features two decades-old cars with lumber and ladders tossed underneath.

Mills believes the government continued its efforts to put him behind bars after his acquittal. One day, a FedEx package was left outside his door that contained a check for more than $19,000 made out to Benton Mills. The check and the accompanying paperwork indicated that it was payment from a California-based business for some cabinetry work. Mysteriously, though, the FedEx package had been sent from a Cincinnati address. Had Mills cashed the check, he would have been guilty of the crime of larceny, and he immediately suspected that this was the intention. Mills drove to the local FBI office and "returned" the check.[10]

Mills lives on a modest annuity he earned and saved apart from fees received from *Guard*—these are not attachable by bankruptcy courts. In 2013, after the Kentucky Supreme Court upheld the *Abbott* summary judgment in full against GCM, Mills stopped drinking.

On an encouraging note, in recent years there has been a relaxation of society's negative attitudes toward the overweight. Since 1997, the percentage of people who find the overweight less attractive has fallen from 55 percent to 24 percent. In 1990, 56 percent of Americans were trying to lose weight, but by 2017, that number had dropped to 49 percent. The once ubiquitous salad bars in fast-food restaurants have all but disappeared. Even more telling, the March 2017 issue of *Vogue* magazine featured a plus-size model on its cover. It is hoped that, in the future, people will no longer be tormented by society's unattainable standards of beauty.

Of the $127 million deposited in the bank accounts of GCM, Chesley, and the Fund for Healthy Living, tens of millions remain unrecovered. Where is the rest? Perhaps it is just as well that it stays hidden forever, as the accursed money has brought disgrace and ruin to nearly everyone who sought to possess it.

Timelines

The Honey Pot Shatters

1983	Fen-phen formula created by Michael Weintraub
1992	*Clinical Pharmacology and Therapeutics* publishes "Long-Term Weight Control Study"
1994	American Home Products (AHP) acquires rights to dexfen-fluramine (Redux)
Aug 1994	Heart abnormalities discovered in diet drug users in Fargo, ND
Nov 1994	AHP obtains FDA fast-track approval for Redux
Feb 1995	Fen-phen article appears in *Allure* magazine
1995–1996	Prescriptions of fen-phen in Kentucky skyrocket from 4,000 to 258,500 a week
1996	AHP launces major marketing campaign for fen-phen; Kentucky relaxes 120-day prescription limit for fen-phen
Aug 1997	Kip Petroff wins first major lawsuits against AHP
Sep 1997	AHP withdraws fen-phen and Redux from the market
Jul 1998	Separate Kentucky lawsuit created (*Guard v. AHP*)
May 1999	Judge Bamberger certifies *Guard* as a class action
Aug 1999	Certification of national class action (*Brown v. AHP*), which consolidates thousands of separate lawsuits
Jan 2000	Chesley inserts himself into *Guard* class action

| Aug 2000 | National class action settled for $5 billion for more than 650,000 plaintiffs |
| May 2001 | *Guard* settled for $200 million |

The Rise and Demise of Gallion, Cunningham, Mills (GCM), and Bamberger

May 2001	Bamberger decertifies *Guard* class action, leaving non-*Guard* opt-outs with nothing
May–Aug 2001	Helmers and team gather settlement signatures, $45 million distributed to 431 claimants, $155 million deposited in attorneys' personal accounts
Nov 2001	AHP sends final $50 million settlement payment, making $200 million total; attorneys' personal accounts: Gallion $54 million, Cunningham $48 million, Mills $17 million
Jan 2002	Gallion and Mills sued by their law partners Baker and Stuart, respectively; Gallion asks Phipps to destroy records
Feb 2002	Kentucky Bar Association (KBA) launches investigation
Feb 2002	Mills confronts Gallion at birthday party; same day, Chesley, Gallion, Cunningham, and Modlin meet with Bamberger, and Chesley brings up *Grinnell* and cy pres doctrine
Feb 2002	Second $28 million distribution approved; attorneys' fees of 49 percent of settlement approved; two days later, Gallion and Cunningham transfer $59 million to Florida bank
Jul 2002	Fund for Healthy Living (FHL) formed with $20 million of settlement funds
Jan 2003	Distributions are roughly as follows: claimants $73 million (two distributions), Gallion $30 million, Cunningham $22 million, Mills $24 million, Chesley $21 million, Lawrence $10 million, FHL $20 million
Dec 2003	Bamberger ends oversight of FHL, retires as circuit court judge to become senior judge
Jul 2004	Bamberger joins FHL board
Nov 2004	Ford files *Abbott* lawsuit

Dec 2006	Bamberger resigns from FHL board, two months after Judicial Conduct Commission launches investigation
Feb 2007	Cunningham's scheme exposed at Florida A&M
Jun 2007	GCM indicted
Aug 2007	Judge Bertelsman denies bail to GCM, sending them to Boone County jail
Mar 2008	Curlin wins Dubai World Cup
Jul 2008	Mills found not guilty; two days later, Bertelsman declares mistrial for Gallion and Cunningham, sending them back to jail
Oct 2008	Kentucky Supreme Court permanently disbars Gallion and Cunningham
Apr 2009	Gallion and Cunningham convicted in second trial
Aug 2009	Gallion and Cunningham sentenced to thirty and twenty-five years, respectively
Jan 2010	Mills disbarred
Sep 2011	Helmers disbarred
Oct 2011	Bamberger disbarred
Aug 2013	KBA president Barbara Bonar publicly reprimanded for actions related to dispute with Chesley

Chesley Agonistes

Nov 2004	Angela Ford files *Abbott* lawsuit against GCM and Chesley on behalf of 382 former *Guard* plaintiffs
Mar 2006	Partial summary judgment in *Abbott* for $42 million; Ford begins distribution of *Abbott* proceeds, including her legal fees
Feb 2011	*Abbott* decision reversed based on Feinberg affidavit
Feb 2011	KBA recommends Chesley be permanently disbarred
Jun 2011	Judge Reeves demands accounting of *Abbott* funds by Ford; Ford transfers $3.6 million to Seth Johnston, which he misuses to indirectly finance synthetic marijuana operation
Nov 2011	KBA general counsel Linda Gosnell fired

Feb 2013	Seth Johnston indicted for wire fraud, tax fraud, and distribution of synthetic marijuana
Mar 2013	Chesley disbarred in Kentucky; gives up Ohio license
Apr 2013	Chesley liquidates law firm assets and moves $59 million to a trust
Aug 2013	Kentucky Supreme Court upholds *Abbott*
Oct 2014	Judge Wehr orders Chesley to pay $42 million *Abbott* judgment
Nov 2014	Seth Johnston found guilty and sentenced to twenty years
2015	Chesley's claimed assets diminish from $63 million (in 2012) to $19 million
Jan 2015	Chesley sues former clients to stop collection; in Ohio, Judge Ruehlman issues restraining order against Ford
Feb 2015	Ford seeks to move *Abbott* collection to federal court (the amount is up to $74 million); Ohio Supreme Court reverses Ruehlman's restraining order
Apr 2015	Chesley refiles lawsuit suing six former clients from Ohio to defeat federal jurisdiction
Nov 2015	Judge Wehr issues arrest warrant for Chesley for failure to appear
Jan 2016	Chesley sues Ford for information on collection and to delay court order
Jul 2016	$10 million IRS tax lien filed against Chesley's assets
2017	Chesley begins liquidating law firm assets and transfers personal wealth to two trusts
Apr 2017	Ford sues to halt liquidation of Chesley's law firm assets
Nov 2017	Kentucky Supreme Court denies Ford's lawsuit against Johnston
Mar 2018	US Court of Appeals denies Chesley's appeal of decision to end restraining order against Ford

Notes

Introduction

1. Daniel Kahneman and Angus Deaton, "High Income Improves Evaluation of Life but Not Emotional Well-being," Center for Health and Well-being, Princeton University, Princeton, NJ, August 4, 2010.

2. Richard Easterlin, "Will Raising the Incomes of All Increase the Happiness of All," *Journal of Economic Behavior and Organization* 27, no. 1 (June 1995): 35–48.

3. Larry Welborn, "The Largest Bank Heist in America Targets Nixon's Millions," *Orange County (CA) Register,* November 13, 2009.

4. Phil Galewitz, "The Pharmacies Thriving in Kentucky's Opioid-Stricken Towns," *Atlantic,* February 7, 2017.

5. Heather Chapman, "The More Opioids Doctors Prescribe, the More Money They Make from Pharmaceutical Companies," *Kentucky Health News,* March 14, 2018.

6. Bill Estep, "Rural Clinics Allege Firms 'Engineered' Drug Crisis for Profit," *Lexington Herald-Leader,* March 24, 2018.

7. Gabrielle Glaser, "The Irrationality of Alcoholics Anonymous," *Atlantic,* April 2015.

8. Christopher Moraff, "Why Drug Rehab Is Outdated, Expensive and Deadly," *Daily Beast,* May 9, 2016.

9. Glaser, "Irrationality of Alcoholics Anonymous."

10. National Center on Addiction and Substance Abuse Disorder, "Addiction a Preventable and Treatable Disease," Annual Report, 2012.

11. Marketdata Enterprises, "$35 Billion U.S. Addiction Rehab Industry Poised for Growth," August 5, 2014.

12. Peter Haden, "How Recovering Drug Addicts Are Getting Bought and Sold by Corrupt Treatment Centers," *Miami Herald,* August 22, 2017.

13. US House of Representatives, Committee on Energy and Commerce, "Examining Concerns of Patient Brokering and Addiction Treatment Fraud," 115th Cong. (2017), https://energycommerce.house.gov/sites/democrats.energycommerce.house.gov/files/documents/Testimony-Tieman-OI-Hrg-on-Examining-Concerns-of-Patient-Brokering-and-Addiction-Treatment-Fraud-2017-12-12.pdf.

14. IRS Form 990, Caron of Florida Inc., July 1, 2014–June 30, 2015.

15. KBA v. Stanley M. Chesley, KBA File 13785, KBA's Response Brief to the Board of Governors, May 10, 2011 (hereafter cited as *KBA v. Chesley*).

16. KBA v. Joseph F. Bamberger, Opinion and Order, No. 2011-SC-000378-KB, October 27, 2011.

17. United States of America v. William Gallion, Shirley A. Cunningham, Melbourne Mills Jr., Docket No. CR 07-39 (ED of KY 2006), May 30, 2008, p. 127 (hereafter cited as *USA v. Gallion et al.*).

18. *KBA v. Chesley*, Report of the Trial Commissioner, February 22, 2011.

1. A Prescription for Disaster

1. Alicia Mundy, *Dispensing with the Truth: The Victims, the Drug Companies, and the Dramatic Story behind the Battle over Fen-Phen* (New York: St. Martin's Press, 2001), 41.

2. Sally Squires, "Newly Approved Diet Drug Promises to Help Millions of Obese Americans, but It Is No Magic Bullet," *Washington Post*, May 7, 1996.

3. Patrice Boussel, *History of Pharmacy and the Pharmaceutical Industry* (Paris: Asklepios Press, 1983).

4. Marian Burros, "Former Surgeon General Begins Push for Americans to Slim Down," *New York Times*, December 5, 1994.

5. Centers for Disease Control and Prevention, www.cdc.gov/nchs/hus/contents2018.htm#table_21.

6. Edward Wyatt, "Weight Loss Companies Charged with Fraud," *New York Times*, January 7, 2014.

7. Kurt Anderson, *Fantasyland* (New York: Random House, 2018).

8. Bobby Lewis, "The Eight Things Media Should Know about the 'Scientifically Dubious' Dr. Oz," *Media Matters*, September 14, 2016.

9. Amber Phillips, "That Time Congress Railed against Dr. Oz for His 'Miracle' Diet Pills," *Washington Post*, September 15, 2016.

10. Lindsay Goldwert, "Children as Young as 5 Suffer from Eating Disorders: 81% of Ten-Year Olds Are Afraid of Being Fat," *New York Daily News*, August 3, 2011.

11. Christina Biesemeier and Susan Cummings, "Ethics Opinion: Weight Loss Products and Medications," *Journal of the American Dietetic Association* 108, no. 12 (2008): 2109–13.

12. Carole Sugarman, "Feeling Fat? Diet Pills Are Back and Everyone Has Something to Say about Them," *Washington Post,* January 3, 1996.

13. "Obesity Declared a Disease," *Science,* March 1, 1985.

14. Marian Burros, "Despite Awareness of Risks, More in US Are Getting Fat," *New York Times,* July 17, 1994.

15. Sylvia Tara, *The Secret Life of Fat: The Science behind the Body's Least Understood Organ and What It Means for You* (New York: W. W. Norton, 2016), 60–62.

16. "Obesity Paradox Evidence: Obese Patients Fare Better than Lean Patients When Hospitalized for Acute Heart Failure," *Science Daily,* January 9, 1997.

17. Katherine M. Flegal, "Association of All-Cause Mortality with Overweight and Obesity Using Standard Body Mass Index Categories: A Systemic Review and Meta Analysis," *Journal of the American Medical Association,* January 2, 2013.

18. Evelyn B. Kelly, *Obesity,* 2nd ed. (Santa Barbara, CA: Greenwood, 2018), 173.

19. Robert Pool, *Fat: Fighting the Obesity Epidemic* (New York: Oxford University Press, 2001), 73.

20. Squires, "Newly Approved Diet Drug Promises to Help Millions."

21. Kitta MacPherson and Edward R. Silverman, "Hot New Diet Pill Redux Facing Heavy Challenges," *Cleveland Plain Dealer,* March 4, 1997.

22. Mundy, *Dispensing with the Truth,* 79–80.

23. Carl Elliott, "Pharma Goes to the Laundry," *Hastings Center Report,* September–October 2004.

24. Judith Wurtman and Richard Wurtman, "Carbohydrates and Depression," *Scientific American,* January 1989, 68–75.

2. Cashing In

1. Alicia Mundy, *Dispensing with the Truth: The Victims, the Drug Companies, and the Dramatic Story behind the Battle over Fen-Phen* (New York: St. Martin's Press, 2001), 52–54.

2. Michael D. Lemonick, "The New Miracle Drug?" *Time,* September 23, 1996.

3. Howard Brody, *Hooked: Ethics, the Medical Profession, and the Pharmaceutical Industry* (Lanham, MD: Rowman & Littlefield, 2008), 274.

4. Sandra G. Boodman, "Diet Drug Danger," *Washington Post,* July 15, 1997.

5. Laura Johannes and Steve Stecklow, "Withdrawal of Redux Shows Drug Regulators' Predicament," *Wall Street Journal,* September 16, 1997.

6. Mundy, *Dispensing with the Truth,* 54.

7. Joseph C. Goulden, *The Money Lawyers* (New York: St. Martin's Press, 2014), 193.

8. Mundy, *Dispensing with the Truth,* 73.

9. Bill Block, "FDA Knew about the Dangers of Redux, but Approved It Anyway," *Life Enhancement Magazine,* December 1997.

Notes

10. Block, "FDA Knew about the Dangers of Redux."

11. Jonathan Bor, "Evidence of Pill Risk Mounts," *Baltimore Sun,* July 22, 1997.

12. Laura Johannes and David Cloud, "FDA Official's Enthusiastic Advice on Diet Pills Stirs Ethical Concerns," *Wall Street Journal,* September 27, 1999.

13. Mundy, *Dispensing with the Truth,* 163.

14. Carole Sugarman, "Feeling Fat? Diet Pills Are Back and Everyone Has Something to Say about Them," *Washington Post,* January 3, 1996.

15. Jim Warren and Valerie Honeycutt, "The Fen-Phenomenon," *Lexington Herald-Leader,* November 17, 1996.

16. Partnership for a Fit Kentucky, "Shaping Kentucky's Future: Policies to Reduce Obesity," 2009.

17. Gideon Gill, "Diet Doctor's License Suspended," *Louisville Courier-Journal,* May 14, 2003.

18. Valerie Honeycutt and Jim Warren, "Sales of Diet Drugs Triple in a Year," *Lexington Herald-Leader,* November 24, 1997.

19. Warren and Honeycutt, "The Fen-Phenomenon."

20. Honeycutt and Warren, "Sales of Diet Drugs Triple in a Year."

21. Valerie Honeycutt and Jim Warren, "New Diet Drug Rules Adopted," *Lexington Herald-Leader,* December 19, 1996.

22. Valerie Honeycutt and Jim Warren, "State Wants Tougher Diet Pill Regulations," *Lexington Herald-Leader,* November 9, 1996.

23. Theodore K. Kyle et al., "Regarding Obesity as a Disease," *Endocrinology and Metabolism Clinics in America,* September 1, 2017.

24. Paul Baldwin, "Diet Pill Combination May Present Heart Risks," *Louisville Courier-Journal,* July 9, 1997.

25. Honeycutt and Warren, "New Diet Drug Rules Adopted."

26. Author's conversation with a former Rite Aid pharmacist.

27. Karen Merk, "Prescriptions for Diet-Drugs Easy to Obtain," *Louisville Courier-Journal,* October 22, 1996.

28. John Hendren, "Woman's Death Raises Questions about Diet Drug 'Cocktail,'" Associated Press, May 7, 1997.

29. Lucian Abenhaim et al., "Appetite Suppressant Drugs and the Risk of Primary Pulmonary Hypertension," *New England Journal of Medicine* 335 (August 1996): 609–16.

30. Kitta MacPherson and Edward R. Silverman, "Hot New Diet Pill Redux Facing Heavy Challenges," *Cleveland Plain Dealer,* March 4, 1997.

31. Mundy, *Dispensing with the Truth,* 108.

32. MacPherson and Silverman, "Hot New Diet Pill Redux Facing Heavy Challenges."

3. It Hits the Fan

1. Kathleen Fockelmann, "Drug Debacle," *Science News,* October 18, 1997.

2. Joseph C. Goulden, *The Money Lawyers* (New York: St. Martin's Press, 2014), 180.

3. "The Problems with Fen-Phen: An Outdated Label May Have Led to a Toxic Combination of Diet Drugs," *MIT News,* August 28, 1997.

4. "Psychiatric Symptoms May Signal Brain Damage from Diet Pills," *Science Daily,* August 28, 1997.

5. H. M. Connolly, "Valvular Heart Disease Associated with Fenfluramine and Phentermine," *New England Journal of Medicine,* August 28, 1997.

6. Tom Humphrey, "Fen-Phen Bill OK'd, Sent to Governor," *Knoxville (TN) News-Sentinel,* May 15, 1997.

7. "FDA Steps up Campaign to Discourage Off-Label 'Fen-Phen' Use with Public Hea lth Advisory," *Pink Sheet,* July 14, 1997.

8. Alicia Mundy, *Dispensing with the Truth: The Victims, the Drug Companies, and the Dramatic Story behind the Battle over Fen-Phen* (New York: St. Martin's Press, 2001), 115.

9. Mundy, *Dispensing with the Truth,* 110.

10. "Study: No Damage from Diet Drug," *USA Today,* April 1, 1998.

11. Mundy, *Dispensing with the Truth,* 181.

12. "The $22 Billion Gold Rush," *Forbes,* March 24, 2008.

13. Goulden, *Money Lawyers,* 108–9.

4. The Master

1. Chuck Martin, "Stan Chesley: The Litigator Champion for the Little Guy," *Cincinnati Enquirer,* May 28, 2006.

2. Terry Flynn, "The Fire that Still Rages," *Cincinnati Enquirer,* four-part series, May 1997.

3. Flynn, "Fire that Still Rages."

4. Flynn, "Fire that Still Rages."

5. Ben L. Kaufman, "Litigation Bulldozed Traditional Legal Routes," *Cincinnati Enquirer,* October 16, 2016.

6. Debra Cassens Weiss, "How a Kentucky Solo Exposed the Fen-Phen Lawyers," *ABA Journal,* September 8, 2009.

7. Lucy May, "Stan Chesley: How a Single Case Dethroned the 'Prince of Torts,'" *WCPC Digital,* May 29, 2013.

8. Martin, "Stan Chesley."

9. Jack C. Fisher, "Silicone on Trial: Breast Implants and the Politics of Risk," *Plastic and Reconstructive Journal of the American Society of Plastic Surgeons* 137 (February 2016): 746.

10. Institute of Medicine, *Information for Women about the Safety of Silicone Breast Implants* (Washington, DC: National Academies Press, 2000).

11. Ted Frank, "Fen-Phen Zen," American Enterprise Institute, April 4, 2007.

12. Sergey Ushynskyi, "Pan-Am Flight 103 Investigation and Lessons Learned," *Aviation* 13, no. 3 (2009): 78–86.

13. Agis Salpukas, "Bankruptcy Petition Is Filed by Pan-Am to Get New Loans," *New York Times,* January 9, 1991.

14. Peter Pringle, *Cornered: Big Tobacco at the Bar of Justice* (New York: Henry Holt, 2014), 287.

15. Paul Barton, "Debate Heats up over Tobacco Settlement," *Cincinnati Enquirer,* June 7, 1998.

16. Robert A. Levy, *Shake Down: How Corporations, Government and Trial Lawyers Abuse the Judicial Process* (Washington, DC: Cato Institute, 2004), 120.

17. Martin, "Stan Chesley."

18. Matt Leingang, "Chesleys Buy Big House," *Cincinnati Enquirer,* September 13, 2004.

19. Howard Wilkinson, "As a Major Fund-raiser, Chesley among the Elite," *Cincinnati Enquirer,* August 17, 2000.

20. David Wells, "Leave the Dogs out of It," *Cincinnati Enquirer,* May 2, 2003.

21. Wells, "Leave the Dogs out of It."

22. Profiles of Cunningham, Chesley, Mills, and Gallion, *LawReader,* December 31, 2016.

23. Pringle, *Cornered,* 45.

24. Lucy May, "Chesley Inc: Famed Local Attorney Got Rich by Breaking Ground," *Cincinnati Business Courier,* December 6, 2004.

25. *KBA v. Chesley,* Report of the Trial Commissioner, February 22, 2011, p. 6.

5. The Troika

1. *USA v. Gallion et al.,* June 6, 2008, p. 107.

2. Author's interviews with Melbourne Mills, August and September 2018.

3. Jim Warren and Valerie Honeycutt, "Attorneys Prepare to File Suits over Fen-Phen, Redux," *Lexington Herald-Leader,* October 3, 1997.

4. Mills interviews.

5. Annette McGee Cunningham, interview by Terry L. Birdwhistell, December 1, 1995, University of Kentucky Oral History Project, Louie B. Nunn Center for Oral History, University of Kentucky Libraries.

6. Author's conversation with a coworker of Cunningham's second wife.

6. Brothers in Arms

1. United States v. Shirley Cunningham and William Gallion, Docket No. CR 07-39, US Court of Appeals for the Sixth Circuit, May 1, 2012, p. 3.

2. *KBA v. Chesley,* February 22, 2011, p. 6.

3. *KBA v. Chesley,* p. 3.

4. *USA v. Gallion et al.,* June 6, 2008, p. 166.

5. *USA v. Gallion et al.,* May 18, 2008, p. 79.

6. After his retirement, Judge Billingsley would go on to publish *LawReader,* an online review and commentary on the Kentucky courts.

7. Kenton County Public Parks v. Modlin, Court of Appeals of Kentucky, April 7, 1995.

8. Andrew Wolfson, "KY Judge Resigns after Public Reprimand," *Louisville Courier-Journal,* February 28, 2006.

9. Shelia Brown et al. v. American Home Products, Civil Action No. 99-20593, ED of PA, 1999.

10. David J. Morrow, "Fen-Phen Maker to Pay Billions in Settlement of Diet-Injury Cases," *New York Times,* October 8, 1999.

11. Kristen Davis, "Lawyer Balks at Fen-Phen Settlement," *New York Post,* September 20, 1999.

12. United States v. Shirley A. Cunningham and William J. Gallion Jr., No. 09-5987/5998, ED of KY, May 1, 2012, pp. 5–7.

13. *KBA v. Chesley,* March 21, 2013.

14. Andrew Wolfson, "Trial: Chesley Testifies in Diet-Drug Lawyers' Case," *Louisville Courier-Journal,* June 17, 2008.

15. Author's interviews with Melbourne Mills, August and September 2018.

16. Jim Hanna, "Strange Secrets," *Cincinnati Enquirer,* November 11, 2007.

17. Howard M. Erichson, "Trouble with All-or-Nothing Settlements," *Kansas Law Review* 58 (2009–2010): 979.

18. Wood v. Wyeth-Ayerst Laboratories, 82 S.W. 3d 849, Supreme Court of Kentucky, 2002.

19. *USA v. Gallion et al.,* June 6, 2008, p. 134.

20. Lucy May, "Chesley Inc: Famed Local Attorney Got Rich by Breaking Ground," *Cincinnati Business Courier,* December 6, 2004.

7. A Very Strange Thing

1. Brief for Stanley M. Chesley on Appeal to the Board of Governors, KBA File 13785, Supreme Court of Kentucky, p. 58.

2. *USA v. Gallion et al.,* May 15, 2008, pp. 83–84.

3. *KBA v. Chesley,* Report of the Trial Commissioner, February 22, 2011, p. 5.

4. Author's interviews with Melbourne Mills, August and September 2018.

5. *KBA v. Chesley,* Report of the Trial Commissioner, February 22, 2011, p. 9.

8. Lowering the Bar

1. Bonar v. Kentucky Bar Association, 000335 KB, Supreme Court of Kentucky, 2013.

2. Debra Cassens Weiss, "Ex-Ky Bar President Is Reprimanded for 'Brazen' Misrepresentations in Office, Conflict in Priest Case," *ABA Journal,* September 3, 2013.

3. Jim Hanna, "Abuse Suit Now a Class Action," *Cincinnati Enquirer,* October 10, 2003.

4. Chrystal Hayden, "Diocese Request Angers Judge," *Kentucky Post,* November 22, 2003.

5. Andrew Wolfson, "Lawyers Clash in Dispute over Fees," *Louisville Courier-Journal,* May 10, 2007.

6. Andrew Wolfson, "Covington Lawyer Loses Fee Dispute Case," *Louisville Courier-Journal,* May 12, 2007.

7. *Bonar v. KBA.*

8. "A Lowered Bar," editorial, *Louisville Courier-Journal,* October 4, 2016.

9. Claire Galofaro, "Attorney Made Millions off Disability Claims; Former Clients on the Brink after Government Yanks Funds," *Lexington Herald-Leader,* December 29, 2016.

10. Eleanor Klibanoff, "Eric Conn: Kentucky's Biggest Con Man," National Public Radio, July 14, 2017.

9. The Deal

1. Linda A. Gosnell and Cary B. Howard, Brief to the Board of Governors of the Kentucky Bar Association, "Counter Statement of Points and Authorities," n.d., p. 15.

2. *KBA v. Chesley,* Report of the Trial Commissioner, February 22, 2011.

3. *KBA v. Chesley,* KBA's Response Brief to the Board of Governors, May 10, 2011.

4. Andrew Wolfson, "3 Lawyers Kept Millions from Drug's Victims," *Louisville Courier-Journal,* May 29, 2006.

5. Abbott et al. v. Stanley Chesley, William Gallion, Shirley Cunningham, Melbourne Mills and the Kentucky Fund for Healthy Living, Fayette County Circuit Court, Case #04-ci-5247, December 30, 2004.

6. Author's interviews with Melbourne Mills, August and September 2018.

7. *USA v. Gallion et al.,* May 14, 2008, p. 164.

8. Abel v. Austin, #2009-CA-000465-MR, Court of Appeals of Kentucky, May 28, 2010.

9. *USA v. Gallion et al.,* June 12, 2008, p. 149.

10. Andrew Wolfson, "Disbarred Kentucky Lawyers Follow Varied Paths," *Louisville Courier-Journal,* January 18, 2014.

11. *KBA v. Chesley,* Counter Statement of Relevant Facts and Proceedings by Judge William Graham, Trial Commissioner, p. 21.

12. *KBA v. Chesley,* Counter Statement of Relevant Facts and Proceedings, p. 22.

13. *USA v. Gallion et al.,* May 21, 2008, p. 10.

14. *USA v. Gallion et al.,* June 6, 2008, p. 21.

15. *USA v. Gallion et al.,* May 23, 2008, p. 95.

16. *USA v. Gallion et al.,* June 18, 2008, p. 113.

17. *Abbott et al. v. Chesley et al.*

18. Hershel Jick et al., "A Population-Based Study of Appetite Suppressant Drugs and the Risk of Cardio Valve Regurgitation," *New England Journal of Medicine,* September 10, 1998.

19. Gina Kolata, "Latest Study Unable to Link Diet Drugs to Heart Damage," *New York Times,* October 1, 1999.

20. Social Issues Research Center, "Another Panic Incited by Bad Science," June 5, 2020.

21. Elisabeth Pain, "Questioning the Validity of Neuroscience Results," *Science,* April 30, 2013.

10. Judge Not

1. Patrick Crowley, "Kentucky's Busiest Judge Just Got Busier," *Cincinnati Enquirer,* July 8, 2002.

2. *USA v. Gallion et al.,* June 6, 2008, p. 22.

3. *USA v. Gallion et al.,* May 30, 2008, p. 250.

11. Bad Times, Good Times

1. Sawyer v. Mills, Supreme Court of Kentucky, August 8, 2009.

2. Andrew Wolfson, "A Breach of Duty: Fen-Phen Case Fees Poured into Racehorses," *Louisville Courier-Journal,* May 30, 2006.

3. Jim Squires, *Headless Horsemen: A Tale of Chemical Colts, Subprime Sales Agents and the Last Kentucky Derby on Steroids* (New York: Times Books, 2009), 122.

4. Andrew Wolfson, "Ky. Lawyer's Florida A&M Pay 'Not Earned,'" *Louisville Courier-Journal,* February 8, 2007.

5. David Damron, "Ousted Dean Says He's Taking the Fall," *Orlando Sentinel,* June 9, 2005.

6. Julie Kay, "Saving the School," *ABA Journal,* January 2, 2010.

7. Ron Matus and Shannon Colaveccio-Van Sickler, "Optimism for FAMU Law School Fades Amid Problems," *Tampa Bay Times,* August 22, 2007.

12. The Alligator

1. Nomination to the Board of Trustees of the University of the Louisville, Alumni Fellow Award, April 14, 2011.

2. Michael Jennings, "2 Social Workers Are Sued in Beating Death of Toddler," *Louisville Courier-Journal,* September 10, 1994.

3. Debra Cassens Weiss, "How a Kentucky Solo Exposed the Fen-Phen Lawyers," *ABA Journal,* September 8, 2009.

4. Andrew Wolfson, "Details Emerge in Dispute over Use of Leftover Settlement Money," *Louisville Courier-Journal,* March 14, 2005.

5. Associated Press, "Fen-Phen Plaintiffs Question Results," *Louisville Courier-Journal,* January 3, 2005.

6. Abbott v. Stanley Chesley, William Gallion, Shirley Cunningham, Melbourne Mills and the Kentucky Fund for Healthy Living, No. 2010-CA-000147-MR, 2012.

7. *USA v. Gallion et al.,* May 23, 2008, pp. 96–97.

8. Andrew Wolfson, "Attorney Denies Wrongdoing," *Louisville Courier-Journal,* February 11, 2007.

9. Andrew Wolfson, "Witness Praises Lawyers' Management of Nonprofit Funds," *Louisville Courier-Journal,* June 6, 2008.

10. Shirley Cunningham et al. v. Abbott et al., Appeal and Cross Appeal, Boone County Circuit Court, No. 2007-CA-000197-MR, 2001.

11. *USA v. Gallion et al.,* May 19, 2008, p. 11.

12. Andrew Wolfson, "Kentucky Judge Resigns after Public Reprimand," *Louisville Courier-Journal,* February 28, 2006.

13. KBA v. Joseph F. Bamberger, No. 2011-SC-000378-KB, October 27, 2011.

14. *KBA v. Bamberger,* Opinion and Order, October 27, 2011.

15. Fernando Alfonso III, "Panel that Investigates Judges Gets Fewer Resources in Kentucky than Nearby States," *Lexington Herald-Leader,* April 20, 2017.

16. Alfonso, "Panel that Investigates Judges Gets Fewer Resources in Kentucky."

17. Linda B. Blackford, "Two Well-Connected Firms Profit," *Lexington Herald-Leader,* September 7, 2008.

18. Edwin Hardin Sutherland, *White Collar Crime: The Uncut Version* (New Haven, CT: Yale University Press, 1983).

19. *USA v. Gallion et al.,* May 30, 2008, p. 46.

20. *USA v. Gallion et al.,* June 12, 2008, p. 149.

21. *USA v. Gallion et al.,* May 30, 2008, pp. 82–83.

22. Andrew Wolfson, "Prosecution's Ethics Challenged in Diet-Drug Case," *Louisville Courier-Journal,* October 10, 2007.

13. The Crucible

1. Author's interviews with Melbourne Mills, August and September 2018.

2. Beth Musgrave, "Judge Sends 3 Fen-Phen Lawyers off to Jail," *Lexington Herald-Leader,* August 11, 2007.

3. *USA v. Gallion et al.,* June 12, 2008, p. 166.

4. *USA v. Gallion et al.,* May 13, 2008, pp. 3–4.

5. Andrew Wolfson, "Lawyer Won't Testify in Fen-Phen Case," *Louisville Courier-Journal,* April 8, 2008.

6. Associated Press, "Diet Drug Judge Threatens Contempt," June 11, 2008.

7. *USA v. Gallion et al.,* May 30, 2008, pp. 84–85.

8. *USA v. Gallion et al.,* May 23, 2008 p. 68.

9. *USA v. Gallion et al.,* June 12, 2008 p. 41.

10. Andrew Wolfson, "Lawyer Defends Payment in Diet-Drug Case," *Louisville Courier-Journal,* June 12, 2008.

11. Andrew Wolfson, "Diet Drug Lawyer Defends Pay," *Louisville Courier-Journal,* June 13, 2008.

12. *USA v. Gallion et al.,* June 13, 2008, pp. 81–82.

13. Andrew Wolfson, "Defendant Wants Judge Out," *Louisville Courier-Journal,* April 8, 2008.

14. Mills interviews.

15. Andrew Wolfson, "Diet-Drug Lawyers Went Too Far Jury Told," *Louisville Courier-Journal,* June 17, 2008.

16. *USA v. Gallion et al.,* June 16, 2008, p. 143.

17. Jason Riley, "Chesley Rakes Drug Trio," *Louisville Courier-Journal,* June 18, 2008.

18. KBA v. Chesley, 393 S.W. 3d 584 (Ky 2013).

19. *USA v. Gallion et al.,* June 13, 2008, pp. 117–18.

20. *USA v. Gallion et al.,* June 17, 2008, pp. 120–21.

21. *USA v. Gallion et al.,* June 11, 2008, p. 63.

22. Andrew Wolfson, "Jury: Diet Drug Case Awaits Verdict," *Louisville Courier-Journal,* June 24, 2008.

23. *USA v. Gallion et al.,* June 13, 2008, p. 3.

24. USA v. Shirley A. Cunningham and William Gallion, ED of KY, Transcript of Sentencing, August 17–18, 2009.

25. Andrew Wolfson, "Mills, 1 of 3 Lawyers Acquitted in Fraud Case," *Louisville Courier-Journal,* July 2, 2008.

26. Jason Bailey and Andrew Wolfson, "Mistrial: Diet Jury Deadlocks," *Louisville Courier-Journal,* July 4, 2008.

27. Jason Riley and Andrew Wolfson, "Deadlock by Diet-Drug Jury Brings Mistrial," *Louisville Courier-Journal,* July 4, 2008.

28. Bailey and Wolfson, "Mistrial: Diet Jury Deadlocks."

14. The Second Bite

1. Andrew Wolfson, "Diet-Drug Case Judge Steps Aside," *Louisville Courier-Journal,* July 8, 2008.

2. Andrew Wolfson, "Bail: Judge Sets Restrictions on Release," *Louisville Courier-Journal,* August 23, 2008.

3. Jim Hanna, "Judge Moves Diet-Drug Retrial," *Cincinnati Enquirer,* July 17, 2008.

4. Adam Liptak, "Fraud Inquiry Looks at Lawyers in Diet-Drug Case," *New York Times,* March 24, 2007.

5. "Supreme Court Hears Arguments in Case against Fen-Phen Lawyers," *Wave 3 News,* June 30, 2006.

6. Daniel Fisher, "Super Lawyer Stanley Chesley Faces Reckoning Tuesday," *Forbes,* June 9, 2011.

7. *KBA v. Chesley,* Motion to Abate Proceedings Pending Resolution of Pending Civil Litigations, and Reservation of Federal Claims, April 29, 2011, p. 5.

8. Associated Press, "Lawyers Found Guilty of Diet Drug Scam," April 3, 2009.

9. *USA v. Gallion et al.,* June 11, 2008, pp. 154–56.

10. USA v. Shirley A. Cunningham and William Gallion, ED of KY, Transcript of Sentencing before the Honorable Danny C. Reeves, August 17–18, 2009.

11. *USA v. Cunningham and Gallion,* Transcript of Sentencing, August 17–18, 2009.

12. *USA v. Cunningham and Gallion,* Transcript of Sentencing, August 17–18, 2009.

13. *USA v. Cunningham and Gallion,* Transcript of Sentencing, August 17–18, 2009.

14. Liptak, "Fraud Inquiry Looks at Lawyers in Diet-Drug Case."

15. *USA v. Cunningham and Gallion,* Transcript of Sentencing, August 17–18, 2009.

16. *USA v. Cunningham and Gallion,* Transcript of Sentencing, August 17–18, 2009.

17. Stan Billingsley, "LawReader Attends 6th Circuit Oral Arguments in Gallion/Cuningham Appeal Case," *LawReader,* January 17, 2012.

15. Cornered

1. Andrew Ross Sorkin, "Dear President-Elect Trump: Here's How to Fix Your Conflict-of-Interest Problem," *New York Times,* November 28, 2016.

2. Shirley A. Cunningham et al. v. Mildred Abbott et al., 2011 WL 336459 (Ky. App).

3. *USA v. Gallion et al.,* June 17, 2008, p. 29.

4. *KBA v. Chesley,* Report of the Trial Commissioner, February 22, 2011.

5. *KBA v. Chesley,* Report of the Trial Commissioner, February 22, 2011.

6. *KBA v. Chesley,* KBA's Response Brief to the Board of Governors, May 10, 2011.

7. *KBA v. Chesley,* Report of the Trial Commissioner, February 22, 2011, p. 27.

8. Dan Horn, "Chesley off Case for Ohio," *Cincinnati Enquirer,* June 17, 2011.

9. Kimball Perry, "Disgraced Lawyer Decides to Retire, Not Fight," *Cincinnati Enquirer,* April 19, 2013.

10. Andrew Wolfson, "Lawyer Ordered to Account for Money," *Louisville Courier-Journal,* July 16, 2011.

11. Angela Ford v. Harold Baerg et al., On Review of Court of Appeals, Kentucky Supreme Court, November 2, 2017.

12. Andrew Wolfson, "Lawyer in Fen-Phen Scandal Faces Drug Charge," *Louisville Courier-Journal,* February 19, 2013.

13. Angelica Ford v. Seth Johnston, Commonwealth of Kentucky, 22nd Judicial District, 2013, "Memorandum of Law in Opposition to Motion," p. 4.

14. *Ford v. Baerg et al.*

15. Martha Neil, "Ex-Lawyer Gets 20-Years for Charges Including $4M Client Theft Linked to Fen-Phen Settlement," *ABA Journal,* September 23, 2014.

16. Stan Billingsley, "Update on the Firing of Linda Gosnell," *LawReader,* November 22, 2011.

17. Because of her ongoing legal battle with Chesley, Ford declined to provide any information to the author.

18. "It's Time to Retire Judge Ruehlman," editorial, *Cincinnati Enquirer,* October 28, 2016.

19. State ex rel. Ford v. Ruehlman, Slip Opinion No. 2016-Ohio-3529.

20. Andrew Wolfson, "Disbarred Lawyer Sues Former Fen-Phen Clients," *Louisville Courier-Journal,* September 21, 2015.

21. *State ex rel. Ford v. Ruehlman.*

22. *State ex rel. Ford v. Ruehlman.*

23. James Pilcher and Sharon Coolidge, "Fen-Phen Attorney Conflicted on Arrest Warrant," *Cincinnati Enquirer/USA Today Network,* November 6, 2015.

24. Kevin Grasha, "Ohio Supreme Court Slams Hamilton County Judge over Chesley Settlement," *Cincinnati Enquirer,* June 22, 2016.

25. James Pilcher, "Fen-Phen Case Draws Stan Chesley Even Deeper into Web of Lawsuits," *Cincinnati Enquirer,* December 27, 2016.

26. Connie McGirr et al. v. Thomas F. Rehme; Waite, Schneider, Bayless & Chesley, No. 17-3518, US Court of Appeals for the Sixth District, May 31, 2018.

27. Andrew Wolfson, "Firm Says Disbarred Chesley Stiffed It on Fee," *Louisville Courier-Journal,* September 27, 2014.

28. Associated Press, "Ex-Attorney Willing to Settle with Ex-Clients over Diet Drug," November 9, 2015.

29. James Pilcher and Sharon Coolidge, "Stan Chesley Speaks: Willing to Settle Fen-Phen Case," Cincinnati.com, November 7, 2015.

30. Alberto Jones, "Protestors Want Disbarred Attorney Stan Chesley to 'Pay Up,'" Channel 9 WICO, May 24, 2017.

31. *McGirr et al. v. Rehme, WSB&C.*

Epilogue

1. Natasha Singer, "Medical Papers by Ghostwriters Push Therapy," *New York Times,* August 4, 2009.

2. Charles Ornstein and Katie Thomas, "Cancer Doctor Didn't Disclose Corporate Ties," *New York Times,* September 9, 2018.

3. KBA v. Helmers, Supreme Court of Kentucky, September 22, 2011.

4. Paul A. Long, "Bamberger Resignation Will Be Costly," *Kentucky Post,* March 1, 2006.

5. Brett Barrouquere, "Judge to Dole out Diet-Drug Settlement," Associated Press, February 24, 2008.

6. Stan Billingsley, "LawReader Attends 6th Circuit Oral Arguments in Gallion/Cuningham Appeal Case," *LawReader,* January 17, 2012.

7. Beth Musgrave, "Supreme Court Approves Revisions to Attorney Code," *Bluegrass Politics Blog,* April 16, 2009.

8. Daniel Desrochers, "Private Gun Sales. Personalized Julep Cups. See What Audit of Kentucky's Courts Found," *Lexington Herald-Leader,* July 12, 2018.

9. Andrew Wolfson, "Lawyer Defends His Fee; Mills Says Most of Case's Millions Are Gone," *Louisville Courier-Journal,* May 30, 2006.

10. Author's interviews with Melbourne Mills, August and September 2018.

Index

Index

Index

Coburn, Tom, 94
Codell, James, III, 141
Codell, James, IV, 141
Codell Construction, 141
Collingsworth, Chris, 56
congestive heart failure, 37
Conn, Eric, 94–95, 140
Connolly, Heidi, 35–36, 37, 113
"Conns Hotties," 94
Continental Insurance Company, 129
contingency fees: *Guard* case and, 8, 71–72, 82, 88, 89, 97, 99, 109
contingency fund: *Guard* settlement and, 78, 81–82, 119
Controlled Substances Act, 27
Conway, Jack, 140
Cook, Trevor, 120
Cooper, Glenn L., 24–25
Corodemus, Marina, 43
Cory Kumler, 194
Courtney v. AHP, 69–71
Covington (KY), 6, 27, 85–86, 90–93
Covington Fire Department, 86
Cox, Scott, 135, 152
Crary, Jack, 35–36, 38
Crawford, Lisa, 183
Crews, Ed, 27, 30–31
Crittenden, Roger, 197
Crouse, Linda, 42–43
Cunningham, James, 28
Cunningham, Pat, 169, 174
Cunningham, Shirley: attempted defense strategy for the KBA investigation and *Abbott* case, 134–35, 138; attempt to cheat Mills on the *Guard* settlement, 106–7; attorneys' fees and reimbursement in *Guard*, 108–9; background of, 7, 64–65, 67; bond amount for, 169; in Boone County jail, 147–48; client contracts and the *Guard* case, 68; conviction of upheld by the US Court of Appeals, 198; Tracy Curtis's complaint about to the KBA, 105–6; disbarment of, 148; entry into the AHP class action, 60, 61; extent of the theft by, 9; FBI wire fraud investigation and, 145; in federal prison, 198; federal

wire fraud and, 106; federal wire fraud trials and, 146, 151, 157, 166–67; Florida A&M law school and, 127–28; Angela Ford and the *Abbott* case against, 131–34; Fund for Healthy Living and, 118, 119; Gallion and, 60, 65, 67; lawsuit against William Bertelsman, 157; marriages of, 65; mediation and settlement in *Guard*, 77–78, 79; meeting with Judge Bamberger and GCM on February 6, 2002 and, 107–9; Mills's settlement with David Stuart and, 129; monetary gains from *Guard*, 9, 82–83, 102, 103, 108–9, 112; personal life and use of wealth from the *Guard* settlement, 124–25, 126–28, 146; race horse Curlin and, 7, 125, 126, 146, 148; settlement with claimants in *Guard*, 101, 103–4; *Stevens* case and, 103–4, 187, 188. *See also* Guard case
Cunningham Summer Academy, 127
Curfman, Gregory, 39
Curlin (race horse), 7, 8, 125, 126, 146, 148, 198
Curlin, Charles, 125
"curse of the monkey's paw," 83
Curtis, Tracy, 105–6, 131
cy pres doctrine, 53, 110–11, 117–18, 138

Daffron Pharmacy, 29
Dante Alighieri, 13
Darla S. Guard et al. v. American Home Products. See *Guard* case
Daubert hearings, 170–71
Daughtery, David, 94
Davidson, David, 146
Davidson, John, 47
Davis, J. Morton, 19
Deitch, Marc, 40
Democratic National Committee, 55
Democratic Party: Chesley and, 55, 56; Eric Conn and, 140
Derby Pie, 28
Deters, Joe, 193
dexfenfluramine, 18, 19–20, 26, 36–38, 41. *See also* Redux
diabetes: fen-phen and, 31–32

Index

Index